Acclaim for Tony Evans's
Two Tribes
Liverpool, Everton and a City on the Brink

'The power of Tony Evans's writing emerges from the juxtaposition of football passion and political insight. A writer who understands that the meaning and beauty of football emerges not from mere tactics and line-ups but from the social context.' **Matthew Syed, author of** *Bounce* **and** *Black Box Thinking*

'Not just a funny and forensic account of the year the city of Liverpool was the undisputed capital of British football, but a proud and unapologetic tribute to how that city stood up, in all its radical beauty, to a brutal Thatcherite pounding. *Two Tribes* is social history of football writing at its finest.' **Brian Reade,** *Mirror*

'Politically charged, and flashing between scenes of gallows humour and improbable sporting achievement, Tony Evans brilliantly captures a city under fire through its rival football teams.' **Simon Hughes, author of** *Men in White Suits* **and** *Ring of Fire*

'Tony Evans is a brilliant writer who knows these teams, this subject, this era, this culture, these themes and this city better than anybody, and this enthralling book makes that so clear.' **Miguel Delaney,** *Independent*

'Thatcher, tumult, tunes. This is more than just a football book.' **Michael Calvin, author of** *No Hunger in Paradise* **and** *The Nowhere Men*

'Highly recommended – not just on Merseyside, but for all who remember that 1985–86 season fondly and for those who wish to recall or understand an era when English football and society existed on a knife-edge.' **Oliver Kay,** *The Times*

'A great read. As a Liverpool fan there is obvious interest. But to me the book goes a lot deeper than that, covering Liverpool City's political climate in the 80s, the growth of football television coverage, etc. Lots of fun.' **Marco Giacomelli,** *Evening Standard*

'The sheer beauty of this book is its ability to take you to the stinking alleyways and crumbling terraces that were the norm for supporters at that time. It's a snapshot of a time when watching football was often a matter of survival – a social history of a highly charged political tinderbox of a city . . . And that's what makes it so good.' **Matthew Crist,** *The Sportsman*

Also by Tony Evans

I Don't Know What It Is But I Love It:
Liverpool's Unforgettable 1983–84 Season

www.**penguin**.co.uk

TWO TRIBES

Liverpool, Everton and a City on the Brink

Tony Evans

BANTAM PRESS

LONDON • TORONTO • SYDNEY • AUCKLAND • JOHANNESBURG

TRANSWORLD PUBLISHERS
61–63 Uxbridge Road, London W5 5SA
www.penguin.co.uk

Transworld is part of the Penguin Random House group of companies
whose addresses can be found at global.penguinrandomhouse.com

Penguin
Random House
UK

First published in Great Britain in 2018 by Bantam Press
an imprint of Transworld Publishers

A CIP catalogue record for this book
is available from the British Library.

ISBN 9780593075920

Typeset in 12.5/15pt Dante by Falcon Oast Graphic Art Ltd..
Printed and bound by Clays Ltd, Bungay, Suffolk.

Penguin Random House is committed to a sustainable
future for our business, our readers and our planet. This book
is made from Forest Stewardship Council® certified paper.

MIX
Paper from
responsible sources
FSC® C018179
FSC
www.fsc.org

3 5 7 9 10 8 6 4 2

To Alisa and Grace.
Words can't explain what they mean to me.

Contents

Contents

Acknowledgements

This book started off as a much narrower idea, focused on football. Just writing about sport did not do justice to the events of the time. What happened in the mid 1980s still has ramifications today. Thanks to Giles Elliott for encouraging the wider view and allowing me to junk the original idea and take on a more ambitious project. He also persuaded me to include some of my personal experiences to give a sense of what it was like to be a travelling fan during the era.

Many people were generous with their time. I'm grateful for the wit and insight of Peter Reid, Neville Southall, Graeme Sharp, Steve Nicol, Jan Mølby, Mark Lawrenson, Craig Johnston, Kenny Dalglish, John Barnes, Tony Cottee, Frank McAvennie, Mark Bright, Ron Atkinson, James Brown, Peter Hooton and Derek Hatton.

Finally, my thanks to Brenda Kimber, who has seen the project through to completion and helped to sharpen the finished product.

Prologue

The big turn-off

10 May 1986

The seconds were ticking away. As 3 p.m. neared, panic began to set in. The time to take risks was arriving.

Some three hundred people – mostly young men – were gathered around gate C and a crush was building. They were the wrong side of the wall and hope was fading. Half a dozen of them climbed on to the small roof attached to the tower, not to flee the growing scrum but to attempt to sneak through the bank of three windows thirty feet above the stairs. It was impossible. The openings were blocked and a policeman stood on the other side. A similar set of apertures ten feet higher was unguarded, though. Teenagers hung out of these upper windows, gesturing to those below to come and join them.

There was only one route upwards: a set of high, spiked railings, eight feet away and at a right angle to the windows. The imploring hands of the youths were surely out of reach.

Then a figure wearing a Union flag around his shoulders hauled himself up to the top of the fence, 40 feet above the surging, baying mob. He looked across to where safety lay: the three small windows that were agonizingly out of reach. Three boys leant out of the thin rectangular openings, gesturing for him to jump. He hesitated. The drop was too far to risk.

Then, the youth on the fence reached out. The boy in the nearest window wore a blue ski hat. He edged forward, his

1

centre of gravity dangerously near tipping point, and offered his hand. The boy clinging to the railings placed his outstretched foot against the wall under the window in a desperate attempt to gain some traction. The teenager in the blue hat placed both hands close to the grasping fingers of his friend. They touched and suddenly their hands gripped: they were committed. It was all or nothing.

The youth with the flag swung. It seemed impossible that the desperate grip could hold but the boy with the green sun hat in the middle window darted forward and grabbed a handful of cloth. It was enough. The lad in the third window moved across to help, his red woollen cap disappearing from view. A huge cheer went up from the crowd as the dangling man was dragged to safety.

Below, four others who were attempting the same route as the boy with the Union flag turned back. There had to be another way.

As the minutes ebbed towards 3 p.m., an increasing mood of hysteria swept across a small area of north-west London. Thousands of young men attempted to scale walls, break down gates and overwhelm security. The police force struggled to maintain its tenuous control over the crowds.

These hordes were not attempting to escape captivity. They were not breaking free of bonds imposed by a restrictive political regime. No, they were trying to force their way into a stadium to watch a football match. What made so many people risk life, limb and arrest to watch 22 players kick a ball around?

'You had to be there,' says Peter Hooton, the lead singer of The Farm. Hooton had a ticket but understands the craving. 'It was unthinkable to miss it. Liverpool *v.* Everton in the FA Cup final? It was the biggest game ever.'

*

Less than two hours later, Peter Reid walked across the Wembley turf wearing a blue-and-white cap and a weak, rueful smile. The stadium remained full and chants of 'Merseyside' and 'Are you watching, Manchester?' rained down from both ends of the ground. Reid would rather have been anywhere else. 'I just wanted to get out of there,' he said.

Kenny Dalglish and his team were on a separate lap of honour and milking the acclaim but they were stunned by the show of solidarity on the terraces. 'Evertonians stayed and applauded,' the Liverpool player-manager said. 'The city came together and stayed together. It was awe-inspiring, especially considering the year we'd just had.'

This was sport at its best. A tense, see-sawing match, an unlikely comeback and a remarkable show of sportsmanship from both fans and players. Just 12 months earlier, football had sunk to its lowest point. Now the game was showing its sunniest face. Liverpool had won but Everton conducted themselves with absolute grace. At least that's what the watching nation saw.

'It was horrible,' Reid said. 'Gruesome. We were all good mates but it was the worst feeling in football.'

The end of the world as we know it

29 May 1985

Liverpool had lost a football match. The players were numb and bewildered as they sat on the coach taking them away from Heysel Stadium. There was usually silence on the journey home after a defeat but this was a different sort of hush. People had been killed on the terraces before the game.

The players knew before the match that there had been significant trouble. The sound of the wall collapsing had penetrated the dressing room. In the long delay before they took to the pitch – the kick-off was almost two hours late – rumour and counter-rumour added to the confusion. Then the Brussels chief of police told the players that people had been killed. They needed to play to prevent an escalation of the trouble. Juventus, they were told, had agreed to participate.

Some of the team did not want to go out and perform in these circumstances. Even their half-hearted involvement would haunt and embarrass some of them for years.

'We didn't want to play,' Craig Johnston, who was on the bench, said. 'We weren't really given a choice.'

Afterwards, the mood was not that of a defeated team. It was the shell-shocked gloom of a group of men who had been unwilling extras in a tragedy. A charge by *their* supporters had caused panic in a supposedly neutral section that was predominantly filled by Juventus fans. As the crowd backed away, the brickwork disintegrated and hundreds of people were rushed. The death toll would reach 39.

Mark Lawrenson was not with his teammates. The centre half started the match but his fitness was always in doubt. He had dislocated his shoulder two weeks earlier and only played because this important match was the last of the season. Within three minutes, he aggravated the injury and was rushed to hospital.

'Normally, you'd be disappointed if you were injured in a big game,' he said. 'I was just glad to be off the pitch. I didn't want to play. None of us did.'

Lawrenson was taken to hospital along with the dead and dying. He awoke after an operation to find the corridors full of angry Italians and an armed policeman protecting his bed. 'When I was leaving the next day with Roy Evans, people were spitting and shouting at us,' he said. 'It was horrible. For the next week, we were just walking around in a daze.'

Bruce Grobbelaar, the goalkeeper, considered giving up his career. 'I said to myself, "I don't want to be part of a club that caused death and destruction in a game." If it would have been any other game than the last one of the season, I would have stopped. As it was, I had the summer to think it over and decided if I knocked it on the head the idiots would have won. I wasn't going to let the thugs destroy me.'

Michel Platini, who scored the winning penalty for Juventus, went on to be president of UEFA. The Frenchman joined his teammates on the lap of honour after the game and celebrated gleefully with the trophy. Asked whether they would have pranced about had they won, the Liverpool players who were there that night invariably respond with a grimace and a shake of the head.

News that Joe Fagan was retiring as manager had broken on

the morning of the game. He was to be replaced by Dalglish, the team's best player. The 34-year-old found himself in charge of a club with its reputation in tatters.

The ramifications of the dreadful night of 29 May in Brussels would extend much further than football. The credibility of an entire nation was on the line.

Liverpool and the club's fans were the focus of the initial contempt and anger in the immediate aftermath of Heysel, but soon the whole of English football would have to share the guilt and punishment. The knee-jerk response by the Conservative government was to act in a draconian manner before they had even begun to explore the causes of the disaster. Under pressure from Prime Minister Margaret Thatcher, the FA withdrew English clubs from European competition within 48 hours of the game's finish.

Thatcher reacted to the disaster immediately. The day after Heysel, she summoned football journalists who had been at the game to 10 Downing Street to get their views about what was wrong with the sport.

Peter Jones from the BBC, the *Daily Mail*'s Jeff Powell, Charlie Burgess of the *Guardian*, the *Express*'s Merseyside man John Keith, Mike Ellis from the *Sun*, the Press Association's Peter Went and the *Sunday Times*'s Brian Glanville are mentioned in Cabinet papers as attending the slightly surreal summit.

'Yes, I was one of the "insignificant seven",' Glanville said with wry humour.

'I was supposed to be flying to Mexico for an England tour but stayed behind to meet the Prime Minister.'

Glanville remembers cycling from his home in Holland Park to Whitehall in a pair of football shorts. At Downing Street, he was told by police to park his bike where Quintin Hogg, the Lord Chancellor, used to leave his bicycle. He then quickly changed into trousers, a jacket and an Old Carthusian tie. He might have looked like another old-school Tory but appearances were misleading. Glanville may have been a former public schoolboy but his views were certainly not those of the Establishment.

'It was a strange experience,' he said. 'Mrs Thatcher talked about getting "ordinary, decent fans" to stop any trouble. I imagined a grandfather saying to a young hooligan "Stop kicking him" and decided she had no idea about the reality of the situation.

'I told her that the troublemakers felt alienated. "I wouldn't use that word," she said.' Glanville is a fine impressionist. He quotes Thatcher in the patronizing, schoolmistress manner that she adopted when talking down to those who did not agree with her stance.

The Prime Minister was reluctant to accept that the troubled economic situation had any impact on hooliganism but, as the Cabinet papers show, the seven journalists made sure they hammered home the point. The notes of the meeting make their views unambiguous, clearly stating that it was 'a social phenomenon rather than a football phenomenon'.

Thatcher's idea that crowds should self-police was rooted in another social struggle, which she misinterpreted as badly as the violence at football matches. The views of 'expert' observers were never going to change the Prime Minister's opinion. Contrary to Glanville's memories, the Cabinet papers suggest the journalists supported the notion that supporters should confront violent offenders. Thatcher would not be the first, nor last, government leader to hear only what suited them and turn the false impression into documented history. 'They endorsed the Prime Minister's attempts to persuade ordinary spectators to make a stand against the hooligans,' the notes say. 'The Prime Minister thought this might prove possible: the example of the recent miners' strike showed that ordinary people were often prepared to stand up and be counted in the face of appalling violence and intimidation.'

That analysis of the miners' dispute is hopelessly one-eyed. Thatcher's biases were all on view at the Downing Street meeting.

Michael Calvin, the columnist and author, is not mentioned in the official documents but was also present. 'I was an insignificant junior reporter at the *Telegraph* then,' he said. 'She had eyes like an owl. She was accompanied by Leon Brittan [the Home Secretary] and Neil Macfarlane [the sports minister]. She was not listening to anyone. She had made up her mind. Brittan tried to steer her in a certain direction but she shut him down quickly. What struck me was how scared of her they were.'

The lady was not for turning. She again made it clear that the FA needed to withdraw from Europe and did the same in a meeting with Bert Millichip, the chairman of the organization. English football's ruling body quickly acquiesced to the Prime Minister.

The decision left those within the game stunned. 'I didn't understand it,' said Ron Atkinson, then manager of Manchester United. 'They pulled the clubs out of Europe and then let the England team play in a tournament in Brazil? I didn't understand. It was a bit hasty, a knee-jerk reaction.' The national team were exempt from the national shame.

There was little logic at work. It seemed clear where responsibility lay for events at Heysel Stadium. 'Most of us thought Liverpool and maybe Juventus should be banned,' Atkinson said. 'No one else.'

UEFA's sanctions against the Italian club were ludicrously light, given their supporters fought with police even before the trouble began at the opposite end of the ground. After the wall collapsed, Juventus fans charged around the running track to attack the Liverpool section. A man stepped from the main Juve terracing brandishing a gun. It turned out to be a starting pistol but it caused panic and fear.

The Turin club were ordered to play their first two European ties behind closed doors. European football's ruling body disbarred Belgium from staging a UEFA final for ten years.

Across the Channel, the British Prime Minister could not wait to spread the blame across English football. Thatcher was on the offensive. She shot down Neil Kinnock's suggestion that unemployment was a factor in hooliganism. The Labour Party leader had spoken earlier in the day and said:

> The problem of football crowd violence is deep-rooted and it has many causes of which one of the most important is long-term unemployment, especially among the young. We cannot hope to tackle this problem so long as we have a government which gives no priority whatsoever to tackling unemployment. And even believes that a certain degree of unemployment is necessary in order to reduce costs and keep [wages] down.

The Prime Minister's response was robust. She stood on the steps of Number 10 and declaimed:

> This is much, much deeper than that. People who have plenty of money to go abroad and have plenty of drink, I do not think you can put it down to unemployment. Indeed if I might say so I think it's rather a slur on those who are unemployed to put it down to that.

This sort of straightforward directness was often used as evidence of Thatcher's clarity of thought. In reality it merely illustrated the so-called Iron Lady's instinct to distil complex problems down to simple black-and-white scenarios. In this limited world view, football in general and Liverpool in particular were part of her 'enemy within'.

Whatever the Prime Minister believed, it was becoming clear

that English clubs would not be competing in Europe in the foreseeable future. UEFA followed the FA's example two days later with an indefinite ban on English clubs and FIFA endorsed the sanctions. The Belgian government also banned all English teams. Common sense was thrown out, too: a team of 13-year-olds from Sheffield planning to participate in a three-day tournament in Zaventem had their invitation withdrawn.

Paranoia and fear were running wild. A bomb was left outside a Marks & Spencer department store in Brussels. The government warned British tourists in Italy to be careful. Europe was in uproar.

Liverpool Football Club reacted to the withdrawal and ban in the only way they could have. 'I think it's a very statesman-like decision,' John Smith, the chairman, said. Representatives of Everton, Manchester United, Tottenham Hotspur, Southampton and Norwich City were less enamoured with the decision. These clubs had qualified for Europe. Along with the Professional Footballers' Association, they took their challenge to the High Court, arguing that the FA should nominate the five teams for entry to European competition, that UEFA should accept them and that FIFA should lift the English suspension. They lost. There was no other course of action. The president of the Football League, Jack Dunnett, labelled the ban 'unjust'.

At Goodison, there was resentment but it was not directed towards Liverpool. Everton, the champions, were not allowed to participate in the next season's European Cup. 'It's difficult watching something unfold and easy to blame the wrong people,' Neville Southall, the goalkeeper, said. 'Thatcher wanted us out of Europe. She didn't want working-class people causing problems abroad. There was another agenda going on that we weren't party to. I'm convinced if she hadn't stepped in we'd have still been in Europe.'

Football hooliganism had long been labelled 'the English

disease' by the British media. It was an outrageous simplification. Violence occurred across the Continent. 'Hooliganism was a problem but it wasn't just English fans causing trouble,' Southall said.

'Everyone always wanted to blame our fans. When trouble happened abroad and the locals were responsible, you'd hardly hear about it. We had all the windows in the coach smashed on a preseason game against Galatasaray in Turkey. There was no mention of that. There were double standards against our supporters. With Britain, it was a one-way street.'

That was true but the record of English clubs and the national side abroad was sullied by repeated examples of violence. British media always focused on the misdemeanours of UK passport holders.

There are too many incidents to detail, but the worst of them made headlines across Europe. Leeds United supporters ripped up the Parc des Princes after their team was beaten by Bayern Munich in the 1975 European Cup final. Manchester United were expelled and then reinstated in the Cup-Winners' Cup in 1977 after trouble away at Saint-Etienne. England fans were tear-gassed in Turin after fighting interrupted a European Championships game against Belgium in 1980 and a year later there were ugly scenes in Basel during and after a defeat by Switzerland. In 1983, there were more pitched battles in Luxembourg. The national side's supporters exported their Little Englander attitudes to Europe and simplistic, right-wing politics and jingoism underpinned much of the aggression. Ironically, most of the troublemakers who followed England and caused anarchy abroad were among Thatcher's most fervent supporters.

The club game continued to have its issues, too. Tottenham, twice, were involved in unpleasant situations. A rivalry with Feyenoord that went back almost a decade erupted in Rotterdam in 1983. The tabloids labelled Spurs 'the shame of Britain'. A year later a supporter of the north London club was shot dead in Brussels. Football had become a national embarrassment for many Britons.

The Merseyside teams had earned a good reputation in Europe. Liverpool had an unbroken run of 21 successive years in Continental competition that stretched back to the mid 1960s. By the late 1970s, young Scousers were travelling in significant numbers to away games across the Channel. They had little patience with right-wing politics – they tended to be left-leaning – and fighting got in the way of their main interests: shoplifting and drinking.

When Liverpool supporters were involved in trouble, it was mostly on the receiving end. UEFA scheduled the 1984 European Cup final to be played in Rome despite the presence of AS Roma in the competition. When the Italian side duly reached the showpiece game, they were matched against the Merseyside club. Before and after the match, Roma fans stabbed, slashed and brutalized the away supporters on a mass scale. It was barely reported in the British press in comparison with the coverage of riotous behaviour by English fans. The festering resentment towards Italian Ultras played a significant role in the build-up to Heysel.

Everton had fewer expeditions abroad but when they played in Europe things passed off peacefully. Two weeks before Heysel, they faced Rapid Vienna in Rotterdam in the Cup-Winners' Cup final. In a city that had a reputation as one of the Continent's hooligan hotbeds, Everton's 3–1 victory passed off peacefully. The enduring memory for most Blues was a massive football match involving the Dutch police in one of the main squares before the game. 'We had such a good time when we went away,' Derek Hatton, deputy leader of Liverpool City Council and an Evertonian, said. 'That's why we were appalled at the way we were punished, too.

'We finally won the league and had a chance at the European Cup and then it was taken away from us. There was some resentment: "That's the only way those red bastards can stop us." It was the sort of thing you'd say to your mates, banter almost. It was disappointing to be banned, though.'

The authorities acted quickly, as if they knew the answers to why things had gone wrong in such a deadly fashion in Brussels. In reality they did not even know the right questions to ask. They groped around in the most foolish manner to try to explain what happened.

Smith, the Liverpool chairman, suggested that the National Front were responsible for the violence on the terraces that caused the crush, pointing the finger at Chelsea fans in particular. It was palpable nonsense. The presence of fascist infiltrators would have been noticed by Liverpool's hard-core support; the right-wingers would have been dealt with long before they reached the stadium. Peter Hooton, the lead singer of The Farm and one of the founders of *The End*, the seminal football, music and fashion fanzine, was adamant from the start that Scousers were at the forefront of the trouble. 'As soon as the police released pictures of the charge, it was clear and undeniable,' Hooton said. 'It was Liverpool. There was no doubt about it. It was ludicrous to say anything else.'

At the other end of the political scale, Cold War paranoia crept in. David Miller of the *Sunday Times* was at an International Olympic Committee meeting in East Berlin less than a week after the catastrophe in Belgium. He wrote: 'The facts are as yet imprecise, but there is grounding for belief that the quite clearly organized assault by alleged Liverpool supporters in the Heysel Stadium had financial and ideological backing from left-wing agencies outside Britain.'

The only thing this analysis had going for it was the recognition that match-going Scousers tended to left-leaning politics.

Crank theories about what had happened were everywhere. In the febrile, furious atmosphere, the madness was not confined to the terraces. The one thing everyone agreed on was that football's future was bleak.

2

The people's game

Football was never the 'beautiful game'. At least not in Britain. It was earthy, its rhythms determined by wind and mud. There, it was the 'people's game', a sport that energized the working class and drew huge crowds as it grew with stunning rapidity in the late nineteenth century. It quickly developed from a social pastime to a lucrative form of mass entertainment.

The seeds of the game germinated on the playing fields of England's public schools and then branched off into various codes. Association Football, soccer, became the most popular. The Football Association was formed in 1863 and set out a series of rules for this arm of the sport. The new ruling body was largely controlled by wealthy businessmen and aristocrats.

Something else was happening, though. At the Newton Heath depot of the Lancashire and Yorkshire Railway, the employees formed a team to play other departments for recreational purposes. At St Domingo's in Liverpool, the muscular Christianity of the Methodist congregation was expressed by church members on the football field. Munitions workers in south-east London got together to create a side. Across Britain, the wealth of the late Victorian age allowed workers and church-goers more free time than they had ever experienced before. They embraced the chance to play sports, especially football. Their co-workers and co-worshippers enjoyed watching their more athletic friends and colleagues compete against other teams. Soon, people from around the district started to take an interest. Newton Heath would become Manchester United, St Domingo's developed into Everton and the group of Woolwich ammunition makers created Arsenal. Similar teams were formed in canteens and churches across the nation. Flat-capped hordes flocked to watch matches as the leagues grew and rivalries blossomed.

Rugby union, another code, had a more exulted social status. Like cricket, it was perceived to be a 'gentleman's' sport. Football grew bigger though, tapping into local pride and a mass market. Its audiences were rowdier and poorer. By the early years of the twentieth century, a snobbery was developing. Football was the game of the great unwashed. By 1985, it was considered to be a downmarket and dangerous activity. It was the sporting equivalent of 'slumming it'. Hooliganism was rife and, in the highest echelons of power in Whitehall, it was judged to be a magnet for British society's most disruptive elements. Heysel was the final proof. It confirmed two Establishment biases: the city of Liverpool and football were both toxic environments that, when mixed, proved explosive and deadly. The game and the region were in their violent death throes in the view of the Conservative government. Heysel offered final, lethal proof.

There was no need to circle the wagons on Merseyside. They had been arranged in a defensive position for some time. In 1985, the city of Liverpool was completely out of step with mainstream life in Britain.

In the 1980s, many people wanted the barriers between Scousers and the rest of the world to be less metaphorical. 'They should build a fence around [Liverpool] and charge admission. For sadly it has become a "showcase" of everything that has gone wrong in Britain's major cities,' the *Daily Mirror* opined in 1982.

This was a region that had fallen on hard times and the events in Brussels reinforced the preconceptions of those who despised the area and its people. Yet the shock and horror of the Heysel Stadium disaster hit home more keenly on the banks of the Mersey than in most places.

Derek Hatton was as appalled as anyone by events. 'I was watching on TV at home,' he said. 'It was shocking, especially as we'd been in Rotterdam with Everton two weeks before and there'd been no trouble. We weren't expecting anything in Brussels, either.'

Once the initial jarring numbness wore off, it became clear that the tragedy in Belgium would have political consequences.

'Margaret Thatcher knew she was on a collision course with the city,' Hatton said. 'The Conservative government were using anything they could to blacken the name of Liverpool. Heysel was used for that, too.'

Peter Reid, who had played in Rotterdam and has a fierce civic pride, agreed. The assault on Merseyside was about much more than football, the Everton midfielder said: 'The Tories were trying to decimate one of the world's great cities. They wanted to destroy us.'

His teammate Neville Southall believes it was a wider attack on an entire section of society. 'It wasn't about football to the Tories,' the Everton goalkeeper said. 'It was an assault against working-class people and their culture.

'It was one way of breaking people's spirit.'

And Merseyside was at breaking point.

At the beginning of the twentieth century, the port of Liverpool was one of the world's most important seafaring centres and considered 'the second city of the Empire'. Its wealth had been built in the slave trade in the 1700s but after this traffic in human beings was abolished in 1807 the burgeoning United States economy ensured that the docklands on this part of the Lancashire coast continued to boom.

Under the surface of prosperity lurked serious social issues. The potato famine of 1846–47 caused the area to be swamped by refugees from Ireland. More than a million desperate, starving Irish came into Liverpool and while most used it as a staging post en route to America or the colonies, enough stayed to change the character of the city's identity. Their poverty brought a new level of squalor to Victorian life. The strong anti-Irishness in England made it easy to dismiss the problems within Liverpool's poorest communities as symptoms of inherent barbarism. *Punch* illustrated the mood of the English with its cartoons depicting the Irish as apes. One of its satires from 1862 said:

> A creature manifestly between the Gorilla and the Negro is to be met with in some of the lowest districts of London and Liverpool by adventurous explorers.
>
> It comes from Ireland, whence it has contrived to migrate; it belongs in fact to a tribe of Irish savages: the lowest species of Irish Yahoo.
>
> When conversing with its kind it talks a sort of gibberish. It is, moreover, a climbing animal, and may sometimes be seen ascending a ladder laden with a hod of bricks.

In London, the immigrants were subsumed into the larger population of the capital. Beside the Mersey they formed new communities, particularly in the North End, an area that ran a mile or so from the city centre to Boundary Street and another mile inland to Great Homer Street. Its main thoroughfare was Scotland Road, which was soon to become a byword for debauchery and anarchy.

Incidents in Liverpool made national headlines where similar crimes elsewhere went unreported. In 1874, on Tithebarn Street where the North End meets the city centre, a man was kicked to death while scores of bystanders watched. The *Daily Telegraph* reacted with horror: 'In all the pages of Dr Livingstone's experiences among the negroes of Africa, there is no single instance approaching this Liverpool story, in savagery of mind and body, in bestiality of heart and act.'

A gang from the streets around Scotland Road, the High Rippers, caused national outrage. Salford's Scuttlers and Birmingham's Peaky Blinders were no less dangerous or disruptive but the whiff of Celtic violence in Liverpool made it more sinister to the general public.

Alcohol played a significant role in establishing the city's reputation as a semi-civilized no man's land. In the same year as the aforementioned murder, 10 per cent of all drunks detained in Britain were apprehended in Liverpool. Dinah Mulock, a Victorian writer, provided a standard view of the place. 'Liverpool is an awful town for drinking,' she wrote. 'Other towns may be as bad; statistics prove it; but I know of no other place where intoxication is so open and shameless.'

Despite what the cold hard facts said, Liverpool was perceived as worse than elsewhere. Biases like this persisted long into the twentieth century and still linger today.

They were fed by the religious divide in the city. Sectarian rioting was a fact of life in Liverpool in the years before the First World War. Catholics and Protestants did come together to fight for workers' rights but that made things worse. During the 1911 Transport Workers' strike, the government sent troops on to the streets and had gunboats on the Mersey ready to shell the city. Soldiers fired into a rioting crowd and killed two men. Viewed from Whitehall and Middle England, it looked like this was a war zone.

Even its politics were alien. The poorest area of the city, the North End, returned an Irish nationalist MP, T. P. O'Connor, to

Westminster from 1885 to 1929. It was in this constituency, in the dense tenement slums around Scotland Road, that the Scouse identity was formed.

Until after the First World War, most of the people in the dockside areas of north Liverpool would have described themselves as Irish. There had been other nicknames for people from the city but they had not stuck. The obsession with dressing and acting like Americans was reflected in the term 'Dicky Sam', dicky meaning fake and Sam from Uncle Sam, the symbol of the United States. Little wonder it didn't catch on. Wack, or Wacker, was sometimes used but rarely in Liverpool. Perhaps it comes from the children's song 'Nick, nack, Paddy-Wack.' After all, the 'old man' who 'goes rolling home' is drunk in this anti-Irish ditty.

At this point, scouse was a type of seaman's stew – a corruption of the Scandinavian word 'lobscouse' – made of the cheapest ingredients. Carts in the Scotland Road area sold the inexpensive gruel to workmen, who were sneeringly nicknamed 'Scousers' by wealthier citizens. The term spread to mockingly describe the residents of this poverty-stricken area but before long the people of north Liverpool were adopting the tag with a sense of pride. Throughout the 1920s and '30s it spread across the city and jumped the religious divide. The *Oxford English Dictionary* claims the first usage of the word Scouse was in 1945. They were 25 years or more behind the times.

Liverpool's status as an outsider in England did not change. Even in the 1980s, parts of the media referred to Merseyside sourly as 'the capital of Ireland'. The relationship between the city and the rest of the country was shaped and defined by this idea of an alien group of people within the body politic of England.

Even before the arrival of the twentieth century, Merseyside's reputation as a violent, drunken place was well established. Then, in the 1960s, against all expectation, Liverpool became the centre of the world, at least for teenagers and devotees of pop culture.

The Beatles took the planet by storm. Their music had a phenomenal effect but it was only part of their appeal. Their irreverent attitude – cheeky, faintly hostile, rebellious – was as quintessentially Scouse as their accents and suddenly everyone wanted to talk with this nasal cocktail of Irish, Lancastrian and Welsh tones. Briefly, Liverpool was the most fashionable place to be. Of course, the Beatles left for London as soon as their bank balance could justify it.

A decade on, things had changed significantly for the worse. Britain's trading outlook switched from the Commonwealth and Americas towards Europe. The docks began to contract and industry relocated. Between 1966 and 1977, 350 factories closed or moved away from Merseyside. More than forty thousand jobs disappeared in the 15 years before 1985. In the year of the Heysel disaster, Liverpool's unemployment rate reached 27 per cent. Nearly half the young men aged between 16 and 24 – the age group that comprised the football clubs' most fervent fans – were on the dole. This did not go unnoticed. The undercurrents of class war were evident in the coverage of events in Belgium. 'Unlike Juventus, the majority of Liverpool fans who travelled to Brussels were recognizably and overwhelmingly working class,' the *Sunday Times* said. 'Even without their team favours, many would be instantly recognizable in their ragged jeans, training shoes and do-it-yourself haircuts.'

Refugees from the potato famine would be more identifiable from this description than the sharply dressed Scallies who followed Liverpool around Europe. Ragged? I set off for Brussels wearing a pair of expensive suede boots from London's Jermyn Street, Levi 501s bought on New York's Sixth Avenue, shrunk to fit in the bath at home and bleached pale in the same tub, a Ralph Lauren polo shirt and a John Smedley crewneck sweater.

As for the haircut, that was the cheapest bit: £6 in Torbo's on Scotland Road. It was not a high-end barbers but it looked presentable enough. The sweeping generalizations had less to do with dress sense than snobbish assumptions. Wilful misunderstanding dominated most of the discourse about Liverpool and football.

If the unemployed were to be sneered at, those who were in work earned little more respect. When they fought for their jobs and refused to accept the terms offered by management and government, they were looked upon as troublemakers. Liverpool's dockers were prominent when the port workers faced down the Conservative regime in 1972. Ford's factory in Halewood became a byword for industrial action. Genuine grievances were dismissed as pointless militancy and laziness by outsiders.

By the early 1980s, poverty was growing and an outburst of social disorder cemented Liverpool's reputation as a grim and forbidding place with a populace of shirkers. In July 1981, long-standing tensions between a heavy-handed police force and the predominantly black community of Liverpool 8 erupted into violence. CS gas was used by the authorities against rioters – the first time it had been deployed in the United Kingdom outside Northern Ireland – even though gas had not been used in Brixton during arguably more severe rioting earlier in the year.

The Conservative government's reaction was to discuss whether Merseyside should be cut loose and left to wither. Geoffrey Howe, the Chancellor of the Exchequer, proposed running down the area as government policy:

> I fear Merseyside is going to be much the hardest nut to crack. We do not want to find ourselves concentrating all the limited cash that may have to be made available into Liverpool and having nothing left for possibly more promising areas such as the West Midlands or, even, the North East.

It would be even more regrettable if some of the brighter ideas for renewing economic activity were to be sown only on the relatively stony ground on the banks of the Mersey.

I cannot help but feel that the option of managed decline is one which we should not forget altogether. We must not expend all our limited resources in trying to make water flow uphill.

It would take 30 years for the public records office release of documents to confirm this but many residents of Liverpool knew they were considered worthless by those at the highest level of politics. They fought back at the ballot box, voting for a left-wing Labour council that immediately set itself on a collision course with Whitehall.

'It was seen as a rogue area because it was resisting the Thatcher government,' Peter Hooton said. 'Every other area complied with the free-markct zealotry.'

Merseyside's one saving grace during this period was football.

'In a city cast as an outsider in its own land, battered by the deliberate economic downturns and clear-outs of the early 1980s, Liverpool Football Club was an enduring source of pride, a magnet for the energies and emotions of a public hungry for success,' wrote David Goldblatt in *The Ball is Round: A Global History of Football*.

Everton had emerged as the other most significant team in the English game in the mid 1980s. The clubs were flagbearers for the city. The players recognized it. 'We all understood the situation,' Graeme Sharp, the Everton striker, said. 'Unemployment was high and you knew the hardship the fans were going through. You'd see all the away fans and think, "How did they manage that?" It made you realize how important football was. We were well aware what people were sacrificing. It gave you great respect for the fans.'

Everton and Liverpool's success lifted spirits in a depressed region and gave people who had little to boast about bragging rights over the rest of the country. The horrible deadly night in Brussels had undermined this.

In among the shame, anger, mourning and confusion, it felt like something special had been ruined. Little wonder Grobbelaar considered walking away from the sport.

3

The story of the Blues

The unholy story of professional football in Liverpool started in a church. In the era of physical protestantism, St Domingo's Methodist Sunday school encouraged its boys to join in the sort of healthy pursuits that would prepare young men to be servants of the Empire. Football was not just recreation but a pastime with a purpose. It taught teamwork and was held to build moral fibre.

The team became popular. Very quickly, non-parishioners wanted to join the fun and in 1879 the club was re-christened Everton. They held matches in Stanley Park until the league demanded that they play in an enclosed area. Everton moved to a pitch off Priory Road.

Football was the mass-participation sensation of the Victorian era. Crowds flooded to see the games and Everton once again found themselves too big for their home. The land's owner didn't like swarms of people on his property, and the club were on the move. Their next home would become famous: Anfield.

Everton were happy at their new ground. They won the League Championship for the first time in 1891 while residents of the growing stadium. The future on Walton Breck Road looked bright. Then, a year later, a boardroom row threatened the future of the club.

Like so much that was controversial in the city, drink was the cause. John Houlding, a local MP and brewer, was one of

Everton's powerbrokers but when he attempted to buy the ground, his enemies on the board opposed him. Houlding wanted to be able to sell his beer to the burgeoning crowds. He got the property but lost the club.

Everton found a new home at Goodison Park less than a mile away and Houlding was left with a football ground, no team and no thirsty customers. The brewer decided to form his own club. He held a meeting in his Sandon Hotel, just yards from what would become the Kop, and created a new entity. Liverpool Football Club played their first game in 1892. The rivalry began immediately.

Everton were the senior partners. They had a glamour that their neighbours lacked, even though each club had won the title five times by the beginning of the 1960s. They were owned by the Moores family, who had become rich running football pools and had built a huge retail empire. Everton were known as the 'Mersey Millionaires'. They spent only four years of their history outside the top flight of English football and have been continuously in the highest division since 1954. As Liverpool became successful in the 1970s, though, Everton struggled.

In 1981, they appointed Howard Kendall, one of their great former players, as manager. He returned to Goodison the same month that Liverpool won their third European Cup. The gloom would deepen before things got better for fans on the Gwladys Street End terraces. For the first time in Merseyside history, a generation of Evertonians had grown up as second-class citizens.

At an Anfield derby in November 1983, the former residents of the ground capitulated meekly to the upstarts who succeeded them. The 3–0 Liverpool victory looked to hasten the end of the Kendall era. The Kop sang: 'Howard Kendall, Howard Kendall, there's a taxi at the gate!'

It was bad enough to have twenty thousand Kopites howling

abuse at you but football is a profession that you cannot leave at the office. It comes home with you. Kendall's worst moment was when his garage door was daubed with the words 'Kendall Out'.

It was the lowest point. The only way was up.

Kendall was on the brink but the same month as the humiliation at Anfield, the Everton manager signed Andy Gray for £250,000 from Wolverhampton Wanderers. It was a masterstroke.

Four years earlier, the Scottish striker had moved to Wolves from Aston Villa for a British record fee of close to £1.5 million. At 27, he had problems with his knees – hence the knockdown price. He was just the man Everton needed to provide an extra dash of know-how to help transform a squad of callow youngsters into serious contenders. 'Andy had passion, desire and drive,' Graeme Sharp said. 'He gave a group of young players experience. He had unbelievable passion on and off the field.'

Still, Everton lived on the brink. The side lurched through the winter and spring, barely surviving a number of crises. Each time Kendall was 'one game from the sack', the team would eke out a result. The various turning points became part of Everton folklore.

At Stoke City in the third round of the FA Cup, the manager opened the dressing-room windows for the players to hear the noise of four thousand travelling fans. 'He just said, "Listen to that. Are you going to let them down?"' Sharp recalled. Everton won 2–0.

Sometimes they needed more than the fans' help. Against Oxford United, a team from two divisions below, Kendall's team were trailing 1–0 and on the verge of a damaging League Cup defeat. Kevin Brock, an Oxford defender, mishit a straightforward back pass and Adrian Heath kept Everton in the competition. They won the replay.

In the FA Cup, Gillingham – who were in the same division as Oxford – had a last-minute chance to knock the top-flight team out in the waning moments of a replay. Tony Cascarino missed the opportunity and Everton progressed after another rematch.

It did not feel like it, but Kendall's team were growing more confident by the week. They reached the League Cup final – against Liverpool, of all people – in March and matched their neighbours in a 0–0 draw at Wembley before being outfought in the replay at Maine Road as Liverpool won 1–0. In the FA Cup, they were unstoppable.

In May 1984, Kendall brought Goodison its first trophy since 1970 when Everton beat Watford 2–0 at Wembley.

It was just the start. The close season of 1984 did little to halt the momentum. In 1984–85, Everton emerged as one of Europe's best sides. In October, they went to Anfield and put down a marker. Sharp scored a spectacular 25-yard strike in a 1–0 victory and the nature of the relationship between Liverpool and Everton changed again. 'We grew up going to Anfield and getting nothing,' Sharp said. 'We were underdogs. We had an inferiority complex.'

After winning the cup, Kendall's side had developed a new attitude.

'We could sense it coming together as a team,' Sharp said. 'The goal at Anfield gave us massive belief. We could challenge Liverpool. We could beat them.'

They stormed to the first division title, leaving second-placed Liverpool 13 points in their wake. They captured the Cup-Winners' Cup, their first European trophy, in Rotterdam in May and were unlucky to miss out on a treble when Manchester United beat them 1–0 in the FA Cup final. There was a growing swagger about Everton. Perhaps with a little less of it, they might have won the cup.

'I've got a picture of me with the Cup-Winners' Cup, filled with champagne on the plane back from Rotterdam,' recalled Derek Hatton, who travelled with the squad. 'It was incredible. Everyone was throwing back the drink and the mood was fantastic. We got back to Speke at 2 a.m. on the Thursday morning. Remember, we were playing Manchester United at Wembley in the FA Cup final on Saturday. If we win, we've won the treble.

'As we walked down the stairs from the plane, Howard turns round and says, "Shall we go to Chinatown?" So off we all go. A couple of the team were getting picked up by their wives and they were fuming that they missed out.'

Liverpool's Chinatown is the second oldest in the western world behind San Francisco's. Its restaurants were notorious venues for late-night eating and drinking.

'When we finally finished, the sun was up and we were all well away [drunk],' Hatton said. 'Kick-off at Wembley was less than 60 hours away.

'The final went to extra time and we got beat 1–0. I mentioned it later to Howard and said how different it could have been. Imagine if the team would have stayed in Rotterdam overnight, got a good night's sleep and done things the way teams do today.

'He said, "Here we go again. If we wouldn't have done things like that, we wouldn't have been the team we were."

'He had a point. The togetherness of the team on nights like this was brilliant to see. I did say, "We could have missed out Chinatown, Howard." He had an answer to that: "I was starving!"'

Kendall's team was hungry for trophies. The future looked gloriously bright. They were going into 1985–86 as England's dominant side. They would represent the country in the European Cup, the Continent's most prestigious competition.

Then came Heysel. For the first time since the precarious days of late 1983, Everton's momentum was halted. And none of it was their fault.

The absurdity of the situation was highlighted when Kendall travelled to Zurich after Everton were named as *World Soccer* magazine's Team of the Year for 1985. João Havelange, the FIFA president, presented the award to a manager whose side were not allowed to compete in international competition.

Peter Reid still struggles to comprehend the thought processes involved. 'People died at Heysel and that put football into perspective,' the midfielder said. 'But it was unjust to ban all English clubs. People who did nothing wrong were penalized.'

Everton were aghast at the injustice of it all, 'We were collateral damage in someone else's war,' Southall said.

'We couldn't believe it,' Andy Gray said. 'We felt cheated. Our supporters had been brilliant in Europe. We'd done nothing wrong. After winning the title, we were excited about playing in the European Cup. In the run-up to Heysel, we were talking about wanting Liverpool to beat Juventus because we wanted to get them in the European Cup. We were imagining getting them in the final and beating them. Can you imagine how good that would have been? That was what we were looking forward to and the opportunity was denied us.'

Gray had been the catalyst for Everton's revival but his career at Goodison was about to come to a close. Kendall reacted to the disappointment of the European ban by spending £800,000 on Leicester City and England's Gary Lineker, who had been the division's joint top scorer the previous season with 24 goals for a team that only escaped relegation by two points. It signalled the end for Gray, who returned to Aston Villa for £150,000 despite petitions from Goodison fans demanding that the striker stay. Whatever the new season would bring, Everton had strengthened their squad. Across Stanley Park, Liverpool were still struggling to come to terms with the enormity of what had happened in Brussels.

*

There is a story, perhaps apocryphal, about Anfield's response to the disaster. A new stadium had been in the planning stages but the blueprints were ripped up after events in Belgium. Instead, Liverpool replaced all the 100 watt bulbs around the ground with 60 watt versions to save money. No wonder their prospects looked dim.

Ever since Bill Shankly arrived in 1959, the club's upward trajectory had seemed unstoppable. They were promoted into the top flight in 1962 and confounded the expectations of fans by winning the title twice, in 1964 and '66, with a first FA Cup final win sandwiched in between.

Things got even better in the 1970s. The floodgates opened: eight titles, an FA Cup, four League Cups and four European Cups ended up in Anfield's trophy room by 1985. Shankly's successors – Bob Paisley and Joe Fagan – had been seasoned in the club's legendary Boot Room and had decades of experience. Paisley was 55 when he took over the reins of the team, Fagan 62.

Kenny Dalglish was 34 with no coaching experience. No one could be sure whether elevating the club's greatest player into the manager's chair would work, even under the best of circumstances. Now, the young manager performed his first duty at the helm of the club: laying a wreath for the dead of Brussels during a service at Liverpool's Catholic cathedral two days after the disaster. The mood was bleak as Dalglish and Bruce Grobbelaar placed down the red and white flowers hung with ribbons in the black and white colours of Juventus. 'We were all still in shock,' Dalglish said. 'No one could have imagined something like this happening. All you could do was try and behave with respect and dignity.'

With Anfield in turmoil, the decision to appoint such a young man to lead the club looked like a huge gamble.

4

Summer of discontent

In the summer of 1985, Scousers were aware of the way in which much of the world perceived Liverpool. It was, in popular imagination, a violent place, full of feckless and angry residents who believed the world owed them a living. The reality was different.

'There was creativity, vitality,' Derek Hatton said. 'This place was energized. People were engaged with politics. People cared. You could taste the pre-revolutionary feeling. I've never seen anything like it since.'

These were the darkest days of Thatcherism. The Conservative government that was elected in 1979 under Margaret Thatcher defined itself by coarse monetarist economics but it was hardly Conservatism. It was as much a revolt against the patronage of One-Nation Toryism as it was an assault on the poor. As one of its architects, Sir James Goldsmith, said: 'Some say the acquisition of wealth is vulgar. Vulgarity is a sign of vigour.'

It was an uprising of the foreman class and those earning middle incomes. Thatcher was a greengrocer's daughter from Grantham in Lincolnshire and the perfect symbol for a political philosophy that said you were responsible for nobody except yourself. She explained it in an interview in the mid 1980s. 'We've been through a period where too many people have been given to understand that if they have a problem, it's the government's job to cope with it,' she said. '"I have a problem, I'll get a grant."

"I'm homeless, the government must house me." They're casting their problem on society. And, you know, there is no such thing as society.'

The selfish and the self-centred loved this notion. It resonated with those dedicated to the acquisition of wealth. This was the age of the Yuppie – an acronym for Young Upwardly-Mobile Professional – where conspicuous consumption was held up to be admired. Anyone with a social conscience was derided.

'It was all about doing well for yourself,' Neville Southall said. 'Stuff everyone else. They wanted you to believe nobody cares about anyone. But they do. People's generosity, people's spirit came through.'

It was a confrontational time. The spectre of the Cold War hung over Europe. Real war had cemented the Thatcher regime's rule in 1982 after Argentina invaded the Falkland Islands, a British archipelago in the South Atlantic. The ten-week conflict cost nearly a thousand lives and harnessed Britain's innate jingoism behind the Conservative government.

There were adversaries closer to home. The Troubles in Northern Ireland rumbled on throughout the 1980s, with images of the ongoing street violence beamed into homes on the TV news on a nightly basis. It was an unwinnable conflict but Thatcher's approach – at least in public – was simplistic. The combatants in the six counties were simply lawbreakers: 'A crime is a crime is a crime,' she said. The government gloried in an unbending, uncompromising image.

The most divisive conflict came on the mainland. Part of the core belief of the Conservative Party is that trade unions have too much political power and their demands for better pay and conditions skew the free market. The National Union of Mineworkers (NUM) was the strongest of the workers' organizations and the Tories were determined to crush the union. The

NUM had effectively brought down Edward Heath's government in 1974. The grudge lingered.

The most significant industrial conflict of the post-war era began in March 1984 with the closure of Cortonwood Colliery in South Yorkshire. The bitter dispute lasted a year. It split the country. The miners, so often considered the backbone of Britain's industrial power, were demonized. Thatcher made it clear that compromise was off the agenda. 'We had to fight the enemy without in the Falklands,' the Prime Minister said. 'We always have to be aware of the enemy within, which is much more difficult to fight and more dangerous to liberty.'

The battle lines were drawn. Police and pickets clashed across the coalfields. The most serious disorder came at Orgreave coking plant in June 1984. The picketing miners were enjoying the sun and having a kickabout when mounted constabulary charged. The fields around the plant resembled a Dark-Ages battlefield. Television news reversed the sequence of events when the trouble was reported, attaching undeserved blame to the striking miners. Fake news is nothing new. Arthur Scargill, the union leader, was left beaten and bloodied as police units ran wild. The *Guardian* later described the day as 'almost medieval in its choreography, it was at various stages a siege, a battle, a chase, a rout and, finally, a brutal example of legalised state violence'.

The miners' dispute became increasingly bitter. The entire apparatus of the British state was galvanized to break the cornerstone of the workers' movement.

What has any of this to do with football? More than it appears. Working-class culture was under assault on all fronts. The prevailing Tory viewpoint sneered at the men down the pitshafts, seeing them as brutish, semi-educated and violent. The terraces were populated by similar lower-class oiks, they thought. The violence at football matches was inextricably linked with the conflict on the picket lines. Good, decent, hard-working people were appalled by that sort of behaviour, so Thatcher believed.

Peter Reid saw it differently. What was happening on the terraces and the streets around the stadiums was a symptom of a wider issue. 'Football wasn't immune,' he said. 'Society was reflected in football. It gave people an outlet for anger. It was the wrong outlet but it was definitely a vehicle for frustration.

'There was a clear agenda against the miners, the unions and the working class.'

On Merseyside, football thuggery and what the Conservative government considered to be industrial sabotage converged. 'A city possessed with a particularly violent nature,' Thatcher declared after Heysel. Not only that, Liverpool had the temerity to elect a council that was at the opposite end of the political spectrum to the Prime Minister.

In the general election of May 1983, the Tories were re-elected in a landslide, increasing their majority from 44 four years earlier to 144. In Liverpool, there was a different sort of electoral avalanche. Labour won 23 of the 33 wards it contested. The party's local appeal was obvious. The Labour manifesto pledged not to cut jobs and services and committed itself to slum clearance and a housebuilding programme. The battle was on.

The council could not carry through its plans with Whitehall slashing the allowances to the regions. So Liverpool set its own budget with a £30 million deficit. Locally, the illegal act went down well with the electorate. Nationally, it was another stick to beat the city with. This seemed to be a town where even the civic leaders had a total disregard for the law.

Nine of the 51 Labour councillors were supporters of the Militant Tendency, a group with Trotskyist leanings. The enemies of the council emphasized the revolutionary beliefs of the group and suggested that the entire Liverpool Labour Party was infected by entryist subversives. The dispute was cast in wider terms: this local council was a threat to the British way of life.

There was division and rancour within the city but the council's stance inspired a significant part of the population. In March 1984, an estimated fifty thousand people took to the streets to support the local authority's stance. The same mood coursed through those who followed the city's football teams. On the trains to London for the 1984 League Cup final between Everton and Liverpool, the more politically motivated fans went down the carriages handing out 'I support Liverpool City Council' stickers in red and blue. They were well received. The concourse at Euston station rang with choruses of 'Derek Hatton, we'll support you evermore' and coins poured into the fundraising buckets of striking miners. At last, Merseyside felt like it was fighting back.

Reid took pride in being part of a team that was the focus for such civic identity and resistance. 'I was definitely conscious of that,' he said. 'We were flagbearers for the city. Football kept people going.'

Many players were middle earners and instinctively voted Tory. Reid was very different. He understood Merseyside's twin obsessions. 'I'm from Huyton,' he said. 'We'd see Harold Wilson walking round. Politics was important to people; so was football.'

Hatton tells a story that explains the link between the teams, politics and the city's pride. 'In the run-up to the League Cup final in March '84, it seemed like everything was on the brink,' he said. 'The battles over the budget were becoming more intense. Whitehall was threatening to get rid of the council and send in a commissioner to run the city and the media were screaming for our blood. And then we had a real crisis. Football.'

The local authority had plans for a parade after the League Cup final. The original idea was that the order of the procession would be decided on merit. 'We thought the winners would take the lead bus and the losers follow on,' Hatton said. 'Then Howard Kendall said to me, "If you think we're going behind those red bastards if we lose, you can fuck off!" He wasn't giving an inch.

'So now we had to convince the Liverpool supporters on the council to use their influence at Anfield to stop this blowing up into a serious diplomatic incident. In the middle of the budget battle, with all this massive economic turmoil, the most important item on the agenda was football. You wouldn't want to underestimate the power of the game.'

Kendall wasn't the only one irritated by 'red bastards'. The government would have loved to crush Liverpool's political leaders.

Thatcher was not prepared to fight on two fronts, though. A month after the League Cup final, Patrick Jenkin, the environment minister, backed down. Extra money would be released for Liverpool. The crisis had been postponed.

Jenkin was hoping the post-agreement publicity would centre on the compromise, with both sides taking a low-key approach. He didn't figure on Hatton. The deputy leader emerged from the meeting in a euphoric mood. On the steps outside the ministry, he beamed for the press and said, 'Victory!'

'It was probably not the greatest strategic move,' he concedes. The bad feeling between the antagonists was intensified. Teddy Taylor, a right-wing Tory MP, told Hatton: 'Don't get too cocky. Scargill [the miners' leader] is our priority. But we'll come back for you later.'

When the Tories came, there would be little support from outside the city. Hatton, in particular, had become a hate figure to those who backed the government. 'The city council were seen as troublemakers,' Southall said. 'Hatton was seen as a typical Scouser because he was so loud. He believed what he was saying.

'The city was fighting a lonely battle. It's happened a few times over the years; 99 per cent of the time it's been right.'

It was not long before Liverpool City Council were the last adversaries left in the political combat zone. The miners' strike finally faltered and collapsed after a year on the picket lines. In March 1985, the colliery bands led the miners back to work, beaten but unbowed. Thatcherism's main offensive had been successful. Thoughts turned to Liverpool.

The assault on the council would have happened anyway but it was easier for the government to go on the offensive in the wake of Heysel. Few people outside the region had any sympathy for a city with murderous football fans and extremist politics.

5

Reaching out

There is a modern school of thought that Merseyside somehow ignored Heysel and avoided the responsibility for the horror of Brussels. It is not true.

Within the city, a deep shame was mixed with a sense of bewilderment. Liverpool club officials had alerted UEFA that the stadium was unsafe and the segregation inadequate. When this was pointed out in the aftermath of the disaster, those who would see the city in the worst light assumed it was Scousers trying to wriggle out of responsibility. Even attempts to reach out to Turin were wilfully misinterpreted by those who were eager to score political points.

Hatton proposed a plan to twin the cities as an act of friendship. Trevor Jones, the head of the Liberal bloc on the council, sneered that this was 'insensitive'.

A delegation comprising Liverpool's senior clergymen – Bishop David Sheppard from the Church of England and his Catholic counterpart Archbishop Derek Warlock – and civic leaders went to the Italian city. The response to their trip was vindictive.

'The conciliatory visit by representatives of Liverpool to Turin a week ago was, by all accounts, shamefully inept and lacking in humility,' wrote David Miller in *The Times*. 'Derek Hatton, deputy leader of Liverpool City Council, made it a blatantly party political platform, devoid of sincere remorse, and David

Sheppard, the Anglican Bishop, who should know better, was a quiescent supporter.'

Hatton is still aghast at the suggestion. 'As soon as I saw that people from the city were one of the causes, I knew we had to go to Turin on a peace mission,' he said. 'How could we ignore them? If we had not gone, it would have looked like we didn't care. We did care.'

Unlike in Britain, the delegation was appreciated in Italy. 'We went to Turin and they made us really welcome,' Hatton said. 'In the cathedral, there was a big service and the families of the people who died were there. They were so lovely to us. It was humbling.'

The politician could not help but feel it would have been a different reaction if the tragedy had been reversed. 'I remember thinking, "Could you imagine if it had been the other way around?" It would have been much angrier in Liverpool, I'm sure. People would have been bricking the coach we were in. We were treated very well and the dignity of the Italians was impressive. It was very moving.'

It did not matter that Hatton and the bishops had actually tried to repair relations, they were still vilified. 'That made it all the more infuriating when opposition politicians accused us of "playing politics" with the situation,' Hatton said. 'It was just a natural human reaction. We had to go to show our sorrow and support.'

The clergymen's statement reflects Hatton's viewpoint. 'There has been a dignity about the way which Liverpool as a whole has felt responsibility for this tragedy,' it said. 'We are prepared to accept whatever blame is ours.'

Whether that was true across the city is something Hatton questions. 'I don't think the people of Merseyside accepted full responsibility,' he said. 'Given all that had gone on, the way the city was viewed by outsiders and the continued assaults from the press for the most trivial of reasons, they were used to having criticism thrown at them.

'There was a sense, "This is just another brick they're throwing at us, just duck and get on with it."'

Miller's article underlines what was happening. It contains the telling phrase 'by all accounts' that should undermine the entire point of the piece. The vast majority of discourse surrounding Merseyside and its problems was irrational and politically charged. It placed the city's advocates on the defensive almost immediately. There was real anger across the region, though.

Two 18-year-olds, Terry Wilson and Steve McDonald, gave an ill-advised interview to *The People* newspaper in which they were quoted as claiming to have led the charge on Heysel's terraces. They suggested their role in the violence would make them heroes to the Kop. Less than 12 hours after the newspaper hit the streets, the pair were in police custody – for their own protection. Furious crowds gathered outside their houses. Once released, Wilson went into hiding. Their parents claimed the boys had been manipulated by the tabloid and threatened to sue.

There were plenty of photographs of the real instigators and a police hotline was available for anonymous whistle-blowers. Within weeks, 27 men were arrested and all but one charged.

There were other attempts to build bridges in the summer of 1985. Peter Hooton, a youth worker in Cantril Farm when he wasn't fronting The Farm or producing *The End*, organized a visit of Juventus fans to Liverpool.

Ironically, the contact between youngsters from the two cities had been planned months before Heysel. 'Where I worked in Cantril Farm there was mass unemployment,' Hooton said. 'The only people in work were on government schemes. There was lots of apathy and no hope.

'We started running youth exchange trips to give the

youngsters some focus. It was called the Liverpool 28 Improvements Committee. It had no political affiliation. It was just about getting young people involved in fundraising and activities to give them a sense of purpose. The year before, we sent a group to Spain.'

After the events in Brussels, it became clear that taking young Scousers to Italy was out of the question. 'We'd planned to go to Turin about six to nine months before we got Juventus in the final. After Heysel, we decided we couldn't do the exchange.'

'Instead, we wanted to invite the Juve supporters' club. A mate of ours from Turin, Mauro Garino, was involved. Kevin Sampson [the novelist who was then managing The Farm] had met him on his travels and we'd become friendly. We were with Mauro in Brussels.'

There were hurdles. 'Mauro had to get the backing of the Ultras,' Hooton explains. 'They had a meeting and the head of the Ultras decided to come to Liverpool. We thought, "Better do something good, then."'

'There was a reception at the town hall, we went to Anfield and they had a picture taken on the Kop, and then we had a meal at Goodison. The highlight was the *Royal Iris*.'

This was a ferry that was licensed for entertainment purposes. It was equipped with a stage and a dancefloor. On a warm August night, the delegation from Turin were treated to a cruise on the Mersey featuring local bands, a poet, a comedian and the Radio One DJ John Peel. The money raised went to the Heysel disaster fund. The show was newsworthy enough for a camera crew from ITV to be present.

The young Torinesi were given an insight into the manic hedonism that existed on Merseyside. Anyone thinking a musical cruise would be sedate had an eye-opening experience. The evening of Thursday, 1 August became one of the most memorable nights of the year. More than five hundred people crammed on to the decks of the *Royal Iris* and the night of madness that ensued became part of local legend.

James Brown, the man who would later go on to create the 1990s lads' mag *Loaded*, was astounded and slightly scared by what he saw. He found that the audience were more akin to a football crowd than the type of people he would expect at a pop concert. 'When you went to gigs in Leeds, the audience was mixed: goths, punks, casuals,' he said. 'The boat was just full of casuals. The place was full of guys in tennis shirts and trainers. Everyone had flick heads and bowl cuts.'

Brown stood out and that made him nervous. 'I'd been on the *Oxford Road Show* and got a Joe Strummer Mohican to go on TV,' he said. 'I was wearing a mohair jumper and combat trousers. I looked like a Clash wannabe.'

It was a look that would not have gone down well with the sort of football fans Brown was more familiar with. 'In Leeds, they were all National Front,' he said. 'The Service Crew sold *Bulldog*, the NF paper. They were all right wing. It was different in Liverpool. I was relieved about that.'

Even so, once the *Royal Iris* cast off, Brown had a small moment of panic. 'I remember thinking as the ship left shore, "I can't leave!"'

Some people nearly missed the boat. Literally. The review in the *Liverpool Echo* told the story. 'The Farm's trombone player, Tony Evans, missed the boat first time round . . . If the Granada people hadn't requested a re-dock at 9 p.m. to get their film footage to *News at Ten*, the arrangements could have been all at sea.' It was the last time I ever said, 'They can't very well start without me.'

Once the show got under way, the real craziness began. Groundpig always guaranteed a good time. They were unlike any other band of the period.

The area's music scene was vibrant and inventive, and groups like Echo & the Bunnymen, Wah, The Farm and numerous others played to rowdy packed houses. The soundtrack to the period was not created by any of these original bands, though, but by Groundpig.

They were unlikely local heroes. They could not have been more idiosyncratic. John O'Connell, the main singer, looked normal enough and had a voice that was so flexible it could lend itself to any style. He could have been a front man for many of the bands in the city. Graham Evans, the other main stage presence, was different. He looked as if he had wandered on stage from a Norman Wisdom sketch. Evans wore a flat cap, a moustache and was the most unlikely pop star of the Scally era. He was a former welder at Cammell Laird's shipyard and, along with his bravura banjo and violin playing, brought a humour to the stage which enhanced the Groundpig experience.

They played a set of other people's songs. During their residency at the Bier Keller, they attracted crowds of nearly a thousand people.

If you closed your eyes, Simon and Garfunkel could have been in the room singing 'The Sound Of Silence' in close, emotional harmony. Groundpig might follow that deeply moving per-formance with the theme from *The Beverly Hillbillies*. Next would be a rousing version of Peter Gabriel's 'Solsbury Hill'. It was unpredictable and the effect was inexplicable. Young girls clambered on to Bier Keller tables and danced Hillbilly jigs while O'Connell and Evans performed a frantically competitive ver-sion of 'Duelling Banjos' on the stage. The mad, frantic energy, the insane vivacity and the sheer exuberance of these gigs were a counterpoint to the bleakness of the economic situation in the region.

Groundpig became the house band of the burgeoning Scally culture. They found their audience in young, match-going fans and transmitted through their music the same feverish excitement found on the terraces. Every gig turned into a massive singalong. People were dancing on the tables on the *Royal Iris*, a dangerous game while afloat, even on the calmest of seas.

Jegsy Dodd, a robust poet, did a set for the appreciative crowd but the night exploded when Ted Chippington appeared on the low stage. Chippington's surreal, deadpan style initially aggravated the crowd, as did his attempts to subvert traditional humour (sample joke: Knock, knock; who's there? Reg Gomez; Reg Gomez who? Stan's brother, you know Stan Gomez . . .).

The reaction was hostile. 'Ted Chippington looked as out of place as me,' Brown said. 'He was dressed like a rockabilly. All the crowd were heckling him, shouting, "Fuck off, Ted."

'He was giving as good as he got. He said, "Where do you want me to fuck off to? We're on a boat."'

It didn't calm the audience. They chanted, football-style: 'Who the fucking hell are you?' for almost five minutes, with Chippington supplying an answer every time they drew breath ('I've told you four times now, Ted Chippington; is the mike not working?'). Brown thought it was great. 'All these wild casuals three feet away from him throwing ale and abuse and he fronted them. And suddenly, the crowd got him and started laughing instead of abusing. He had them eating out of his hand.'

The mood swung and the night became wilder in the best sense. The Italians were treated to voluminous amounts of beer and were dancing alongside their hosts.

The Farm closed the night. The *Echo* described them as 'bringing with them their current street credibility. That includes suede shoes, cords, fairly naff shirts and pullovers. A sort of Scally wardrobe by courtesy of the Burton's catalogue . . . by now it wasn't just stand on the tables time. They were bouncing up and down on the deck.' At least the *Echo* had a slightly better grip on the way Scousers dressed than the *Sunday Times* after Heysel.

'There was another look going on, too,' Brown said, endorsing the *Echo*'s view of the band's fashion sense. 'Some of the lads were wearing tweed and corduroy jackets. Imagine a geography teacher meets Sherlock Holmes and goes to the match.'

The Italians were seeing a different side of Scouse drunken behaviour and were enjoying it. 'They couldn't believe the scenes on the boat,' Hooton said. 'It was a brilliant night.'

'We had a song called "No Man's Land" about the First World War. Basically, it was about how in different situations people on opposing sides would be friends. That's what the trip was about.'

There were no recriminations or finger-pointing on this visit. It ended with embraces and tearful goodbyes.

'They were emotional,' Hooton said. 'They were physically moved by it all. They didn't blame us. There were myriad reasons for the disaster.'

Such attempts at reconciliation received barely any coverage outside Merseyside. There was an easier narrative. In that summer, almost every public event was framed against the background of Heysel.

Little more than a fortnight before the fundraiser on the *Royal Iris*, there was another musical charity appeal – on a much larger scale – that took place at Wembley Stadium, 'the home of football'. Live Aid was inspired by the dreadful television pictures of the famine in Ethiopia in 1984. Bob Geldof, the singer with the Boomtown Rats, organized a charity single, 'Do They Know It's Christmas', for the festive season and followed it up with overlapping concerts in London and Philadelphia. Rock 'n' roll's great and good turned out for the cause and it became one of the most memorable events of the decade. *The Times* chose to interpret its significance not in terms of the effect in starving Africa or the urge of the British people to be compassionate even at the peak of 'no society' Thatcherism. The paper saw Live Aid through the prism of Brussels.

'Although its ostensible purpose was to bring balm to a far-off people, at times the Wembley leg of Saturday's extraordinary Live Aid concert felt like the healing of our own nation,' Richard Williams wrote. 'After the weeks of troubled self-examination that followed the tragedy in the Heysel Stadium in Brussels, here the British seemed to be proving that their young people could gather peacefully in great numbers, drawn as much by a "good cause" as by the chance to worship the gods of popular entertainment.'

Few had any faith that football supporters could behave when brought together in significant numbers. Or Scousers.

6

The trouble with football

The climate of fear surrounding football was established a long time before Heysel. Violent disorder had flared up around matches for as long as the sport had been played. The game had always been a working-class pursuit. When young men from this background were placed in confrontational situations – often with alcohol as a combustible catalyst – there was potential for trouble.

Mass away travel began in the 1950s as Britain experienced a post-war boom. Harold Macmillan declared, 'Most of our people have never had it so good.' The perk of the prosperity hailed by the Conservative Prime Minister was that there was more disposable income to spend on leisure pursuits like football.

Everton and Liverpool were at the forefront of the new age and their away fans soon earned the nickname of 'Mersey Maniacs' for their behaviour. The newly invented 'football excursion trains' were often the focus for disorder, and train-wrecking became a regular feature of British life. The 'football specials' – often dilapidated rolling stock with minimal facilities – were frequently vandalized.

As early as 1956, Everton fans made the pages of *The Times* after a Saturday match away to Manchester City. 'Nearly every train coming into Liverpool after 8.15 [p.m.] had some damage. It will take several weeks to repair the coaches,' an official was quoted as saying. The last train from Manchester arrived at 11.20 p.m., according to the article. The game kicked off at 3 p.m., would have been over around 4.40 p.m. and the journey between the two cities could hardly have taken longer than an hour, even in the 1950s. The suspicion is simple: the later the train, the more drink its passengers would have taken.

There were also early indications that Scouse travelling supporters were less interested in violence than theft. 'Shopkeepers lock up when Everton are in town,' said a report in November 1964.

Increased television coverage brought disorder inside grounds into the public consciousness. One of the most significant moments in the history of football hooliganism occurred in May 1967 and did not involve the Merseyside teams.

Manchester United were chasing the title when they went to Upton Park to play West Ham United. Mancunians, who were rapidly developing a reputation for being disruptive at matches, arrived in massive numbers to see their team win the championship, and the police lost control. There was fighting all over the terraces. United had the upper hand on and off the pitch.

Four months later, West Ham hosted the champions early in the new season. This time, the East Enders approached their meeting with the Mancunians with a less hospitable attitude. Hooliganism in its modern form was born within the sound of Bow Bells. Another brutal afternoon on the terraces at the Boleyn Ground heralded the age of segregation in British football stadiums.

The 1970s were a period when Manchester United's fans became the most notorious in the country. They arrived at away games in huge numbers and anarchy ensued. This was particularly true of the season the club spent in the second division. In 1974–75, United's Red Army terrorized small-town England. Vivid television coverage of their antics and hysterical newspaper reporting turned football violence into a source of modern moral panic.

Back at West Ham, something else was happening. In the wake of the 1967 incidents, the disparate East End gangs had developed a degree of cooperation against outsiders on match days. Their reputation for toughness increased during the skinhead era. As the 1970s ended, a new phenomenon began.

Groups of supporters started going to away games on the normal scheduled trains rather than the 'football specials'. They were able to afford it because of a marketing campaign by Unilever, the Anglo-Dutch conglomerate. The company entered into a deal with British Rail to allow them to offer two-for-one prices on rail tickets as part of a promotion. Advertisements centred on Persil washing powder asked, 'Did you know Persil are giving away millions of free train tickets to help you the next time you want to take a break or visit a friend?' Customers could post three tokens taken from the packaging of a host of Unilever cleaning products to the company and receive a voucher in return. When a passenger purchased a train journey and presented the voucher, they were given two tickets for the price of one.

Special trains, put on for football fans, were cheap but comprised the oldest and nastiest rolling stock. They were slower than scheduled services and closely policed.

Travelling as a normal passenger was more expensive and unaffordable for many of the young, wilder supporters who were in thrall to hooliganism. Persil vouchers halved the price for a pair of troublemakers. Across the country, tough young delinquents began to take an interest in their mothers' laundry habits.

Taking the timetabled trains rather than the excursions put on for football had another advantage. It allowed potential mischief-makers to make an earlier start to away games and arrive at their destination before the police had a chance to seal off the station and arrange an escort to the ground. Hooligan gangs prided themselves on being able to operate under the radar of the authorities. They would turn up four or five hours before kick-off, slip out of the station into town and enjoy some pre-match 'entertainment'.

The idea of Manchester United fans being the 'Red Army' was a generic term, referring to the travelling fans as a whole. The West Ham boys who took the service trains – and similar groups across the country – saw themselves as distinct from the main body of their away support. They were the elite.

The hysterical tabloid coverage of hooliganism brought a perverse glamour to fans who liked a ruck or two. The East Enders recognized that and played up to the image. They christened themselves the Inter City Firm (ICF) and printed calling cards to leave with their victims that read 'Congratulations, you've just met the ICF'.

The media lapped it up. The myth of 'organized' hooliganism was up and running.

Unlike the Red Army, the ICF and their ilk did not wear club colours. The age of the scarf-wearing bovver boy was over. The new delinquents dressed smartly and initially could have been mistaken for clean-living, respectable young men. Their unexpected arrival times and unremarkable clothing gave them an initial element of surprise and added to their notoriety.

Newspapers bought into the mythology. *The Times* claimed they 'hold regular meetings to plan their campaigns' and talked of 'military-style precision'. The *Sunday Express* agreed, suggesting they 'often meticulously plan the trouble and start it'. It was all nonsense. There was little planning, barely any organization beyond discussing what train they would get and the 'meetings' were generally a few pints in the pub. But the public lapped it up. The ICF embraced the publicity. The way they dressed even had a name: Casual. They would have liked to claim they invented it, but its genesis took place 200 miles north.

★

Something big was happening in 1976. In London, punk was developing. Its style of contrived shabbiness and deliberately mismatched clothing would soon become world famous. There was always an art-school, middle-class vibe to the scene and if it had its roots in the capital's lower classes, it soon left them behind. What was happening on the streets of north Liverpool took longer for the fashion magazines to recognize but has had a much more enduring effect on British fashion.

Things were changing. As much as the punks down south were tired of the long-hair-and-flares look of the 1970s, the youth in the tenements around Scotland Road were groping for a different identity. They got it largely by accident.

Adidas Samba training shoes were already the footwear of choice among Liverpool's teenagers. They are superb all-purpose trainers and were versatile in a district where games of street football were common and running from the police not unusual.

Like the East End of London, the area just north of Liverpool city centre was in flux. It was still dotted with bomb sites that had never been rebuilt after the Second World War. The slum clearances of the late 1960s and early 1970s left even more swathes of open land – the demolished houses had not been replaced. The building of the Kingsway Tunnel under the Mersey – it opened in 1971 – exacerbated this.

Arden House, a huge, gothic Salvation Army hostel, stood close to Scotland Road and the vast expanse of wasteland adjacent to the building made it an attractive stopping-off point for long-distance lorry drivers who could park their vehicles there and sleep in an inexpensive bed. The informal car park became the birthplace of a youth fashion. Local residents referred to this lorry parking area as 'the Loadies'. They were more interested in unloading the goods, however. Break-ins were an occupational hazard for the sleeping drivers.

In the summer of 1976, one of the wagons was carrying adidas

T-shirts. An enterprising thief broke in and stole the consignment. Within days, they were circulating around the Tate & Lyle sugar factory – the district's biggest employer – and were snapped up eagerly.

Many of the young boys in the area were presented with the T-shirts, which had round necks, a trefoil on the chest and three stripes down the short sleeve. They were similar to the adidas jerseys Brugge had worn against Liverpool in the UEFA Cup final the previous spring. Everyone aged between ten and 16 in the Scotland Road area seemed to be wearing one of these shirts, even if the entire consignment appeared to come in a single colour: orange.

Hairstyles were changing, too. A much shorter cut with a side parting and ears exposed was becoming fashionable. Some have pointed to the influence of David Bowie's *Low* on the haircuts of the era but the album was not released until 1977 and the real reason for the trend may be more prosaic.

In the summer of 1976, ITV's counter-programming to the Montreal Olympics was the American mini-series *Rich Man, Poor Man*. The haircuts of the main characters – especially the pugilist Tom Jordache played by Nick Nolte – sent the male adolescents of the Scotland Road area rushing to the barbers. In a district where being a hard man was most boys' ambition, everyone wanted to look like this television tough guy. At the beginning, hairstyles were based more on the stylized TV interpretation of post-war America than Bowie's Futurism, though the Thin White Duke's influence would grow over the next couple of years.

By the first months of 1977, the move from flared jeans to straight-legged trousers was under way. The new look was starting to develop at a more rapid pace. Lois and Lee Riders jeans were popular. Kickers were an alternative to Samba – my first pair were bought for £16 in the summer of 1976. Clarks Nature Trek shoes, known as 'pasties' due to a design that looked like a

Cornish pasty, were popular and suede chukka boots began to be seen around. Sheepskin jackets and snorkel parkas were the outerwear of choice for the freezing football season.

When the Scotland Roaders went to the match – either Liverpool or Everton – people from other areas began to copy the fashions.

It became known as 'Scally'. The older generation liked to call young upstarts 'scallywags'. It was a term of disdain uttered with contempt by the adults but it was soon appropriated by the new generation of young fans. It became the buzzword of the era on Merseyside. Looking 'Scal' was very desirable.

It was still driven by theft from the Loadies. In the summer of 1977, brown Fred Perry polo shirts fell off the back of a lorry. Their appearance had nothing to do with a Mod revival that was beginning to develop in the south, though the Scally style did have a similar element of dandyism.

That showed increasingly in the haircuts. The wedge – with its pageboy-style mushroom of hair on top, short sides and boun-tiful quiff – was a common sight across the city. It gave the youngsters a deceptive, almost feminine look. At away grounds, the locals stared on with mocking disbelief. It looked like these young Scousers were easy victims. The reality came as a shock to the old-school hooligans.

The fashion might have withered at this point, with punk in the ascendant and the mod revival on the horizon, if it hadn't been for Liverpool's football success.

In 1977, Bob Paisley's team won the club's first European Cup in Rome. It was a magnificent, trouble-free night and the young boys who made the trip to Italy enjoyed the experience so much that they were keen to do it again. When the team started their defence of the trophy for the new season, scores of young men were determined to follow their path across the Continent.

The big problem was money. How could the youth of a city

where unemployment was rampant and school-leavers had little chance of work afford the trip? The more brazen bunked the trains and ferries to Europe. Most headed to a company called Transalpino, who offered cheap European travel for those under 26. The company expected most of their customers to be students, so the offices were in Myrtle Parade, near the university. They suddenly experienced an upsurge of business from young Liverpool fans who were looking for a different sort of education.

Persil vouchers and Transalpino would only get you so far, though. Trips abroad needed spending money, which many of the youthful tourists did not have. The answer was simple. The expeditions needed to be self-financing.

Once on the Continent, some of the travellers shoplifted. The wide and colourful range of adidas training shoes had obvious resale value. There were no Fred Perry tennis shirts but Lacoste polos were similar enough. When the crocodile-logoed shirts got back to Liverpool, they sold rapidly.

Later, talented forgers would take Transalpino inter-rail tickets and change them from the cheapest priced category to the more expensive versions, allowing longer and wider travel without the danger of being thrown off the train. The destinations – and the clothes these boys brought back – became ever more exotic. Bold, vibrant colours were in demand.

The movement could not stay underground for long. Robert Wade Smith, an enterprising controller of adidas's concessions in Top Man stores in the UK, spotted that a revolution was under way. In 1979, he watched the sales of the Stan Smith tennis shoe go from six pairs a week to more than 20. Liverpool's Top Man sold more than twenty thousand ST2 kagoules between 1979 and 1981. The city loved the adidas brand and Wade Smith grabbed his opportunity.

The shoe company believed it was a short-term fad and would

pass quickly but Wade Smith talked his bosses into importing 500 pairs of the Wimbledon tennis shoe. These were top-of-the-range footwear and priced accordingly at £29.99 (more than £130 in today's terms), a third more expensive than the Stan Smith series. They flew off the racks.

Wade Smith upped the ante. The new trend demanded rarer and more exclusive trainers. Adidas had imported 500 pairs of the gold-striped Forest Hills shoe. Their prohibitive price tag, £39.99, meant they sat in a warehouse for a year. Once Wade Smith got his hands on them, they sold out in three months. The 21-year-old realized it was time to open his own business.

He rented a store on Slater Street in Liverpool city centre but found that many of his potential customers were wearing more exotic training shoes than were on offer in the shop. When he asked where they had acquired their footwear, they invariably said Brussels. Wade Smith shut the store and set off for the Belgian capital.

It was an unsuccessful trip. He was unable to find the sort of styles he was looking for. The turning point came at Ostend, where the putative retail king bumped into a group of Scallies with their Head bags brimming with stolen goods. After a bargaining session, Wade Smith bought 25 pairs of shoes, mainly the popular and colourful Trimm Trab. He also learnt where the best place to find rare specimens was actually located.

Back in Liverpool he sold 23 of the 25 pairs in a single morning, hired a van, collected a wad of Deutsche Marks and headed for Aachen. Once there, he bought 475 pairs of shoes from the main adidas dealer in the German city. They sold like wildfire and the trip to West Germany became a regular run. Trimm Trabs became so popular that 'trab' is still used as a generic term for any training shoe around Merseyside.

Sportswear had already become streetwear but retailers like Wade Smith pushed the fashions further. Fila, Ellesse and Kappa clothing became popular, often in vivid primary colours. Match-going youths were the spearhead of the fashion. It took quite a while for the public to associate the style with hooliganism.

At away games, legions of young Scals would be subjected to abuse from the denim-wearing seventies Neanderthals that still dominated football crowds. Even the ICF held on to their post-skinhead flying jackets too long. Scousers were setting the agenda on the terraces and on the streets. The London-based media would not discover the new movement until well into 1983, when Kevin Sampson wrote about the groundswell of style for *The Face*.

Punk, for all its sound and fury, has become an historical sideshow. The anonymous thief who forced the lock on a truck outside Arden House in 1976 was opening the door on a youth culture that still defines streetwear in Britain and across the world.

7

No vision

The prurient obsession with football violence was huge across the country. Interest in the actual game was at an all-time low. No wonder. The two months before Heysel were particularly gruesome. In March, on a fraught night at Kenilworth Road, Millwall fans invaded the pitch during an FA Cup tie against Luton Town and chased away the police. The game turned into a full-scale riot.

A month later, at Goodison Park in the semi-final of the FA Cup, Liverpool and Manchester United supporters fought in every section of the stadium. Magnesium flares were fired at close range into opposition crowds, golf balls hammered through with six-inch nails were hurled across divides and Stanley knives were the weapons of choice on an afternoon where it was clear this was not just hooligan gangs clashing. Large sections of supporters on both sides were involved in the violence. All bets were off and no one was safe. There were no 'civilians'. Those who were there still speak of the day with awe. The ferocity of the fighting in and around Goodison was shocking. It was surprising that there were no fatalities.

Deaths came on the final day of the season. Leeds United and Birmingham City fans fought at St Andrew's and a wall collapsed amid the madness. Ian Hambridge, a 15-year-old, was killed. It was a horrible precursor of what was to come at Heysel. The death in Birmingham was overshadowed by events in Bradford, though, even if the shocking news from Yorkshire had nothing to do with hooliganism.

Bradford City were enjoying the end of a successful season when they hosted Lincoln City at Valley Parade. The home team and fans celebrated receiving the third division trophy before the game and the match was meandering towards half-time when the first wisps of flame were spotted in the main stand. Four minutes later, the entire structure was ablaze. Supporters ran for their lives. Those who headed for the pitch made the right choice; those who went back into the stands towards the exits were doomed. The gates were locked.

Fifty-four Bradford fans were killed and two Lincoln supporters died, bringing the death toll to 56. More than two hundred and fifty people were injured in a stand that had already been condemned and was due to be demolished. It looked like football had hit its lowest point. That notion would last a mere 18 days until Heysel.

How could the sport rebound from this series of events? Attendances had been declining rapidly for a decade. The Thatcherite middle classes saw the game as beneath them and new, glamorous, family-friendly activities like American football were attempting to make inroads into Britain's sporting culture. There were plans in place to play gridiron at Wembley in 1986 and a sell-out and widespread TV coverage was guaranteed.

And here, at the lowest point in its history, football decided to pick a fight with television. The clubs blamed the decline at the turnstiles on the cameras. Instead of addressing the dangerous, decrepit, uncomfortable stadiums and countering the threat of hooliganism, those running the sport fell back on their traditional prejudices.

There had been a two-year experiment with live league matches shown on Friday nights and Sunday afternoons and it was felt that screening entire games encouraged the public to watch from the sofa instead of the terraces. Football League chairmen wanted to cut back on 90-minute programming and increase the highlights packages. The broadcasters did not agree.

The offer on the table from the BBC and ITV was £19 million over four seasons to show 14 league games and two League Cup semi-finals as well as recorded highlights. The clubs offered ten live games. 'Recorded football is a dead duck as far as the viewer is concerned,' John Bromley, the TV negotiator, said. Graham Kelly, the secretary of the Football League, articulated the clubs' position. 'The more live games there are the less likely people are to go through the turnstiles of their local club,' he said. The new season would start with a total TV blackout.

There were plenty of people who were happy to see the game kept off the screen. 'It is television which has largely fanned the fire of self-indulgence, a self-indulgence epitomized by players who can spend £800 on a fashionable pair of leather trousers,' David Miller wrote in *The Times* as the row began to develop.

The game was committing suicide and even those who were supposed to be its biggest advocates were intent on helping it end its own existence. Football journalists, chairmen and the game's administrators were all complicit.

Even the players felt conflicted. They loved their jobs but some sections of 'polite society' regarded the profession with the same scorn as they did the fans on the terraces. 'It was a time when it wasn't cool to say you were a footballer,' Mark Bright said. The striker was in his early twenties and playing for Leicester City in 1985. People looked askance when he admitted his profession. 'You didn't say you were a footballer when you went on a night out,' he said. 'You could get away with it because there was no wall-to-wall TV and people didn't recognize you. You could say you were an accountant and get away with it. Being a footballer put a lot of people off.'

It was a problem fewer players were experiencing. In the weeks after Heysel, teams were cutting staff loose in anticipation of declining revenues. The Professional Footballers' Association, the players' union, said that 250 of its members were without a club. It was the highest number of unemployed footballers since the Second World War. The dole queues were getting bigger across Britain and football, arguably the biggest expression of working-class culture, was not immune to Thatcherism.

The *Sunday Times*' verdict after the Bradford fire seemed to be the prevailing view. Football was 'a slum sport played in slum stadiums increasingly watched by slum people, who deter decent folk from turning up'.

The attendances in the opening weeks of the season seemed to endorse this view. The game was leaking its lifeblood: supporters.

What was it like to be a young football fan in the summer of 1985? In Liverpool, it was difficult.

At 24, I was a veteran match-goer, a good example of one of the 'slum people'. In the tenements between Scotland Road and Vauxhall Road, playing and watching football was the main pastime for most young men. It was not an affectation. Everyone you knew went to the match. No one chose it. It was something everyone did.

When Liverpool and Everton reached cup finals, most families decorated their flats with red or blue. Concrete street bollards were painted to look like fans wearing hats and scarves. In 1965, when Liverpool reached Wembley, the bollards in Burlington Street looked like a row of Kopites; a year later when Everton reached the cup final they had changed their allegiance, the fresh blue paint covering the faded colour of the previous year.

For people my age, hooliganism was part of the normal backdrop to the game. A sense of danger heightened the enjoyment of away travel. Trouble was not quite as pervasive as the hysterical headlines suggested. In more than a decade of following Liverpool around England and Europe, I'd experienced a handful of serious incidents. There was plenty of posturing, charges and counter-charges across streets, but very few blows were thrown or landed – even in scenes where there appeared to be a full-on riot in progress. Generally, you could avoid trouble unless you were determined to find it.

Conflict ratcheted up in 1984. Confrontation was everywhere. The entire philosophy of the government was to crush the opposition. It was easy to dismiss the link between social disorder and poverty but Britain had been growing more spiteful as the divide between north and south and rich and poor grew wider.

On Merseyside, we felt close to the bottom of the pile.

No one knew at this stage that the British government had discussed the 'managed decline' of the city at Cabinet level but you did not need access to the corridors of power to feel the resentment towards Scousers. It even permeated pop culture. The Bangles, an American group, had a minor hit with a record called 'Going Down To Liverpool'. The song had been written by a band from Cambridgeshire, Katrina and the Waves. Its lyrics could have been conceived anywhere in the affluent south of England. The simplistic and crude words talked about going to the city 'with a UB40 in your hand . . . to do nothing'. The UB40 was the form used when signing on to receive a social security payment. The feckless, workshy image of Scousers was deeply ingrained in the popular imagination. In December 1985, the BBC started filming a sitcom set in the Dingle, an area on the banks of the Mersey. The basic premise of *Bread* concerned a Catholic family with no visible means of support and a loose attitude towards the law. They lived hand to mouth but managed to accrue cars and even cordless phones despite being on the dole. It became massively popular – at one point attracting 26 million viewers. Its writer, Carla Lane, rejected accusations that it stereotyped Scousers, because she was from the city. It helped present an image much at odds with reality. Being poor was no fun.

The Conservative Party's attitude to unemployment was simple. Norman Tebbit, the Secretary of State for Trade and Industry, thought the answer was easy. 'I grew up in the thirties with an unemployed father,' he said. 'He didn't riot. He got on his bike and looked for work. He kept looking until he found it.' It is a trait of the very worst politicians that they cannot imagine an experience other than their own and then apply their principles to other people. Middlesex, where Tebbit grew up, is in close proximity to London. The job market in the capital and the Home Counties has never plumbed the depths that Merseyside did in the 1980s.

Plenty of people 'got on their bikes' and left Liverpool looking for employment. That brought Scousers into contact with wider English society. Yet the biggest interaction most young residents of the city had with other places was through football. From late summer to spring, thousands travelled up and down the country to watch Liverpool and Everton. A faintly hostile, suspicious view of Scousers was common.

Trying to spend a £20 note was an adventure. Publicans would not take them from people like me because of a rumoured spate of forgeries. In shops, servers who greeted customers with a smile would clam up and become surly when they heard the Liverpool accent. Away fans from all regions were susceptible to this sort of treatment but a special contempt seemed to be reserved for Scousers.

After Heysel, it got worse. Those of us who were there in Brussels had a difficult cocktail of emotions. There were many Liverpool supporters who went to Belgium and behaved in a civilized and normal manner. Many of the younger, hard-core travelling support had overstepped the mark.

David Geey, a barrister who had been at the club's previous European Cup finals, was having lunch in the Grand-Place in the Belgian capital. 'You could see things turning ugly early in the afternoon,' he said. 'There was a restaurant with a glass frontage and Liverpool fans were urinating on to it with people sitting inside eating. It was horrible.' Geey, who was in the stands and had a clear view of the collapsing wall at the stadium, left Heysel before the match kicked off after realizing the gravity of the disaster.

Others did not have such a clear view. It was obvious that something very ugly had happened but when the match kicked off, many of us on the terraces behind the goal assumed that things were not too bad. Our rationale was that the game would not have been allowed to go ahead if there had been fatalities.

When Michel Platini and his Juventus teammates pranced around the running track with the trophy, pursued by hundreds of celebrating fans – many of whom had a clear view of the deadly events at our end – it confirmed the impression that the situation was not as awful as originally suspected. We'd all drunk too much and behaved like idiots, most of us thought, but no real harm was done. It was not until 6 a.m., on the boat heading back to Dover, that the gravity of what had happened became clear when BBC news reported the death toll. It came as a shock for most people on the ferry.

In the next weeks, there were a wide range of reactions. Some people gave up football and never went again. There was a strong undercurrent of shame and embarrassment.

There was no denial. Even though it was accepted that the stadium was not fit to host a match of this stature, the catalyst for tragedy had been the behaviour of Liverpool supporters. 'It was a shock to the system,' Peter Hooton said. 'I'd seen trouble like that umpteen times on the terraces.'

We all had. It had never ended in mass death, though.

'London's chief fire officer went to the stadium and said it was an absolute disgrace,' Hooton said. 'He said he would not have held an amateur game there. That wasn't what Thatcher wanted to hear. The report got buried.'

Even that did not completely explain how things got so out of hand so quickly. There were suggestions that the violence was provoked by bottles and missiles thrown from the neutral section into the Liverpool end but few of us believed that. Hooton's version of the build-up to tragedy contains the ring of truth. 'Flares were being fired from our section,' he said. 'Four or five went over in quick succession.' The Farm's singer thinks this event, more than the brawling in the neutral area, provoked the stampede. 'That's when the crowd moved back,' he said. 'When you're standing in a crowd, you can't see much of what's going on around you. Fights like the ones in Z section don't cause the sort of panic you saw there. The people in the crowd would have seen the flares firing into them.'

One of the most disappointing aspects of the day is that many of us recognized that adequate policing would have saved lives. 'I remember thinking, "How could it get to this point?"' Hooton said. 'Ten Liverpool police would have sorted it out in minutes.'

In this maelstrom of conflicting emotions, a mood of defiance grew quickly. 'If they'd stood their ground, they'd be alive' was a common refrain. However, that sort of flawed rationalization could only go so far.

Liverpool's first game after Heysel was a preseason friendly against Burnley, who were then in division four, the lowest tier of English professional football. Those of us who went to the game were expecting a hostile reception.

Instead, we were surprised at the reaction. A couple of dozen of us were sitting on the train at Preston station waiting for the connection to Burnley to depart. Passengers and staff stared at us with mute disgust. One Liverpool fan said, 'Look at the way the bastards are looking at us.' Another older and wiser character replied with a resigned note in his voice, 'They've probably never seen mass murderers before.'

We all laughed, because bravado was about all we had left. It was a horrible way to start the campaign. No one knew what to expect from the new season. For the first time ever, we weren't looking forward to it.

8

Kick-off

Everyone was apprehensive, not just in Liverpool. West Ham United warmed up for the big kick-off with a preseason friendly game against Orient, another division-four side. Heysel had ruled out exotic foreign summer adventures, so West Ham made the journey to Brisbane Road, just 20 minutes from Upton Park. John Lyall's team had flirted with relegation the previous season and another year of struggle seemed on the cards, especially after Orient beat their illustrious neighbours 3–1.

After the match, an angry West Ham fan burst into the changing room and exploded in fury. 'He went mad,' Tony Cottee, the Hammers striker said. In the *Boys of '86* by Tony McDonald and Danny Francis, Tony Gale quotes the outburst in detail. 'What the fucking hell's going on here?' the defender remembers the fan saying. 'We're going right down the pan, you bunch of tossers. We had a shit season last year and now we've lost to fucking Orient. Where do we go from here?'

Cottee laughs when the rant is read back. 'That'd be about right.'

The mood was already glum for the 20-year-old. 'It was a bad year, 1985,' the striker said. 'Not just Heysel but the Bradford fire and Millwall rioting. It was so depressing. I'm a football fan, so it was upsetting. As a player, you knew it could cost you the chance of playing in Europe.'

It was six days before the season began. West Ham were a shambles.

'Against Orient, we weren't very good,' Cottee said. 'It was not a positive way to go into the new season.'

There were few positives for West Ham. Their goal was scored by a new face of whom few on the Upton Park terraces knew much about. Little was expected of this £340,000 signing from St Mirren with a vivid blond mullet. Frank McAvennie's arrival had gone largely unnoticed and he would remain under the radar for some time to come.

Few people were excited about the new season. For the fans, there was a severe clampdown on alcohol in stadiums and on transport to grounds.

Under the 1985 Sporting Events (Control of Alcohol) Act, intoxicating liquids were banned inside grounds and on public transport to and from games. Coach operators were threatened with having their licence revoked if drink was found on board their vehicles.

Football, of course, was the only sporting event that the act applied to. Even today it is a crime to drink beer in view of the pitch while a match is being played. At rugby and cricket, fans have always supped away happily in the stands while watching the action.

Of course, even in 1985 there was a two-tier system at football. If you mixed in the correct circles, you could still get a drink in the stadium. Clubs were allowed to sell alcohol for two hours before and an hour after games in their executive lounges.

Over their gin and tonics in the boardroom, many of the club chairmen and owners eagerly embraced the Thatcherite view of football fans. David Evans, the Luton Town chairman and soon to be Conservative MP for Welwyn Hatfield, banned away fans from Kenilworth Road. There was little outrage. The rioting by Millwall fans on the pitch at Luton was still fresh in the public consciousness.

Evans's heroine in Downing Street was planning a wider application of the policy and began working towards a compulsory ID card scheme that would be enforced on the 92 Football League clubs. Reading agreed to run a trial of the system at Elm Park while government strategists looked into the feasibility of introducing such a draconian measure.

The season kicked off with the Charity Shield. Everton, the champions, played Manchester United, the FA Cup winners, in a repeat of May's cup final. It was a subdued affair that the Merseyside team won 2–0. There was much more interest in Liverpool's start to the league season the following week.

There was a nervous mood across the entire Football League. In the previous five years, only 36 of the 92 clubs had turned a profit. The changes in stadium safety demanded by the Popplewell Inquiry into the Bradford fire were expensive and there was a real possibility of many of England's historic clubs going under. All the omens were bad.

The *Sunday Times* conducted a Mori poll with a sample of more than two thousand people. A quarter said they stayed away from matches because of fears of hooliganism; 28 per cent said they would rather watch on TV, appearing to back up the FA's conviction that television would kill the sport. Two-thirds of those polled said the players were overpaid – nothing changes – and 84 per cent said they never went to the match.

Interestingly, 15 per cent said admission prices were too expensive – at Old Trafford, watching Manchester United cost £2.60 on the terraces and £4.80 for a seat – and only 5 per cent complained about poor facilities.

People may not have wanted to watch football, but they were keen to see how Anfield would handle Liverpool's first competitive game since Heysel. The match against Arsenal would also be Kenny Dalglish's first meaningful outing as manager. The 34-year-old not only had the challenge of taking charge of England's most successful team but also had to rebuild the reputation of a club under the glare of worldwide publicity.

Dalglish arrived at Anfield in the summer of 1977. He replaced Kevin Keegan, who had delivered Liverpool their first European Cup the previous May. Keegan was a Kop hero and had been the dominant force in a team that had begun to show signs of being the best side on the Continent. The Englishman played the pivotal role in Liverpool's 3–1 victory over Borussia Mönchengladbach in Rome that made the team European champions. He appeared irreplaceable.

When Keegan signed for Hamburg SV for £500,000 in 1977, the sceptics thought Anfield's momentum would stall. Instead, Bob Paisley, the Liverpool manager, took the money to Scotland to purchase Dalglish's services.

The Scot had trained at Melwood as a 15-year-old but was too young for the move south. He felt homesick and returned north. Celtic were the beneficiaries and Dalglish's impact was nothing short of sensational. At 26, he was ready to try England again.

Paisley bid £400,000. Celtic demanded an extra 10 per cent. Liverpool wavered just long enough for the Scottish club to believe that they had pushed their English counterparts to the brink and then did the deal. The £440,000 transfer was agreed and Paisley whispered to Peter Robinson, the club secretary, 'We'd better get out of town before they realize what we've done!'

It was the deal of the century for Liverpool. Dalglish would become the greatest player in the club's history and heap a fair amount of misery on Everton. Howard Kendall, who would become the Scot's great sparring partner as a manager, later said he could have derailed Dalglish's signing.

Kendall was approached by Paisley, who sought his advice about Trevor Francis. The future Everton manager had played with the young Englishman at Birmingham City and Paisley was keen to hear Kendall's opinion on the striker, who was one of the alternative choices to replace Keegan.

Kendall assured the Liverpool manager that Francis would be a good choice, although he also mentioned that the Birmingham forward was prone to injury. Paisley plumped for Dalglish. Later, Kendall must have wished he had performed a harder sell on Francis's abilities. Dalglish would come to haunt Everton.

The Scot was a revelation down south. Keegan was forgotten almost instantly. Within five minutes of his league debut against Middlesbrough at Ayresome Park, Dalglish scored a beautiful, curling chipped goal from an acute angle. When he repeated the feat against Newcastle United in front of the Kop four days later, Anfield had found a new love.

Dalglish had an eye for goal but there was much more to his game than scoring. He was unselfish on the pitch and had the knack of making teammates look better.

Alongside Graeme Souness and Alan Hansen he formed a Scottish backbone that drove Liverpool to three European Cups, five league titles and four League Cups. It was a period of unparalleled success. Then, on the morning of Heysel, the news broke that Dalglish would take over from Joe Fagan as Liverpool manager. He would become the first player-manager in the club's history.

The Scot was not just a talented footballer. He had other qualities. He was born in Glasgow's East End and grew up a Rangers fan. It meant that when he signed for Celtic he crossed the religious divide. That required both mental and physical toughness in a violently sectarian environment. He developed a quick wit and a forceful style of dealing with opponents and teammates alike. The Scottish triumvirate imposed their will to win and ethics on the rest of the Liverpool squad.

'The Scots set the tone in the dressing room,' Craig Johnston said. 'They decided who and what were funny, what was acceptable, who played well, who played badly. They were like strict schoolmasters even though they were playing. They understood how you had to behave if you were a group of men who wanted to win things.'

There was no place for shirkers. 'They were warriors,' Johnston said. 'There was a bit of the *Braveheart* culture about them. They were clansmen.

'If you were tired, not contributing or slacking, they didn't want to know you. The Jocks kept everyone in line. They kept the rest of the team professional. They were savage about getting the job done in the most direct way.'

Souness left to join Sampdoria in 1984 and Dalglish became the undisputed leading voice in the dressing room, with the younger Hansen as his junior partner. Dalglish embraced the Darwinian football philosophy of Bill Shankly. He also inherited the Boot Room brains trust created by his fellow countryman Shankly. 'The Scots had a rough, working-class ethos,' Johnston said. 'Particularly Kenny. He was a winner and a leader.'

As his playing career came to an end, Dalglish became the natural replacement for Fagan. But making the leap from teammate to boss over the course of a summer was unusual, especially at Anfield.

'It was a gamble,' Jan Mølby, the midfielder, said. 'I'd never come across the concept of a player-manager in Denmark. I never imagined a club like Liverpool would do it, even though some other English clubs had one. I wondered whether it would work.'

Steve Nicol, another of the Scottish crew, had no doubts. 'No, not at all,' he said. 'The transition was seamless. He called me up and told me he'd got the job. I started laughing. He said, "What's so funny?" I said, "Nothing." Then he said, "If you've got anything to say, say it now." So I asked what I should call him. "Boss, gaffer, anything. Just don't call me Kenny."

'He was like a gaffer anyway. Everyone looked up to him.'

Not quite everyone. Phil Neal took the appointment badly. The veteran full back had applied for the position too and was miffed when he was passed over for the Scot. 'Phil struggled with it but he thought he might be in the running for the job,' Nicol said.

Even the smoothest change of regime can be difficult. 'It was hard,' Mølby said. 'He was my mate. We had to change the way we dealt with him. Even so, you'd never relate to him like you did to Joe Fagan.'

Craig Johnston agreed. 'It was a shock,' the Australian said. 'One minute he's your mate and next you've got to change your mindset. It was like, "Ke . . . I mean, Boss." Most of us got used to it pretty quickly.'

Mark Lawrenson felt the transition was more difficult for Dalglish than the players. 'It felt almost harder for him than us. Me, Jocky [Hansen] and Dizzy [Gary Gillespie] – the Southport crew – had driven into work with him every day. Then he was the boss. That was it.'

The Boot Room framework that had been so important to Shankly, Paisley and Fagan's success gave the new regime strong foundations. Ronnie Moran, the club's sergeant-major figure, remained in place, as did Roy Evans, the much-liked coach. The most important fixture around Anfield was Paisley, whose success gave him huge authority and whose football wisdom was unparalleled.

'Kenny's very astute and Liverpool were very astute at the time,' Mølby said. 'The game's about decisions and this was the right one. Bob Paisley was around and he helped. He was always there if advice was needed.'

Dalglish agrees and credits Paisley's presence as one of the crucial factors in his transition. 'Bob never told me what to do,' Dalglish said. 'But every now and again you'd see him round and about more than usual. I'd say, "Bob, you want to tell me something?" He'd mumble in that Northumbrian accent and say, "No, son, it's fine but I was just thinking . . ." and then he'd suggest something. He never made me feel he was telling me what to do but it was the best advice a young manager could get.'

Even the great Paisley could not counsel on the correct etiquette for laying wreaths after Heysel and acting diplomatically in front of a global press corps whose main interest was not football. Now, as the first game of the season loomed, Dalglish had more on his plate than a rookie manager should expect.

'It's the most pressure I've ever felt,' Lawrenson, a veteran of European Cup finals and numerous big games, said about the mood before the match against Arsenal. 'There were something like a hundred Japanese journalists there. It was massive pressure. I felt sorry for Kenny. It was the first time he'd managed the team in a league game and the scrutiny was intense.

'Kenny just had this air about him that he didn't feel it. I don't know how he did it.'

Mølby felt the same way. 'The game was on trial. We knew that we were the accused. We were very conscious of it.

'We had a low-key start with friendlies at Burnley and down south. We knew the game needed to send out the right signals. That was as important for the players as the supporters.

'Once the season starts, you get wrapped up in the day-to-day stuff and move on – it's only natural. But we knew the spotlight was right on us at the start.'

This was emphasized by the *Liverpool Echo*. 'With the eyes of Europe on Anfield, it is vital for football everywhere that this game provides a memorable afternoon's entertainment,' wrote Ian Hargreaves.

It got off to a bad start. There was a short ceremony 'of prayer and dedication' scheduled for before the match. The Order of Service was listed in the programme and the city's three religious leaders – the Catholic Archbishop Worlock, Bishop Sheppard of the Church of England and Reverend John Williamson, Moderator of the Free Churches – said brief prayers in front of the Anfield Road End. After this, the plan was to sing 'Abide With Me', the hymn associated with FA Cup finals at Wembley.

Unfortunately, the public-address system failed. The tannoys at Anfield were barely audible at the best of times but now the prayers and hymn were drowned out. The inevitable last-minute influx of supporters into the Kop, some 80 yards distant, meant that many of the latecomers were unaware that any observance was under way.

Even those with programmes found the service difficult to follow. The situation got worse when, after the first verse of 'Abide With Me', the Kop assumed the hymn was over and began singing 'You'll Never Walk Alone'.

The newspapers decided it was an act of disrespect. Even the reliable Brian Glanville, so often a lonely sane voice in defence of supporters among the press, was aghast. Liverpool, he wrote, were 'cursed with some of the most savage fans in England'.

The match that followed was much less newsworthy. The home side won 2–0 but the hangover from Heysel was a long way from dissipating.

The downbeat mood was widespread. Attendance across the Football League programme was 412,603, the lowest for 40 years. The next weekend's turnout dipped under the 400,000 mark.

West Ham opened the season away to Birmingham City. This was another match that was closely watched by the media after the death of 15-year-old Ian Hambridge following a wall collapse at St Andrew's the previous May.

West Ham's visit was clearly a flashpoint game. The ICF were Britain's premier hooligan crew – at least in PR terms – and every effort was made to ensure the game passed off peacefully.

The London club had suspended the official Irons Travel Club and started the season by refusing to sell tickets for away games. It rather missed the point of the ICF. Few in the game understood the forces that were driving disorder at and around matches.

Birmingham and the local police insisted the match kick off at 11.30 a.m., three and a half hours earlier than the usual time. Just 11,164 people turned up to watch on a warm, sunny day in the Midlands, a few hundred east Londoners among them. It was a completely unremarkable game that the hosts won 1–0. West Ham appeared to be setting out on another season of struggle.

Things started going wrong early. John Lyall's preferred strike force paired Tony Cottee with Paul Goddard, a stocky and efficient forward and the club's record signing. The duo had scored 26 league goals between them the previous season and were the established first-choice forward line.

Just before half-time, Goddard dislocated his shoulder after a robust challenge. The West Ham manager shuffled his side and pushed Frank McAvennie up from midfield to play with Cottee. The partnership did not produce on the opening day but Lyall had just stumbled on a combination that would change the course of West Ham's campaign.

McAvennie had played up front for St Mirren but he was expected to operate in the midfield at Upton Park. The Glaswegian was never shy about coming forward, though. 'I was lucky Paul Goddard got injured,' McAvennie said. 'Things weren't working up until then. It might have worked eventually but it was fortunate for me we had to change and I moved up front.'

The 25-year-old came to football late. He had dug roads, painted and decorated and worked in a garage while struggling to get by on Clydeside. Spells on the dole were not unusual. When he came to London, McAvennie embraced the lifestyle with gusto.

In his autobiography, Lyall recalled bringing the Scot from the airport after the move south was completed. 'We drove back through the centre of London,' Lyall wrote. 'He wanted to see the King's Road. I was to learn he was a fashion-conscious lad, very concerned about his appearance. I could tell he was thrilled to be in London.'

McAvennie's sense of style was hardly West End. He had dyed his red hair bleach blond and the spiky, backcombed hairdo looked like a relic from the previous decade.

'We drove through the city, where the traffic was particularly heavy,' Lyall continued. 'Passing on the opposite side of the road was a convoy of black limousines with police motorcycle escorts. Sitting in the back of one of the cars was Princess Diana. She passed within a few feet of us. Frank was impressed.'

McAvennie remembers the incident slightly differently and his version is a more accurate depiction of the new signing's attitude. Far from being awed, Frank was cocky. 'All the roads were blocked for royalty,' he recalls. 'I said, "Even the Queen's coming out to meet me." I think it was the moment that John Lyall realized he'd bought a character.'

That is an understatement. Far from being dazzled by the royal family, McAvennie wanted to make a big impression on the capital. Soon, he would be king of the East End and football's first anonymous superstar.

Perhaps the only game that had a real buzz of anticipation about it was Leicester City's home opener against Everton. The defending champions were among the best teams in Europe but one man made this a must-see match in the East Midlands city: Gary Lineker.

The striker was a local hero. He had scored 24 goals for Leicester the previous season and had become the hottest property in English football. A move to a bigger club was inevitable. The champions were the obvious destination.

The fixture computer sent Everton to Filbert Street on the opening day of the season, providing Lineker with a quick return to his boyhood club. Leicester was agog with excitement.

'It was massive,' Mark Bright said. 'The newspapers went mad. I thought, "I've got to get in the team for this one."'

Bright was 23 and had signed for the Foxes from Port Vale the previous summer. He understood his role at Leicester. 'When I signed, I asked, "Where will I play?" because Gary was the main man. They said I'd be his understudy and I'd learn a lot from him. I did. As we got towards the end of the season, it became clear that he was going to leave. I was sad to see him go. He'd been very helpful. He always looked to help me.'

Bright was suddenly starting the season as the first-choice forward. Like most people in Leicester he was pleased to see his friend return to Filbert Street. 'Gary got a great reception,' he said. 'After all he'd done for the club, he was always going to be welcomed back and he's a local boy. I thought it was inevitable that he'd score.'

The afternoon turned out to be less predictable. Lineker's league debut for Everton proved to be memorable for someone else – the understudy now recast in the starring role.

'I scored two of the best goals of my career and nobody except those in the ground saw them because of the TV blackout,' Bright said ruefully. 'I turned [Kevin] Ratcliffe and hit it with my right foot past Neville [Southall] for the first.'

On the Everton bench, Howard Kendall looked on in shock as the unknown striker powered the ball into the net. 'Adrian Heath was substitute and Howard, sitting on the bench next to him, asked, "Who the hell is that?" Inchy told him. He knew all about me from his time at Stoke when I was at Port Vale.'

The Everton manager was dismissive. 'He'll never score another one like that,' he said. Kendall spoke too soon.

'Alan Smith nodded a ball on and this time I lobbed Neville for the second,' Bright said. Leicester went on to win 3–1, leaving the prodigal son disappointed.

'At the end, Gary hugged me and said well done,' Bright said. 'I wound him up and said, "2–0 to Brighty" and he laughed. He reminded me of it at the end of the season when I was stuck on six and he'd scored a few more.'

The champions and Lineker were off to a slow start. There was talk of a 'Heysel hangover', as if the disappointment about not being able to compete for the European Cup was having a lingering effect at Goodison. Neville Southall dismisses the notion. 'Once we got into preseason, all we were thinking about was playing,' he said. 'Once you're in that bubble, you don't think about anything else. You have to be self-centred.'

Leicester was just an off day for Everton. Lineker, like McAvennie, failed to make an instant impact. Better times lay ahead for both.

9

Black September

The other main contenders for the first division title had a straightforward start. Manchester United swept past Aston Villa 4–0 in front of the biggest crowd of the day, 49,743. Ron Atkinson's side was led by Bryan Robson, the England captain. They lost the season opening Charity Shield to Everton but optimism was high at Old Trafford. There was an increasing sense that the Red Devils were ready to break the Merseyside stranglehold on the title.

The craving to win the league was huge at Old Trafford. United had not won the title since 1967.

Liverpool-born Atkinson had a swaggering confidence. Nicknamed Big Ron, the 56-year-old was the most flamboyant personality at Old Trafford. He had shot to prominence as the manager of West Bromwich Albion and was something of a groundbreaker. His West Brom side featured three black players: Brendon Batson, Laurie Cunningham and Cyrille Regis. It was rare to find a black face in the top flight in the 1970s. A trio in the same side was unprecedented. They were nicknamed 'the Three Degrees' after the American female soul singers. The media embraced the moniker despite its obvious layers of racism. Black players of the era were considered to be less tough than their white counterparts. They couldn't handle rough treatment, the popular theory went, and their manliness was frequently questioned. It was often claimed they did not like cold weather or hard work. Batson, Cunningham and Regis undermined any crank white-supremacist dogmas.

It was a breakthrough. A decade earlier, a Member of Parliament for Wolverhampton South, a handful of miles from the Hawthorns, gave an inflammatory speech to the West Midlands Conservative Association that pandered to fears of immigration. Enoch Powell's racist fantasy became known as the 'rivers of blood' speech, though those words were never spoken. Ever keen to show off his classical education, the pretentious and snobby Powell alluded to Virgil. 'Like the Roman,' he said, 'I seem to see the River Tiber foaming with much blood.'

Well, Batson, Cunningham and Regis helped break the dam. Powell feared race war but all he got, if he ever noticed, was a flood of superb black footballers.

Atkinson let the trio loose on a league unprepared for their impact and they were a revelation. Things were changing in Britain, and in the ethnically diverse West Midlands, West Brom caused a sensation. Twice in Atkinson's three seasons at the Hawthorns the Baggies finished above United. 'For a while, we were the best team in Europe,' said Atkinson, never a man to undersell the exploits of his teams. In the early days of 1979, he was not far wrong. 'We were top of the league in mid January. We'd beaten Valencia in Europe and then the big freeze happened. We didn't play for three weeks. The next game was at Anfield and we were rusty and lost 2–1. Then the fixture pile-up happened and we ran out of steam.'

West Brom played 17 times in March and April, finished third in the league and reached the quarter-finals of the UEFA Cup. The two teams above them were the European Cup holders at the beginning of the season – Liverpool – and the team who would become Continental champions at the end of the campaign, Nottingham Forest. Batson, Cunningham and Regis continued to draw most of the attention but a 22-year-old midfielder whose career had been dogged by injury was beginning to emerge as West Brom's most influential performer. Bryan Robson was beginning to make his mark.

Atkinson had the Baggies punching way above their weight. It earned the outgoing Scouser a move to Old Trafford in 1981, where he made headlines almost immediately by returning to the Hawthorns to sign Robson for £1.5 million, breaking the British transfer record in the process.

'After every game at the Hawthorns, I'd pull Robbo into the office and ask him a simple question: "Who's tapped you up this week?"' Atkinson said. 'He'd always tell me. Lots of clubs approached him. In those days, you always went to the player and got it sorted with them before going to their club.

'One time he said United had been on to him. I shot it down. "The only way you're going to Old Trafford is if I get the job there," I told him.

'On my first day as manager of United, I got a call from Robbo. He said, "You know what you told me about United?" Let me get my feet under the bloody table! But he was the first player I wanted. What a signing.'

This was now Atkinson's fifth season at United. They had won two FA Cups but the club and fans were obsessed with winning the title. Their pain was sharpened by Liverpool's domination and Everton's emergence as a power. Manchester's rivalry with Merseyside was toxic.

After losing the Charity Shield, United stormed into the season like a juggernaut. By the end of August, they were top of the league with a five-game 100 per cent record. They had scored 12 goals and conceded two and if the media and public loved any team in football it was the one from Old Trafford. 'United were all about show,' Steve Nicol said from his jaundiced viewpoint at the other end of the East Lancs Road. 'The papers were full of them. It was all, "What's going on with Big Ron this week?" Our attitude was: "Keep talking, we'll keep playing."'

Nevertheless, United's bullish start to the campaign heaped more misery on an area that was under political, economic and social pressure. Football, at least until Heysel, was Merseyside's saving grace. Manchester would have liked nothing better than to remove any straw of comfort from the sporting arena.

Life was difficult for black players. There were more of them in the league than ever before but racism was still widespread. Every touch of the ball would be greeted with jeers, and monkey noises were often directed at anyone with Afro-Caribbean heritage.

Racial slurs were common on the terraces and it was not unusual for opponents to try to unsettle black players on the pitch with bigoted jibes. There was little sympathy for those who complained about such behaviour. The best approach, most people in the game believed, was to suck up the insults and pretend that the comments were not hurtful.

Mark Bright suffered his share of abuse playing for Leicester. His manager's advice was to act as if nothing had happened. 'Gordon Milne said not to say anything to the papers, it would only make things worse,' Bright recalled. 'The only answer was to puff your chest out and score goals.'

It was bad when opposition fans made racial taunts but even more sinister when supporters turned against a player on their own team. Paul Canoville was on the receiving end of such treatment throughout his Chelsea career. While warming up to make his debut against Crystal Palace at Selhurst Park in 1981, the winger had to run the gauntlet of hate from the away fans. He described the moment in his autobiography. 'As I'm stretching and running, I hear loud individual voices through the noise: "Sit down, you black cunt!" "You fucking wog – fuck off!"

'They were all wearing blue shirts and scarves – Chelsea fans, my side's fans, faces screwed with pure hatred and anger, all directed at me . . . I felt physically sick. I was absolutely terrified.'

The National Front and the even more sinister Combat 18 had made inroads on the terraces of Stamford Bridge. Bright was aghast at the treatment Canoville received from elements in the Shed.

'There were very few black players and we all knew each other,' Bright said. 'I played against Chelsea and Paul was getting massive abuse from his own fans. I said, "How can you play here?" Paul just said, "I love this club."'

Canoville's experience was not an isolated one. After John Barnes scored a brilliant solo goal for England in the 2–0 victory over Brazil in the Maracaña in June 1984, the Watford winger was castigated by racist fans of the national team on a plane to Chile. The group had National Front insignia on their flag and, within earshot of Barnes, frequently repeated their opinion that England only won 1–0 'because a nigger's goal doesn't count'.

'No one did anything,' Barnes said. 'Never mind the FA, the press were all on that plane and could have stepped in and said something. There was nothing in the papers about what happened.'

Margaret Thatcher thought the answer to hooliganism was 'decent people' standing up to the thugs. There was no chance. On a flight loaded with officials and newspapermen, everyone turned a blind eye while the bigots made snide comments about one of England's best players. There was little will to confront racism.

'That's the way society was,' Barnes said. 'You expected to get racist abuse.'

No black footballer could expect any real support from the game's authorities, the press or the police. They were largely on their own.

Even teammates could be a problem. Howard Gayle, who started his career at Liverpool but was playing at Sunderland in 1985, detailed in his autobiography how Tommy Smith was particularly vindictive to his young black colleague at Melwood. The 'Anfield Iron' was overtly racist but snide remarks that passed as 'banter' were almost as bad. Gayle went to a Liverpool players' party where there was a stripper present. The girl dusted her breasts with talcum powder and rubbed herself against Gayle's face. Roy 'Chubby' Brown, the coarse comedian providing the entertainment, said, 'Try walking through Toxteth now.' It was the sort of quip that black players could expect. If they took offence, they were told it was only a joke and they needed to develop a sense of humour.

Dressing rooms were still uncomfortable places for black players. There were plenty of people on the pitch and on the terraces who still resented their presence.

Football is as good a barometer of the nation's psyche as anything. The Swinging Sixties made London feel like the centre of global attention and, sure enough, England obliged by winning the World Cup in 1966. As a darker, more divisive new decade dawned, Harold Wilson's Labour government were thought to be certainties to win the general election in June 1970. Four days before the voting booths opened, England were beaten 3–2 by West Germany in a World Cup quarter-final match after leading 2–0. The public's mood soured and the Conservatives won the election. Huddersfield Town-supporting Wilson believed that the defeat in Mexico contributed to his eviction from 10 Downing Street.

In the malevolent September of 1985, football reflected society's frame of mind. Not even the England team could unite the country. The BBC did not show the World Cup qualifying tie against Romania live. The match was part of a separate TV deal and the national broadcaster had the rights to screen the game. However, the BBC said that there was 'not sufficient interest'.

The Wembley crowd echoed this. Just 59,500 people turned up for the 1–1 draw that left England a point away from sealing qualification.

Bobby Robson was perhaps the only man in football who might have welcomed the Heysel ban. The England manager may have thought that the lack of European competition would leave his players fresher for the next summer's tournament that would take the World Cup back to Mexico. Colombia had originally been scheduled to host 1986 but FIFA were forced to move the finals because of political turmoil in the South American nation.

Robson was aghast when the Football League filled the weeks left vacant by the absence of European fixtures with the Super Cup and Full Members' Cup in a misguided attempt to generate more revenue. The England boss said he was 'sad and disappointed'. Disappointment was just about the only growth industry for vast swathes of the UK that autumn.

September was a dreadful month for international football. Wales faced Scotland at Ninian Park with both nations still in contention for a place in Mexico. The BBC had passed on the England game but ITV eagerly embraced this British showdown. The match was screened live – a rare treat these days for the viewing public.

The Scots needed a draw but were 1–0 down at half-time. Jock Stein, the Scotland manager, found out at the break that Jim Leighton, his goalkeeper, had lost a contact lens during the first half and had travelled to Cardiff without any replacements. With World Cup qualification on the line, there was uproar in the dressing room. It was a footballing crisis that could break the hopes of a nation.

The 62-year-old Stein was used to pressure. He had built the Celtic team that brought the European Cup to Britain for the first time in 1967. He had been feeling the strain in the run-up to the match, though. He looked pale and had little appetite, which was unusual.

With nine minutes left, Scotland were going out and Wales advancing. The Scots threw men forward. Graeme Sharp nodded the ball into the opposition penalty area and David Speedie knocked it on in a hopeful but aimless manner. David Phillips, a Welsh defender, unwisely closed the striker down with his arms in the air and the ball hit his elbow. The Scottish team appealed and the referee awarded a spot-kick.

Davie Cooper, on as substitute, scored the penalty and sent Scotland through to a play-off against Australia. That controversial moment should have been the night's talking point but it was overshadowed by what happened next.

Stein mistook the referee blowing for a free kick for the final whistle. He moved to shake hands with Mike England, the Wales manager, and barked angrily at photographers who were gathered to capture the moment of triumph and defeat. What the snappers got was unimaginable. Stein suffered a massive heart attack and despite speedy medical attention was dead within minutes.

Stein was one of the great triumvirate of Scottish managers who dominated the post-war game in Britain. Along with Matt Busby at Manchester United and Bill Shankly at Liverpool, 'Big Jock' was in the game's top rank of managers. At Celtic, Stein created sides that were feared all over Europe. His loss at an early age was keenly felt across British football.

An even more tragic World Cup story caused headlines barely more than a week later. A massive earthquake hit Mexico City, where the final was scheduled to be played in just ten months' time. More than five thousand bodies were recovered from the rubble but estimates of the death toll were as high as forty-five thousand.

FIFA announced within three days that the disaster would not affect the 1986 tournament. It had already moved once and was going to go ahead whatever the circumstances.

The night England were edging towards Mexico, Handsworth in Birmingham was burning. Racial tension had been building all summer and heavy-handed policing in the area sparked three days of rioting less than half a mile from the Hawthorns. Two people died and Enoch Powell's dangerous fantasy began to be talked about again. Things then got worse.

At the end of the month, Brixton was aflame, too. Days later, Broadwater Farm in Tottenham achieved infamy when police constable Keith Blakelock was hacked to death during ferocious violent disturbances on the council estate. In an echo of Thatcher's delusional stance on football hooliganism, the Prime Minister's advisors Oliver Letwin and Hartley Booth wrote a memo on the 'real' causes of social disorder. They were quite a pair to claim they had their fingers on the pulse of urban Britain. Letwin, who later became an MP, was educated at Eton and Cambridge, the perfect places to gain an understanding of ghetto life. Booth was a Methodist lay preacher. It is worth quoting their opinion at length.

> The root of social malaise is not poor housing, or youth 'alienation', or the lack of a middle class. Lower-class, unemployed white people lived for years in appalling slums without a breakdown of public order on anything like the present scale; in the midst of the depression, people in Brixton went out, leaving their grocery money in a bag at the front door, and expecting to see groceries there when they got back.
>
> Riots, criminality and social disintegration are caused solely by individual characters and attitudes. So long as bad moral attitudes remain, all efforts to improve the inner cities will founder.

*

The Tories had found their answer. It was black people and their 'bad moral attitudes'.

Football is a reflection of society. Little wonder the black players making their way in the game were finding life tough.

10

Blond ambition

Frank McAvennie's moral attitude was straightforward. The West Ham striker wanted to have fun. He bleached his naturally ginger hair blond, believing he would get more attention. 'I didn't bother with toner; I just used bleach,' he said. 'I was determined to get myself noticed in London.'

What got noticed in the dressing room is that things didn't quite add up about the new signing. 'We found out in the showers,' Tony Gale said. 'Downstairs he was ginger. He had ginger pubes. We nicknamed him "Lulu".

'Then we found out his immaculate teeth were false. They were all capped.'

To carry off such a look in the East End – and in Upton Park's dressing room – required the Scot to deliver on the pitch. In his home debut against Queens Park Rangers, the new boy scored twice. Yet as much as the goals, it was McAvennie's work rate and attitude that endeared him to the 15,530 fans inside the Boleyn Ground. The striker was keen to make his mark early in the game – on opposition defenders. He won the crowd's approval when he whacked QPR's Ian Dawes with a late challenge and sent the defender flying into the East Stand's wall.

'I wasn't very big,' McAvennie said. 'I was bigger than TC [Cottee] but that's not hard. But I got stuck in. You're a centre forward. You've got to put yourself about.'

The crowd loved this. On the pitch, there was nothing artificial about the Scot.

As August turned to September, McAvennie's name, if not his face, became increasingly familiar. He scored nine league goals and one in the Milk Cup. Everyone was keen to know who this goalscoring sensation was.

ITV's *Saint and Greavsie* programme eventually got him on television. A camera crew and reporter took McAvennie across Waterloo Bridge – where he went unnoticed – and then asked members of the public what they knew about West Ham's new goalscorer. After hearing their answer, the presenter introduced the player to the surprised interviewees.

He was quickly a familiar face in the capital's nightclubs.

Despite bringing a fiancée to London – a model, of course, who operated under the name Anita Blue – the striker was as determined to score as often off the pitch as on it. 'I enjoyed myself,' he said, remembering those days with relish. 'It's not often you get to do anything in life you enjoy so much.'

That applied to football even more than carousing but more than one wag observed that Stringfellows was as much McAvennie's club as was West Ham.

Soon, many of the Page 3 girls and wannabe glamour models who thronged Stringfellows were on intimate terms with McAvennie. By December, the goals were still flowing – 18 in the league – and the Scot made his own TV blackout-busting appearance on *Wogan* just before Christmas. The BBC chat show attracted as many as 15 million viewers at its peak.

Dressed in Gucci clothes and Cartier shoes, McAvennie was interviewed alongside Denis Law. The exchange with Terry Wogan illustrated the curious mix of confidence, wit and vulnerability that served McAvennie so well when on the pull. 'Your name's on everyone's lips,' the host said. 'Why?'

'Because it's so hard to say?' the West Ham striker shyly offered in response.

'It was embarrassing,' he said. 'The state of me! Khaki suit, tie, shoes . . . I looked stupid.' For a Glasgow boy, there was always going to be an element of self-consciousness in the environment of a massive talk-show appearance but the effect of such exposure was huge. 'It was life-changing,' he said. '*Wogan* was a turning point. All the women who didn't read the back pages knew me now. I loved it.'

Wogan was just the start. Before long, McAvennie was being pictured on the set of *EastEnders*, the most popular BBC show of the era. The soap opera was regularly watched by more than 20 million viewers and its cast had rapidly become tabloid sensations. A new kind of celebrity was developing and McAvennie muscled his way into the spotlight in a manner no other footballer was even close to doing.

Soap stars became household names in a matter of weeks. Leslie Grantham, the actor who played 'Dirty Den' in *EastEnders*, leapt from obscurity to become one of Britain's most famous men almost overnight. Grantham was pictured heading a ball with McAvennie in the Queen Vic pub on the soap-opera set. The two men indulged in a bout of celebrity one-upmanship. 'You're the Frank McAvennie of the acting profession,' the Scot said. 'No,' replied the thespian, 'you're the Dirty Den of football.' Either way, the pair were more than famous. They were notorious.

Late nights, gallons of beer, jeroboams of champagne and more women than he could remember might have affected McAvennie's appetite for football but his lifestyle did not disrupt his game. 'We were mates but never socialized together, so I didn't see what he got up to,' Tony Cottee said. 'But he was a great trainer whatever he'd been doing the night before. He never turned up pissed for training.'

The wild lifestyle would eventually have a negative effect on McAvennie's career. Drink and cocaine addictions lay in the future but in the autumn of 1985 he developed a celebrity status that transcended football. He brought a rough-edged glamour to the game. As well as the West End, McAvennie and his team-mates gathered at the Phoenix Apollo, a Greek restaurant on Stratford Broadway. It seemed a rather unglamorous venue but it was where the West End came when it went east. It became McAvennie's headquarters.

EastEnders actors like Nick Berry frequented the nightspot, as well as other sportsmen like Frank Bruno, the boxer. The inevitable legion of Page 3 girls were always present. McAvennie's fame drew people to him. The time of footballers pretending to be accountants had well and truly passed.

'I loved going to the clubs,' McAvennie said. 'There'd be Elton John, Rod Stewart, George Michael. It was a great time to be in London.'

The attention occasionally caused friction. At the West Ham annual Christmas party, the club broke with tradition and invited wives and girlfriends. It unbalanced the laddish atmos-phere of team get-togethers and McAvennie was at the centre of the awkwardness. One of the women reacted to the striker's 'banter' by pouring a pint of beer on his head. Another was ac-cused by her husband of flirting with the Scot and delivered her spouse a slap on the face by way of reply.

Showbiz and sport were intersecting and the West Ham forward was perfect fodder for the red-top tabloids and their gossip columns. He leapt out of the sports pages on to the front sections of the newspapers in a way few players had done before. Billy Wright had flirted with non-football celebrity when he married Joy, one of the Beverley Sisters, in the 1950s. The Wolves and England captain was close to the end of his career, though, and the 36-year marriage was solid. There was no salacious aspect to Wright's crossover fame.

George Best had become a symbol of the Swinging Sixties. The Northern Irishman was the most talented player Britain had produced and his 'El Beatle' nickname illustrated the

Manchester United forward's cultural and global impact. Best had already earned fame and glamour on the pitch before the headlines became more concerned with his private life than his football life.

McAvennie came from nowhere. Five months after arriving from Scotland, he was the most notorious footballer in the English game. For many people – among them the tabloid newspaper editors – the goals were almost immaterial. The his-and-hers topless photo sessions with model girlfriends and the tales of a wild, high life were an end in themselves. The age of instant celebrity was beginning.

Some thought McAvennie was prosecco to Best's vintage champagne but he was an indication that the game was not dying. Football was merely mutating and the Scot was a harbinger of the quick-hit stardom that would come to characterize the game.

If McAvennie's star was on the rise in the autumn of 1985, there was little to lift spirits on Merseyside. Manchester United's winning start to the season continued, with Liverpool and Everton trailing in their wake. Liverpool were nine points behind Atkinson's side after ten games. It was worse for Everton.

The champions had lost three times and trailed the leaders by 13 points. Long-term injuries to Peter Reid and Derek Mountfield meant Howard Kendall's resources were stretched. At least the Everton manager was not struggling as badly as Liverpool City Council.

The city was fast running out of money. Because the council had refused to set and collect a legal rate, the coffers would be empty by Christmas. To buy time and forestall legal action against the councillors, the decision was taken to issue 90-day redundancy notices to local authority employees.

It was a public-relations disaster. Despite every effort to make it clear to the recipients that the notices were merely a ploy and livelihoods were not being threatened, their arrival caused panic and dismay across the city. The situation was exacerbated because the council used a taxi firm to deliver the messages. In the short term, it meant that the council could keep its credit lines open and its members would not be surcharged. Unfortunately for Derek Hatton and co., many people misunderstood and mistrust of the local politicians grew stronger.

Within a week, the district auditor removed the 49 councillors from office and fined them £106,000, the lost interest for the period during which rates had not been set.

Worse was to come as the party conference season began. Neil Kinnock, the Labour leader, used his keynote speech in Bournemouth to lambast Liverpool Council and launch an assault on the Militant Tendency.

Kinnock dismissed the city's attempt to confront Thatcherism as a quixotic dream:

> I'll tell you what happens with impossible promises. You start with far-fetched resolutions. They are then pickled into a rigid dogma, a code, and you go through the years sticking to that, outdated, misplaced, irrelevant to the real needs, and you end in the grotesque chaos of a Labour council – a *Labour* council – hiring taxis to scuttle round a city handing out redundancy notices to its own workers.

As a piece of rhetoric, it was a masterpiece. The repetition and emphasis of 'Labour', the use of 'scuttle' and the contemptuous Welsh tones made it perhaps Kinnock's greatest speech. In Liverpool – and in Downing Street – it was seen as the final surrender of socialism and resistance to the government.

'The speech changed everything,' Hatton said. 'Before it, we were going to meetings all over the country – Sheffield, London,

Manchester – and getting crowds of two, three thousand. None of the local politicians were getting crowds anywhere near this and they wanted us on the same platform. It felt like we were at the forefront in the fight against Thatcherism.'

The battle was over. 'From that moment, Labour leaders didn't want to know. Kinnock convinced the party that his way was the only way to get rid of Thatcher. Well, we all know how that turned out.'

On Merseyside, even those who opposed Hatton and his colleagues were downcast. The mood of the dominant south of England was summed up in an editorial in *The Times*:

Nothing must let the Liverpool councillors off the hook they fashioned for themselves two years ago when they announced their intention to 'confront' [the government]. Liverpool, this sad city, must be an object lesson of the consequences of irresponsible administration: if its people return a Militant-dominated council, they must be first witness of the result.

Later, Hatton bumped into Teddy Taylor, the Conservative MP who had warned that the government would come looking for Liverpool after the miners had been quashed. 'Taylor was laughing,' Hatton said. 'He said, "Margaret got the shock of her life when Kinnock did her work for her."'

Liverpool, the city that fought back, was beaten. The struggle would continue but there was never any doubt after Kinnock's speech that the Militant era was over. The city council's quest to build houses and maintain jobs and services had been fatally undermined.

Peter Hooton, who had seen the council's good work first hand, was appalled. 'It was a proper people's council,' he said. 'They addressed the problem of housing, cleared the tenements and built real houses for people.'

It was not about dogma, despite Kinnock's words. Hatton may have been the face of local Labour politics but Tony Byrne, the chairman of the finance and housing committees, was the brain. He was a clever strategist and even the *Spectator* called him 'a splendid financier'. When forced to sell off council houses to tenants by the government, Byrne sold the mortgages to a French bank and used the money to build more civic accommodation.

'Tony Byrne had a regeneration strategy and cleared the slums,' Hooton said. 'At elections, turnouts were high and Labour kept increasing their share of the vote. Instead of seeing this as a template for resisting Thatcherism, Kinnock attacked it. The national Labour party was trying to undermine the local party.'

These were bleak times for the city but one correspondent found humour in the situation in a letter to the *Echo* by evoking football and the great wide players of Anfield and Goodison's past.

'I reckon Neil Kinnock is very inconsiderate attempting to deprive Liverpudlians of our left-wingers,' wrote a G. Ormesher. 'After all, we have not had the privilege of being entertained by men in that position since the days of Eglington, Liddell, Thompson and Morrissey.'

But even football was piling on the pain. The only thing that could make things grimmer on Merseyside was Manchester United winning the league and it increasingly looked like that was going to happen.

In the midst of this political chaos, Everton faced off against United but it was the most underwhelming trip to Old Trafford in the history of this Lancashire rivalry. On Wednesday, 18 September, they played their opening match in the Super Cup, the tournament sponsored by a company called ScreenSport.

Only 33,859 attended the game that no one wanted. Howard Kendall's team talk summed up the attitude to this newly invented competition. 'What a waste of time this is,' the Everton manager declared. 'Out you go.'

The Blues won 4–2. As if anyone cared.

Liverpool had played Southampton the night before. Dalglish, in his programme notes, tried to lift spirits:

> We have every incentive to get through to the final . . . it could produce another all-Merseyside meeting at Wembley, or a Merseyside–Manchester confrontation. We're taking on crack opposition from our own league and we all want to show who's boss. It may not be the European Cup, but it's still there to be won.

It did not accurately reflect what the player-manager was thinking. 'What else was I supposed to say?' he asked.

For Steve Nicol, this was the moment the enormity of Heysel hit home. 'I wasn't mature enough to take it all in at the time,' he said. The 23-year-old could not comprehend the horror of events. 'The older fellas felt it more. I was just too young.'

Nicol had not even grasped the impact that Brussels would have on his career until the Super Cup loomed. 'It didn't hit me until the season started and the European competition began,' he said. 'We were playing in a Mickey Mouse competition they invented.'

The Super Cup featured the six teams who would have qualified for Europe. The public hated it. The Full Members' Cup, created for the other clubs in the two top divisions, fared even worse. Only five teams from the top flight – Chelsea, Coventry City, Manchester City, Oxford United and West Brom – took part. Six clubs from division two could not be bothered to participate.

In all, 21 teams started the competition. The Southern section

comprised four groups of three teams. In the North, they struggled to form groups. Group one was a mini-league of three teams;
group three had just two, who played on a home and away basis;
and groups two and four consisted of two sides playing one-off
matches. It was ludicrous. Fans, players and managers had no
interest in the new tournaments. These new cups were no solu-
tion to the game's problems.

Power play

After the nadir of the Super Cup came a game that set the blood racing for fans of Everton and Liverpool. The 133rd Merseyside derby took place at Goodison Park on a wild, rainy day. These were arguably the best two teams in Europe. They were certainly the finest sides not involved in Continental competition.

The two groups of players drank and socialized together. They were mates. Until the derby loomed.

'Off the field we got on great,' Graeme Sharp said. 'A lot of us lived near one another in Southport. We'd see each other when we were out and we'd send drinks across to each other. I lived next door to Ronnie Whelan, a great fella. We'd avoid each other derby week but otherwise we were all mates.'

As an Australian, Craig Johnston might have been dispassionate about a match like this. Instead, he got caught up in the tension, emotion and drama as much as any local. He dreaded derby days as much as he embraced them.

'I'd be shitting myself,' he said. 'I was sick with worry. If you do something good, then great. But if you lose the ball, all the Blues are laughing at you and all the Reds are moaning. It's the most frightening place in the world. There's 50,000 Scousers howling abuse at you.'

In the away dressing room at Goodison, while the maelstrom began to crescendo, Johnston found a way to dampen his fear. 'I looked around. I had Hansen to my left, Dalglish in front of me,

Rush to the side. I'd been thinking about Peter Reid trying to cut me in half. Then I thought, "What the fuck am I worried about? Imagine if I was sitting in the Everton dressing room?"'

Mark Lawrenson did not enjoy the hullabaloo around these games. 'They're horrible,' the centre half said. 'The worst thing is the fear of getting beat. It didn't matter where anyone was in the table, top or bottom, it was brutal.'

Defeat was unthinkable. Losing meant a player's life was miserable until the next derby. 'I had a car sponsored by Skyway Ford in Halewood and it had my name all over it,' Lawrenson said. 'If we lost, I hated stopping at traffic lights. You couldn't look around because there'd be an Evertonian gloating or giving me two fingers. If someone beeped you, you learnt not to look up. When we got beat, I used to use my wife's car. It was easier.'

Graeme Sharp came down from Scotland and was quickly made aware how much this match mattered. Initially, the Everton striker was surprised: 'Fans would come up to you and say, "I can't go into work if you lose." You'd think, "Is that really true?" It was.'

Everton were confident. They had won three derbies in a row. Before the game, Howard Kendall was presented with his Manager of the Year award from the previous season. The accolade had gone to a Liverpool boss eight times in the previous 12 years. With Dalglish as first-year manager, it felt like a changing of the guard was taking place.

Dalglish sprung a shock with his team. Jan Mølby, the midfielder who Brian Glanville once described as 'corpulent enough to be playing darts for Denmark', was deployed as a sweeper in an attempt to neutralize Everton's pace. No one was more surprised than the Dane.

'Kenny was a great student of the game,' Mølby said. 'He loved Italian football. He was very versatile in his tactics. Half an hour before the derby, he said to me, "Go and play between Hansen and Lawrenson and keep an eye on Lineker."'

It was a daunting task. The slowest man in the Liverpool team was assigned to watch the whippet-like Lineker.

Bobby Robson, sitting in the stands, was shocked. The England manager turned to the journalist John Keith of the *Daily Express* and said, 'Liverpool playing with a sweeper? When did you ever see that?'

The action came at the other end, though. Everton kicked off with their usual ploy, punting the ball towards the opposition's corner flag so that their midfield terriers could press the defence deep in Liverpool territory. Alan Hansen was waiting for the ball and headed it back to Bruce Grobbelaar. The goalkeeper took one touch and then passed it out to Steve Nicol. The full back controlled the ball, looked up and banged a long pass 60 yards down the pitch towards Ian Rush, who was lurking in the inside-right position on the edge of the Everton box.

Rush had his back to goal and was closely policed by Kevin Ratcliffe. The Welsh striker flicked the ball back towards Dalglish and, as the defence backpedalled, the player-manager curled a shot into the far corner of the net from 20 yards to record his first league goal of the season. The Park End, where the Liverpool supporters congregated, erupted. The visitors were leading 1–0 after 25 seconds. All around the stadium, groups of Reds celebrated. In the enclosure near the corner flag where we were standing, there was a short, sharp brawl. The friendly derby has its comradeship tested at moments like this. Liverpool were on top.

Everton looked stunned. Rush, Goodison's nemesis, doubled the lead 15 minutes later. Gary Stevens made a hash of a defensive header and Ronnie Whelan and Rush were left clear on goal. Neville Southall charged to the edge of his box but as the goalkeeper arrived Whelan slid the ball to Rush to place into the empty net. Kendall's side were in disarray. Just before half-time, Liverpool added to their lead. Dalglish, under pressure on the edge of the opposition box, pulled the ball back to Steve McMahon, who rammed home a shot from 20 yards.

McMahon had come through the Everton youth system but felt underappreciated and underpaid at Goodison. He left to join Aston Villa and was a very recent arrival at Anfield. Liverpool paid £350,000 for his services three weeks before the derby. When the new signing was introduced to the crowd before the Watford match, he was greeted with chants of 'Everton reject' from the Kop. Now he leapt high in celebration, punching the air in joy. He would never be jeered again by Liverpool fans.

At half-time, Kendall tried to staunch the wounds. 'Howard was never a ranter but he was unhappy,' Southall said. He was not the only one. Losing dressing rooms are rarely comfortable places but being routed in a derby led to some furious exchanges between players. Ian Marshall, a centre half making his debut, was out of his depth and was replaced by Adrian Heath, a forward, as Kendall shuffled his side. It was a different Everton in the second half.

Seven minutes after the restart, McMahon got caught in possession, allowing Paul Bracewell to shoot. The effort was blocked but Graeme Sharp jumped on the rebound and hammered home: 3–1.

The diminutive Heath was nicknamed 'Inchy', after the cartoon detective show *Inch High, Private Eye*, but the striker's intelligence and movement gave Everton another dimension.

'Inchy was important to them,' Lawrenson said. 'He made things happen. He could always find angles.'

Sharp always felt better with Heath on the pitch. 'He was the best partner I had at Goodison,' the striker said. 'He was intelligent and the partnership came naturally. We had an almost telepathic understanding.'

Heath found room in the box to shoot with seven minutes left and his cross-cum-shot was turned into the net by Lineker, who scored his eighth goal of the season. At 3–2, Everton were on top and pouring forward towards the Gwladys Street End in search of an equalizer. Liverpool were dangerous on the break, though, and twice Dalglish shot wide when one-on-one with Southall. At the final whistle, the players of both sides collapsed exhausted.

Kendall was generous afterwards and had a playful dig at Dalglish. 'My great disappointment is that their manager refused my hospitality and didn't accept the offer of a traditional drink before the kick-off. Can't think why.'

The Liverpool boss joined the mood of levity when asked about his missed sitters. 'Disgraceful,' he said. 'The manager is not happy.'

Everyone else was. The plaudits came pouring in. Veteran reporter John Keith wrote it was 'the greatest collision between Everton and Liverpool I have seen in almost 30 years'. England manager Robson concurred: 'I have been in football for 35 years and I don't recall seeing a better game in my life.'

Stuart Jones in *The Times* gushed: 'It was extraordinary by any standards. If there is a finer game anywhere across the Continent, let alone the first division, this season, it will be a rich privilege and a rare pleasure to see.'

They saw it in Egypt, where the game was broadcast live, and in numerous countries across the world. In Britain, only those inside the stadium were able to witness the spectacle. Those of us who were there were breathless.

Weeks later, a VHS cassette arrived in the post at our house, a copy of an Australian highlights package featuring the derby recorded by friends Down Under. It did not play properly on our recorder and the action was almost obscured by greenish ghosts on the screen. Still, people were desperate to see it. It was lent around the city and numerous copies made. Even those who had been in the ground wanted to relive the experience. Football needed television back and it needed it soon.

Liverpool's derby joy was slightly tainted by results elsewhere. Manchester United racked up their tenth consecutive league victory by beating Southampton. Behind the scenes, though, rivalries were being put aside in pursuit of revenue. The so-called 'Big Five' – Liverpool, Everton, United, Arsenal and Tottenham Hotspur – were beginning to realize that their earning power was much greater than that of other clubs. Their attendances were higher than the rest and their potential for growth was bigger. They had not been impressed with the creation of the Full Members' Cup, which had been railroaded through by Chelsea's Ken Bates and Ron Noades of Crystal Palace. Arsenal, the only one of the Big Five eligible to play in the Full Members' competition, declined to get involved. 'They didn't give a reason,' Noades said. 'I think they thought it was beneath them.' It was.

At the League Management Committee's autumn meeting, the Big Five made their power play. They demanded a smaller first division and threatened a breakaway league. 'The big clubs are very, very impatient for many reasons,' Liverpool's John Smith said at the time. 'We are suffering financial hardship because there is no television agreement, we are not in Europe, gates are declining and altogether the state of our national game is in disarray. It is up to legislators, like ourselves, to do what we can to bring common sense back to it.' The road to the Premier League was beginning.

It did nothing for the mood of the frustrated five when talks with the TV companies broke down again in November. At that point, only the FA Cup and Milk Cup finals were scheduled to be shown, as they were part of a separate agreement.

The FA and Football League bigwigs seemed to be operating in a different world to the television executives and putative reformers of the game. When Bert Millichip, the FA chairman, deigned to talk about potential sponsorship of the FA Cup, he chose the lunch before the annual Oxford and Cambridge University fixture. The people's game indeed.

The ruling body had turned down a £9 million sponsorship deal for their premier competition. The FA knew their price. 'A £10 million deal over five years would be hard to resist,' Millichip said. 'Although I'm totally against it, as I believe the FA Cup is sacrosanct and dominated by the old amateur spirit, I don't think the time for sponsorship can be far away.'

There was huge scepticism about the public's appetite for live football on TV. Brian Glanville doubted that the audience's attention span would hold, especially after the diet of highlights the viewers had been served by two decades of shows like *Match of the Day* on the BBC and *The Big Match* (and its regional variations) on ITV. Glanville asked: 'How long will the public respond to live football on the screen?' He thought he knew the answer:

> The whole essence of televised football seemed to me the brilliance of the filming and editing, whereby even the dullest game could be made palatable. There is nothing they can do with a dull live game, which in any case lacks both the atmosphere and the panoramic view of the real thing. Once the novelty wears off, will the public really want 'live' football?

The events of the previous few years had left many with similar reservations.

The craving to see Manchester United was as strong as ever. As win after win was chalked up, the possibility of a first title for Old Trafford since 1967 was hyped up more and more by the newspapers. 'It's All Yours, Ron,' said one of the more memorable headlines.

Atkinson was not so sure. 'We knew it wasn't over. Liverpool had a good start,' he said. The United manager had learnt his lesson not to underestimate Anfield the hard way. 'Our best chance to win the league was 1983–84,' Atkinson said. 'Liverpool kept slipping up and instead of taking advantage we'd do the same. We reached the semi-finals of the Cup-Winners' Cup against Juventus and on the day of the game Robbo got injured and the season unravelled.

'We finished fourth. How do you finish fourth in a two-horse race?' The question still haunts Atkinson.

Competition was even more intense now. Even though United had the lead, Liverpool knew that titles were won in May, not November.

'We weren't bothered,' Steve Nicol said, reflecting the mood at Anfield. 'We were not interested in anyone else. We were more concerned with sorting ourselves out.'

Even after the derby victory, Liverpool still saw Everton as their biggest rivals for trophies. 'They were a real team,' Nicol said. 'A great team. We knew who was going to stay the course. Everton wanted to play.'

That was the difference for Nicol. Kendall's team were committed to winning. The Scotland defender was not so sure about what drove United onwards.

'There were some other teams that pandered to the idea of being professional,' Nicol said. 'It was like they had a ten-year-old's view of what football was like and just imagined the benefits without the hard work.

'United were like that. They forgot they had to win to get the sort of status they expected to be given.'

It is harsh criticism but some United players were exempt. Bryan Robson was the best English player of his generation and already skipper of the national team. When 'Captain Marvel' was in the side, United were a significantly more dangerous proposition. The midfielder was prone to injury, though. He broke his leg three times in his early years at West Brom. His relentless playing style did not help, either. 'He was fearless,' Atkinson said. 'Too fearless for his own good sometimes.'

There was class in the United squad but little depth. Paul McGrath was a superbly stylish centre back and his partner Kevin Moran – who had broken Kenny Dalglish's cheekbone at Anfield the previous year – was ruggedly effective. Both picked up too many injuries.

Jesper Olsen and Gordon Strachan were talented but light-weight in midfield. In attack, United were a little short of firepower and pace. Mark Hughes and Norman Whiteside gave the team ferocity and youth but they were still developing. After his front-line players, Atkinson's squad looked thin.

There was a culture of heavy drinking at Old Trafford. Robson, as usual, led the way. McGrath was not far behind. The captain could sink umpteen pints and still train as hard as anyone. Some of the others in the team were less able to cope with drinking and training sessions.

United were not the only team where heavy drinking was encouraged as part of a team-bonding exercise. Until Dalglish changed things at Liverpool, the backroom staff would fly into a fury if they caught the players having a round of golf. Numerous rounds in the pub were, however, acceptable. It was believed walking the course tired out the legs and swinging a club caused back injuries. Long, boozy afternoons after training drew no rebukes and the Boot Room staff liked to listen to tales of the players' drunken debauchery.

At Everton, Howard Kendall led the way, often stopping the coach on the way back from away games for an impromptu booze-up. Teetotallers were looked upon with suspicion at every club.

'It was a matter of pride,' Jan Mølby said. 'You wanted to be top of the league and top of the boozing league.'

Alcohol could never be used as an excuse for United's failings. Whatever the reasons, they were beginning to slow down.

They drew their 11th league match 1–1 away to Luton Town, on the notoriously awkward Kenilworth Road plastic pitch. That meant they failed to equal Tottenham's top-flight record for a perfect start to the season, set in 1960. Then United beat Queens Park Rangers 2–0 at Old Trafford but Robson picked up an injury. He was missing for the rather tame 1–1 draw with Liverpool, which appeared to be a better result for Atkinson's men than Dalglish's trailing team. The captain was also unavailable for wins over Chelsea and Coventry City. The unbeaten start had now run to 15 games and into November. On the morning of United's trip to Hillsborough to play Sheffield Wednesday, a red-top tabloid ran a banner headline 'Give It To Them Now'. Robson was back, the Red Devils were ten points clear of Liverpool and Dalglish's side were due to play Coventry City that afternoon and had a relatively poor record at Highfield Road. Everton, the champions, were 17 points adrift of United.

Ron Atkinson's team lost 1–0 to Wednesday. Liverpool won 3–0 in the Midlands. 'We knew they would come back to us at some point,' Nicol said. 'We were waiting for it.' The headline writers would be more restrained for a while.

The meltdown continued. United took only one point in the following two league games. Next up after that was a Milk Cup tie which sent them to the last place a troubled, struggling team needs to go: Anfield. What occurred on 26 November in front of the Kop became part of Liverpool legend.

Jan Mølby never thought he would see the goals he scored against United in the fourth round of the Milk Cup. The second, and winning, goal was straightforward enough. It was a penalty. The first, though, quickly became regarded as ranking with Anfield's epic moments. With no television broadcast available, all anyone in the crowd could do was rely on their memory and use their descriptive talents to convey the beauty and brutality of Mølby's strike.

The hour mark was approaching with Liverpool trailing to a Paul McGrath goal when Mølby won the ball 15 yards inside his own half with a juddering challenge on Norman Whiteside, the notoriously tough Belfast youngster. The Dane set off upfield as United players flocked towards him to exact revenge. The Liverpool midfielder burst through their assaults, flattening his opponents like an unstoppable juggernaut heading towards the Kop. With white-shirted defenders scattered around him, Mølby lined up his shot and the ball exploded off his foot so hard it sent Gary Bailey, the goalkeeper, into a cowardly defensive crouch to avoid being seriously injured. It was, to hear the pub recollections, the most spectacular expression of Scouse power ever seen against the most-hated enemy. I know, because I missed the match and had the tale of the goal recounted to me on numerous occasions.

The Farm had been recording a BBC radio session for the *John Peel Show* in London. Normally, with Peter Hooton, the singer and leader, and Kevin Sampson, the manager, being massive Liverpool fans, we would work any engagements around the fixture list. The BBC were not going to let us shift the session for a football match.

It was not a game anyone wanted to miss. While incidents of football violence had seemed to drop off after Heysel, any time Liverpool and United met there was invariably trouble and the threat of disorder generated a frantic atmosphere that always gave the fixture a frisson other games lacked. There is a deep rivalry between Merseyside and Manchester that goes way beyond football. Its roots are economic and cultural.

Manchester had to use the port of Liverpool to export the cotton that its mills churned out. The service came at a price and the inland city's businessmen decided the port's charges were too high. Against massive opposition from Liverpool, a ship canal was built linking the landlocked mill town with the sea. Manchester became master of its own economic fate.

Both City and United have a sailing ship on their badge. That the clubs use such vessels as part of their iconography feels like an insult to Scousers.

The two cities are little more than a day's walking distance from each other but feel remarkably different. They frequently judge their achievements – in music, fashion, politics, the arts and literature – in comparison to each other rather than London. Merseyside assumes the upper hand in music, courtesy of the Beatles, and can claim to have invented terrace fashion. Manchester has produced better literature, has a more vibrant artistic scene and was developing groundbreaking radical political ideas when Liverpool was still an Establishment bastion nicknamed 'Torytown'.

Most fans on both sides would not have been able to articulate why the hatred existed; they just learnt to mistrust their enemies from an early age. My first away game was at Old Trafford in September 1972. On the forecourt outside the ground, I remember asking my dad about the Mancunian accent. 'How do they speak?' I said. 'With forked tongue,' came the terse reply. There were bloody clashes in the Scoreboard End before the game and the fighting spilt on to the pitch as the teams came out before the match. Liverpool lost 2–0. At the age of 11, I already knew who the enemy were and was enthralled by the rivalry.

Both cities were suffering badly under the Thatcher government but that hardly lessened the antagonism that existed over football. This was United's first time back on Merseyside since the FA Cup semi-final at Goodison six months previously. The levels of violence on that day in April exceeded anything that had gone before in encounters between the teams. The expectation of another titanic clash – on and off the pitch – was high.

It was the biggest flashpoint of the domestic season so far. Peter Robinson made a plea for calm from the Liverpool boardroom: 'Any incidents could have a major bearing on when we are allowed back into Europe. Both United and ourselves are eager to get back into European competition as soon as possible and it would be a tragedy if a flare-up of any kind delayed our return.'

Tragedy was perhaps the wrong word given what had gone before but the mood was tense. Police warned that they would confiscate offensive banners. The dark undercurrents made anticipation of the game even more exciting.

United were – and still are – the biggest club in England and one of the world's premier football teams. They had won the European Cup in 1968 – nine years before Liverpool – and had a wider fanbase. The global awareness of United was rooted in real tragedy. In February 1958, while returning from a European Cup quarter-final against Red Star Belgrade, the team's plane crashed while taking off after a refuelling stop at Munich. Twenty-three people on board were killed, including eight players and three of the club's staff. Matt Busby, the manager, survived with serious injuries. The team had won the title in the previous two seasons and had acquired the nickname 'the Busby Babes' for their youthfulness and brilliance. One of the best sides in English football history was destroyed in the disaster.

The initial outpouring of sympathy towards United was as strong on Merseyside as anywhere else. Two decades after the crash, a generation was growing up who had not been born in 1958 and believed that the horrific air disaster was fair game to chant about at matches.

The 'Munich' songs grew louder throughout the 1970s. Liverpool – and Everton – supporters began making flags that simply read 'Munich 58'. It did not matter that Busby had been a much-admired captain at Anfield. The sick ditties talked about him waking in an oxygen tent after the crash.

The flags went everywhere Liverpool played and were always prominently displayed. They could be picked out on the live television coverage of the World Club Championship in Japan in 1981 and 1984 alongside the 'On the dole, drinking sake, Tokyo' banners. Munich flags were visible at Heysel, too.

The police could confiscate the banners but it was impossible to stop the chanting. United's fans tried to hit back by singing 'Shankly 81' to mock the great man's death that year but their response never caused the fury the Munich songs generated. During the 1–1 draw at Old Trafford a few weeks before the Milk Cup tie, supporters in the away end threw inflatable aeroplanes into the no man's land between the two sets of fans and the Liverpool end cheered wildly when they nosedived into the ground.

When the Milk Cup draw was made, the clubs immediately talked about setting up closed-circuit television and showing the match at Old Trafford. A potential crowd of 90,000 across the two stadiums was mooted. In the end, 7,200 Mancunians watched the game on a big screen. At Anfield, more than 41,000 saw a match where the noise 'was laced with a disturbing amount of animosity', according to *The Times*.

Mølby's goal sparked a pitch invasion but things never quite got out of hand. The tie passed off relatively peacefully. It was just as well. UEFA sent representatives to monitor the match. Serious trouble would have inflamed an already tense situation.

That should have been that. The goal became the stuff of legend, elevating the Dane's exploits to epic status. Kopites trapped in Maida Vale studios thought themselves accursed they were not there.

Then we learnt that there was a tape of the game. United had a video from the closed-circuit footage. My brother found this out from his mate during athletics training at Kirkby Sports Centre. The friend, Alasdair, was the son of Jim McGregor, the United physiotherapist. Within a week or so, we were watching the tape. As great as it was, the goal was a disappointment after all the hyperbole.

Mølby does not clatter Whiteside. He cleverly whips the ball off the Northern Irishman's toes. He turns upfield and, rather than being gang-tackled by a bunch of Mancunian bruisers, he accelerates towards goal, leaving Clayton Blackmore in his wake. The shot is indeed powerful but not quite the cannonball of popular legend.

It was perhaps the best argument for keeping football off television. The feats on the pitch and the exploits of players become even greater in the imagination and memory.

After a few months, someone I knew who lived on the same estate as Mølby on the Wirral asked to borrow the tape to show the midfielder. Another few weeks passed and Mølby's neighbour suggested I accompany him to get the video back and perhaps have a drink with the great man, who had indicated he would be up for a beer. When we got to the semi-detached house on a new-build estate, Big Jan came to the door bare chested. He handed the tape over and communicated that he was busy by pointing to a blonde girl sitting on his couch.

Mølby does not recall the incident but said, 'It sounds like me.' He had forgotten who had provided the tape. 'I remember seeing it and having it but I thought Ron Atkinson got it for me.'

The memory of the goal is sharp, though, as he recalls the moment. 'You act on instinct,' he said. 'Nothing goes through your mind. Well, almost nothing. I was worried about Whiteside because you took your life in your hands going past him. But once I was clear, it opened up and I just did what came naturally. I was playing well and in a confident mood.

'You have moments in your life when you *know* something

special has happened. This was one of them. Driving home that night I knew it was a moment that would be hard to beat. It was my first goal in front of the Kop, too. It made it doubly special.'

United's good start to the season had sown some doubt on the Kop and Mølby feels the victory was an important step in rebuilding confidence within the team and on the terraces.

'The fans needed it, too,' he said. 'It was a time of change and youngsters had come in and replaced some of the players who'd been important for so long. Phil Neal and Alan Kennedy [long-serving European Cup winners] had gone, Kenny was the manager and it was a time of transition. We needed to step up and prove we could fill their shoes.'

United's awful November was nearly over. All that was left was one more stumble, a 1–1 draw at home to Watford. Liverpool appeared to be hitting their stride. There was a long way to go, though.

12

London calling

While United's ten-game winning start to the league season had garnered all the headlines, there were other teams that got off to a great opening. In division three, Reading were sweeping all in front of them.

It was one of the unlikeliest stories in the Football League. The Berkshire club had a tiny support base and were susceptible to the Thatcherite doctrine that only entities that made a profit had any worth. On the balance sheet, Reading were a disaster.

In the early 1980s, they were treading water at the bottom of the division and fewer than two thousand people were coming through the turnstiles on average.

Predators were circling. Robert Maxwell, the corrupt tycoon who was building a media empire, acquired Oxford United in 1982, picking up the club when the previous owners could not service their debts to the bank. Oxford were one of Reading's nearest neighbours and in the same division. To the fans, that meant a rivalry. To Maxwell, it suggested something different: a business opportunity.

The Czech-born former Labour MP cared nothing for the social component of football clubs. He imagined only profit. His idea was to merge and grow. A year after taking control at the Manor Ground he unveiled his big idea: to consolidate Oxford and Reading into the Thames Valley Royals, basing the new club in Didcot between the towns and creating a bigger catchment area for supporters.

Maxwell's footballing philosophy would have earned Thatcher's approval. 'Everything in the world that cannot pay its way must go the way of merger to combine into stronger units,' he said.

Reading fought off the hostile approach. In 1984, having been unable to amalgamate two clubs into a bigger entity, Maxwell flexed his ambitions even further. He tried to buy Manchester United. Luckily for all at Old Trafford, he was unable to make the deal work.

Reading looked extremely vulnerable in the post-Heysel world. Elm Park's capacity was reduced from 27,000 to 6,000 and the local council denied an application for the club to build new, revenue-raising social facilities.

Reading did curry favour with the government, though. The club volunteered to be the guinea pig for Margaret Thatcher's much-reviled computerized identity card scheme for football fans. The plan, in its infancy at Reading, required supporters to carry photo ID cards and only those with this proof of identity would be allowed to attend away games.

Ian Branfoot, the manager, had little interest in politics. He imagined an opportunity. Branfoot had seen Watford and Wimbledon, two small teams from London's commuter belt, rise through the divisions with remarkable speed. Watford had finished second in the league to Liverpool in 1983. With good and prudent management, advancement was possible without merging.

Reading had a striker in Trevor Senior who excelled at this level. They also kept clean sheets. They kept pace with United with ten victories to start the season and when Ron Atkinson's team drew with Luton, Reading had a chance to equal Tottenham's 1960 record of 11 wins to open a season. Local businessmen clubbed together and promised the club the princely sum of £4,500 should they exceed Spurs' start. They passed with ease, winning their first 13 league matches.

During the run, they kept seven clean sheets and Senior clubbed in with 11 goals. Their first dropped points were in the 2–2 draw away to Wolverhampton Wanderers in late October. It did not spark a crisis. Reading would go on to win the third division title with four games to spare and Senior would score 27 league goals over the season. United's fate was not so straightforward.

There was more to West Ham than Frank McAvennie. Against all expectations, the East London club were one of the unseen attractions of the tail end of 1985.

'We had Phil Parkes, who was the world's most expensive goalkeeper when he moved to West Ham, Mark Ward and Paul Goddard were class players and Alan Devonshire was coming back from injury and that was like a new signing,' Tony Cottee said. 'There were good players all over the pitch.'

West Ham were another club that started as a works team. In 1895, they were formed at Thames Ironworks, on the instigation of a foreman from the foundry and the company's owner. Initially, they took the character of the firm's Oxford-educated boss, wearing a kit that copied the university's shade of blue. By the time Thames Ironworks morphed into West Ham United they had adopted the more egalitarian claret and blue shirts, colours that would come to be associated with the East End.

The 1960s were West Ham's glory years. They were the second English club to win a European trophy – the Cup-Winners' Cup in 1965, two years after Tottenham had achieved success in the same competition – and had won three FA Cups in their history. They had never come close to winning the league, though. Their proudest boast was they provided the core of England's World

Cup-winning side in 1966. Bobby Moore, the captain; Geoff Hurst, who scored a hat-trick in the final; and Martin Peters gave the world champions a claret-and-blue hue.

The club had a reputation for playing in an entertaining style but also for being a soft touch. Bill Shankly summed them up in the era of two points for a win: 'Lovely club, great people, great football, four points.' Teams like Liverpool expected to beat the Hammers whenever they played them. Inconsistency was in West Ham's DNA.

By the mid 1980s, they were more famous for their fans. Alf Garnett, the bigoted racist character from the BBC sitcom *Till Death Us Do Part* was the best known but his notoriety was being surpassed by the ICF, a group of wide boys on the make who had spotted a way to turn hooliganism into a nice little earner.

In true Thatcherite fashion, many of the ICF were parlaying their notoriety into a business opportunity. Some even used the media glare to create their own fashion range. It never caught on but many of the people dismissed as 'thugs' went on to successful careers in writing, music and the arts. The popular press always found folk devils easier to deal with than the reality of terrace culture. Having said that, groups like the ICF also generated their fair share of bouncers, drug dealers and armed robbers. The East End always had a tradition of producing gangsters, regardless of whether they were West Ham fans or otherwise.

'The Irons' are the Cockney club. Most away fans from the provinces refer to all Londoners the same way. 'Shit on the Cockneys' was as likely to be sung at Stamford Bridge in SW6 as it was at Upton Park. The East Enders, born in the area traditionally within the sound of the bells of St Mary-le-Bow in the City of London, thought themselves a breed apart. When the legend of the Bow Bells developed in the nineteenth century, the ringing could be discerned as far away as ten miles to the east if the wind was blowing in the right direction. With modern tower blocks and traffic, the radius for Cockneys had shrunk but West Ham's association with working-class East End life lingered longer than the peal of the bells.

McAvennie fitted in with the flash Essex-boy aesthetic that was developing. The barrow boys of the Cockney heartland largely bought into Thatcherite ethics. Like Frank, they wanted blondes, champagne and piles of cash. They would get their chance very quickly. Since 1983, the Conservative government had been planning the deregulation of the financial markets in the City of London. The 'Big Bang' of 1986 was a two-pronged assault – to loosen the restrictions on stock market activity and to destroy the elitist 'old school tie' networks that had dominated the Square Mile. This was not Conservatism. It was radicalism.

West Ham's mindset was undergoing a radical overhaul, too. The team were starting to believe that they could become England's best side. They were not all flash. Alan Devonshire, the delicate, talented midfielder, was a forklift truck driver until he was 20, when he was spotted by a scout and finally found himself a professional footballer. Devonshire never learnt to drive anything larger than the forklift and used to take the Tube to Barking Station, where he was picked up by Tony Gale for the last part of the journey to training. Despite playing in the first division, Devonshire would take public transport each morning, have a fry-up and read the *Racing Post* while he waited for his teammate to arrive with his lift.

Gale, a Londoner from Pimlico, was one of the big characters in the dressing room. He was nicknamed 'Reggie' after one of the Kray twins, the East End's most famous gangsters. The defender was tough and the rest of the squad feared his cutting tongue. Along with Alvin Martin, Gale gave West Ham a defensive meanness that the Irons had sometimes lacked over the years. Mark Ward, a quick, clever winger, had the combination of skill and vigour that knitted the team together.

'Mark Ward was the cog,' McAvennie said. 'He was a great buy. He made all the difference.'

And what a difference it was. 'West Ham fans tended to go to the match hoping the team would win but not really expecting it,' Tony Cottee said. 'Same with the players. That season, supporters and players went to every game expecting to win. For one season, we competed.'

Cottee developed a fine partnership with McAvennie but it took some time to gel.

'It took a while for me and Tony to get used to each other,' the Scot said. 'When I was shouting at him, he thought I wanted to fight him all the time. At first he didn't understand it was just that I was desperate to win.'

McAvennie's work rate also put the young Londoner to shame. It was noticed by the rest of the team and there was talk among the players that Cottee was not pulling his weight. Martin, the captain, a rugged Scouser from Bootle, thought the mood was unhealthy and called a team meeting where the striker was told about the concerns to his face.

'I don't remember much about it,' Cottee said. 'It's the sort of thing that needs to happen. Frank would be chasing defenders down but I was only 20 and thought goalscoring was all I had to do. It cleared the air and things went from strength to strength. No one was complaining at the end of the season.'

'It's very rarely you go to every game and think you're going to score,' McAvennie said. 'This was one of those seasons.'

As Manchester United faltered, West Ham became the talk of the game. By the turn of the year, McAvennie had scored 18 league goals while his junior partner tucked in with nine. Despite all the excitement, they were in fifth place in the table but with a game in hand that could see them leapfrog Liverpool and Everton in fourth and third place respectively. In second place, just two points behind a faltering United, were another surprise London package: Chelsea.

Ken Bates would have loved financial deregulation. The Big Bang came too late for the Chelsea chairman's career in banking. At least he had football.

Bates is a force of nature. Few people in the game have ever exuded such energy, pursued their aims so ferociously or been so open to comic parody. He could have personified the Thatcher era. He was the living essence of vulgarity as a sign of vigour.

He was born in west London and began his career in haulage. By the 1960s, he started to see that football presented an opportunity and became involved at Oldham Athletic. Grubbing around in the lower regions of the English leagues was a mere cottage industry. Bates had bigger ambitions.

More Arthur Daley than Gordon Gekko, Bates dipped his toe into banking. He attempted to buy an island in the tax haven of the British Virgin Islands but local resistance led to the sale being thwarted. Instead, he went to Dublin and set up the Irish Trust Bank, an institution that went bust causing numerous small investors to lose their money.

By 1980, he was back to football and became co-owner of Wigan Athletic. They got promotion from the fourth division to the third but two years later a better opportunity arose. Chelsea, who were treading water in the second tier of the game, became available.

The team were struggling but the club had plenty going for it, especially off the pitch.

Stamford Bridge sits on some of the most expensive land in London. When Bates got the chance to take control of the club – for £1 – he jumped at it.

If anyone ever suggests to Bates that he bought Chelsea for a pound, he is eager to correct them. 'I assumed the debts for a quid,' he says in a characteristically aggressive style. The businessman was never a Chelsea fan and had not hitherto shown an altruistic approach to investment in the game. What he did have were good connections in South Africa, the United States and Israel.

Bates likes to see himself as a visionary. From the comfort of the Premier League, two decades after taking control in SW6, he told the *Guardian*:

> When I took over the club, I thought to myself, we've got 12 acres of land here in the most valuable part of London and it is only open for business 25 days a year. What business can survive on that? So, ever since, I have been trying to make it work 365 days a year.

The reality was that television money would transform the game, not footfall on non-match days. Bates was an implacable enemy of cameras in grounds. He fought the TV companies viciously.

Part of it was ideological. Like the Thatcher government, Bates had an instinctive dislike of the BBC. He regarded the television licence, paid to the public broadcaster, as an assault on freedom of choice. The duopoly of the BBC and ITV, the privately owned, advertising-funded alternative to the national television service, not only drove down the prices for football on the small screen but represented a cartel that imposed a restriction on competitive bidding for the TV rights.

Bates was big on freedom. When it suited him. He resented the power of the Big Five, whom he saw as the aristocracy of the game, keeping down the middling and smaller clubs. Along with Ron Noades, he rallied football's have-nots. They knew that television was only interested in a small clique of big sides. 'There are only about eight teams in the first division that are attractive to the nation,' John Bromley, the head of ITV Sport in the 1980s, told Anthony King for his book *End of the Terraces: The Transformation of English Football*. Casual viewers did not tune in to watch the 'lesser' clubs.

The blackout widened the gap between the Big Five and the rest. The phrase 'Big Five' was a new phenomenon. It only came into popular usage in the early 1980s – King could not find an instance of its use before 1981 – but the comments that came from the boardrooms of this privileged handful warned Bates what to expect.

'We cannot continue forever and a day to divide our money among 92 clubs,' Philip Carter, the Everton chairman, told *The Times* in November 1985. 'We are starting a long road of change and there will be problems for some clubs.'

Bates might have been all for the harsh Thatcherite economics of survival of the profitable if he was in Carter's shoes but he would not let Chelsea suffer without a fight. And Ken knew how to fight.

In both business and his personal life, Bates used boorishness as a weapon. Chelsea had a notorious reputation for hooliganism in the early 1980s and their chairman defended the fans vigorously in his programme notes. Then he installed electric fences at Stamford Bridge. A combination of local-authority opposition, health and safety rules and good sense meant that current never flowed through the wires on a match day. Much to Bates's regret.

Results started to improve. Chelsea bought wisely and John Neal, the manager, was allowed to bring in players like Kerry Dixon, David Speedie, Pat Nevin, Nigel Spackman and Eddie Niedzwiecki. The team stormed into the top flight.

The first season back in the big time brought success. Chelsea finished sixth in the table but Neal retired because of poor health. He was replaced by John Hollins, one of the club's finest players.

Hollins got off to a good start. Without the sort of flashy

goalscoring exploits of McAvennie or Manchester United's all-conquering start, Chelsea were in third place in the table by the time they went to Anfield on the last day of November. A 1–1 draw with Liverpool underlined their credentials. It was a match that kicked off at midday in an attempt to avoid trouble. Not only had there been violence in games between these clubs over the previous decade but John Smith's blame-throwing over Heysel still rankled with Chelsea fans. They were not responsible for the disaster in Belgium and any suggestion that they were involved was ludicrous. There was friction in the air when the teams met. Chelsea left Anfield having scored more than a point.

A month later they closed out 1985 in second place in the first division, two points behind United. They had beaten the champions Everton at Stamford Bridge and Dixon had banged in 12 goals while Speedie had bagged ten. Bates, who had set himself up as the flagbearer of the Football League's strugglers, was beginning to think about crashing the big-time five. He was an increasingly strong voice within the FA and Football League.

If Bates was fixated by finance, so were Liverpool City Council. They managed to fight off the district auditor's attempt to unseat the councillors but D-Day was 21 November. Wages were due to be paid to 31,000 local authority workers. There was no money in the bank. Merseyside was about to collapse. It was then Tony Byrne produced a stroke of genius to outwit their enemies. The council had borrowed £30 million from Swiss banks. The crisis was averted. The workers were paid and a legal rate set.

Effectively, Liverpool City Council had borrowed against its property, confounding for the moment a government that was encouraging its citizens to take out mortgages and put themselves into debt to buy council houses. For now, Merseyside had avoided bankruptcy.

★

Others playing games of financial brinkmanship fared less well. Six days before Christmas, football caved in to television. The deal was only until the end of the season and ITV and the BBC paid £1.3 million for the right to screen nine first division and league cup games live, plus highlights. The broadcasters had originally offered £19.2 million over four years.

A separate deal was agreed for the FA Cup. The first live game was Charlton Athletic against West Ham in the third round in early January. Armchair viewers would finally get a glimpse of McAvennie.

The West Ham striker had nothing but contempt for the game's authorities. 'The figures they were arguing about were pathetic,' the Scot said. 'The miserable sods running football didn't have a clue. The money was going to them, anyway, not the players.'

The face-off with television was over but the civil war between the clubs ratcheted up a notch. The Big Five were determined to change the distribution of wealth within the game. A committee of leading figures from the sport had been working on how this could best be accomplished and they delivered their verdict in December. They handed the clubs a ten-point plan as a basis for discussion. The main suggestions were these: that the first division be reduced from 22 to 20 clubs by 1988; play-offs should be introduced to decide the final promotion place; the top flight should receive half the television and sponsorship income, the second division 25 per cent and the third and fourth tiers share the remaining 25 per cent; the Football League levy of 4 per cent of gate receipts earmarked for redistribution across the 92 clubs should be reduced to 3 per cent; and the voting system should be reformed to give more power to the bigger clubs.

Everton's chairman, Philip Carter, made the threat explicit, telling *The Times*: 'If we [the Big Five] do not get the support, then the first division clubs will have to look at their future again. We hate bringing out the idea of a Super League or breakaway. But if things stay the same there is no way the major clubs will allow themselves to be dragged down into obscurity.'

Football's most dangerous year was finally over. One thing was certain. Nothing would ever be the same again.

So the cameras came back into the stadiums and on Sunday, 5 January 1986, the nation finally got a chance to see Frank McAvennie in claret and blue on a pitch rather than on an interviewer's couch.

West Ham had drawn Charlton Athletic in the third round of the FA Cup and, in a drab set of ties, the chance to show the Hammers was too good for the BBC to ignore.

Charlton were a tier below their rivals but riding high in the second division. Two years earlier, the club had gone into administration and barely survived. Things got worse after the dreadful events of 1985. The Football League deemed their ground unsafe after the Popplewell Report.

They barely had the cash to scrape by from week to week and were unable to make the improvements demanded to stay at the Valley, one of English football's iconic grounds. Too many areas of the stadium were dangerous.

Their last game at their home was in September and they were forced to move to ground-share with Crystal Palace. The first televised match of the new era took place at Selhurst Park.

The nation must have wondered what all the fuss was about for the majority of the game. McAvennie was quiet and Charlton held the high-flying Hammers for 88 minutes until West Ham's striking duo eventually gave a glimpse of their ability. McAvennie reacted first to a sliced clearance and gained half a yard on his marker. Despite the close attention of a defender and the sight of the onrushing goalkeeper, the Scot toe-poked a delicate chip towards goal. It looked too delicate. On the mud patch that comprised the Selhurst goalmouth, it was unclear whether the shot had the pace to bounce in before a defender arrived. Cottee removed the doubt by slamming the ball into the back of the net. The Englishman was on the scoresheet but McAvennie's contribution to the goal showed the viewers what his game was all about – uncanny anticipation, a blinding five yards of pace and the vision to select the right type of contact when shooting goalwards. 'Frank was a superstar,' Cottee said. 'No one had seen us because of the TV blackout. Now it was a chance for everyone to see what we could do. We wanted to perform in front of the cameras to show everyone that West Ham's form wasn't a fluke.'

13

Holding out for a hero

Frank McAvennie had scored 18 league goals by the time the new year arrived. Many in football would regard 1985 as the bleakest of years but it was the Scot's prime time.

By the time the West Ham striker went on *Wogan*, it appeared that he was a certainty to be the division's leading goalscorer. Gary Lineker had just 11 league goals to his name. The Everton striker's own Yuletide extravaganza was about to unfold, though. In the three matches over Christmas, Lineker netted five more times. The Englishman's influence on the season had been underestimated but that was about to change.

He was overlooked a little because the spotlight was on the new boy in the East End. After all, the football public already knew what Lineker could do. Going into 1986, the England striker had scored 16 in the league but he had also notched five more in the cup competitions.

Lineker was the child of a greengrocer in the East Midlands – something he had in common with Margaret Thatcher – but their family businesses were at opposite ends of the fruit and veg trade. In Grantham, Thatcher grew up with a father who was a lay preacher, an alderman and eventually the town's mayor. The Linekers were market traders, operating in a much earthier environment. They were relatively well off but certainly not wealthy.

Gary was a fine sportsman, excelling at cricket, but football was his vocation. His teachers did not agree. A school report suggested he 'concentrates too much on football' and predicted that he would not make a living playing the game.

After leaving school, he joined his hometown club, Leicester City, and made his debut two years later in 1979. He played seven times before the end of the campaign.

The following season he had 20 first-team outings as Leicester won the second division and earned promotion to the top flight. He was deemed too raw for City's season in the big time and was selected for a mere nine games as the team fought a losing battle against relegation.

His first three seasons gave few clues that a brilliant goalscorer was evolving. His strike tally for those three campaigns was one, three and three. Lineker came of age in 1981–82 in the second division, when he scored 17 league goals and two in the FA Cup as the team reached the semi-finals.

With the improving striker as a cutting edge, Leicester won promotion 12 months later with Lineker leading the way with 26 goals. He had two seasons with Leicester in the top flight, breaking the 20-goal barrier in each campaign. In 1983–84, his 22 strikes made him second leading scorer behind Liverpool's prolific Ian Rush. The next season he shared the top-scoring title with Chelsea's Kerry Dixon, both men notching 24 times.

Leicester were never going to be able to hang on to such a splendid talent and in the summer of 1985 Lineker was in demand from England's leading clubs. Liverpool considered a bid but they still had Rush. The Welshman had been the subject of a remarkable £4 million offer from Napoli in the summer of 1984 and had been unsettled in the subsequent season, scoring only 14 times. Dalglish was betting on his strike partner's return to form, though. Manchester United and Everton were much likelier destinations for Lineker.

'I tried to sign him for United,' Ron Atkinson said. 'We had a deal lined up with Leicester for £600,000. The board said yes but I'd have to sell one of my strikers to raise the money.' The United manager could not shift any of his players quickly enough to get the cash together. 'Howard sold Andy Gray to Aston Villa and got in first,' he said ruefully.

Howard Kendall was indeed quicker on the uptake. He set in motion a deal to send Gray back to the Midlands while negotiating with Leicester.

It was a bold move and not a popular one. Gray had been one of the players instrumental in turning around Everton's fortunes. His arrival at Goodison was the catalyst for the team's revival. It would not be a stretch to say that the 30-year-old had saved Kendall's job. The manager, however, had no sentiment when it came to improving the side.

Gray was expecting to stay on Merseyside. He was moving into a new house in Formby when, on a Sunday morning, Kendall realized that he had secured Lineker for Everton. He went round to his striker's new property and saw that a fitter was installing a cooker in Gray's kitchen. Not quite sure how to tell a man who had changed the course of the club's history he was surplus to requirements, Kendall got straight to the point. The manager gestured towards the workman and said, 'Tell him to stop.' Gray got the message immediately. He was on his way out of both house and club.

Kendall had added the first division's best up-and-coming goalscorer to his battle-hardened title winners. It made an already powerful team more formidable. The price, set by a tribunal, was cheap: £800,000. The British transfer record was £1.5 million and Leicester might have expected to raise more cash for their prize asset.

Atkinson was left to ponder what might have been. 'Lineker would have made the difference for United,' he said. 'The one thing I never had was blistering pace in the side, someone who could run in behind defences. If we'd have got Gary, who knows . . .'

As United's season continued to fall apart, Lineker's was going from strength to strength.

Everton were England's best side. No team relished playing the Blues.

Kendall had put together a squad that balanced skill, physical power and mental toughness perfectly. They came very close to winning a treble in 1985. They had already sealed the Cup-Winners' Cup and the first division championship when they were beaten 1–0 in the FA Cup final by Manchester United, the winning goal coming after 110 minutes of an attritional match at Wembley.

Their ambition was to bring the European Cup back to Goodison. Lineker's recruitment was plotted with this aim in mind. Heysel changed that. Now it was all about domestic dominance. They had the team for it.

Everton had been known as the Mersey Millionaires in the 1960s but the club had fallen on harder times since. It took Kendall three years to mould a group of players into a team that could challenge their neighbours for honours.

Money was tight but the board at Goodison were professional. The directors were mostly connected with Littlewoods, the pools and retail business created by the Moores family. The club would give Kendall a budget and target attendances, which covered wages and expenses. Any gate receipts above the agreed mark – and profits from cup runs – would go into the pot to buy players.

The problem in the early days of Kendall's tenure was that gates were poor. In the bleak days of 1983 and 1984, they often dipped below 15,000, well beneath the break-even point. 'Times were hard,' Peter Reid said. 'It wasn't a lack of support. People just couldn't afford it.'

When Kendall arrived at Goodison, Bryan Robson was top of his wish-list. There was no possibility that the club could pay the £1.5 million it took to take the midfielder to Old Trafford.

Money was tight but Kendall had good people around him. His right-hand man was Colin Harvey, his one-time midfield partner and now closest lieutenant. Harvey demanded perfection and was a constant complainer about the standards of training at Bellefield. He kept the players on their toes. 'In training, Colin was a nightmare,' Neville Southall said. 'He wanted to be the best player. He hated losing. It was always a battle in a good sense. It was never nasty. He never let his standards drop, so you wouldn't let yours slip.'

'With Colin it was good cop, bad cop,' Sharp said. 'Howard was more jovial. Colin was the studious type and the taskmaster.'

While Kendall dealt with bigger issues, his assistant micro-managed individuals. After a game, Harvey would sit and rewatch the match on a VHS machine, note the counter numbers and sit down with players to show them their mistakes or suggest improvements.

Kendall's methods were different. 'He was a players' manager, very approachable,' Sharp said. 'Howard knew what he wanted. He wasn't the bullying type. He very rarely lost his temper.

'He'd be great mates with you and then drop you without a second thought. You'd be angry and try to kick him in training. He never minded.'

The Everton manager's preparation was always thorough. Sharp recalls the build-up to the pivotal Anfield derby early in the title-winning season. The 1–0 victory against the European champions gave the Blues the belief that they could go on and win the league and Kendall's attention to detail gave his players an edge. 'Liverpool used adidas Tango balls,' Sharp said. 'Everyone else used Mitre. All week we trained with the adidas ball.'

During the game at Anfield, Sharp was 30 yards from goal

when the ball dropped into his path. Normally, he would have taken it under control but he saw his chance. 'The Tangos were lighter and you knew they'd fly. When the ball sat up for me, I thought, "I'll have a go here." It sailed in.'

That victory made the Everton players feel that the tide had turned on Merseyside. They were a tough and committed group. The team ethos came from Kendall, Sharp believes. 'Howard said, "You're mates on the pitch and off it. Act like it. Act like someone picked on one of you in the pub."'

Southall was the best goalkeeper in the first division. He was not an athletic netminder – he appeared overweight and would lumber on and off the pitch – but his movements were remarkably quick when a ball was heading goalwards. His unkempt, just-out-of-bed demeanour belied his single-minded work ethic in training. The Welshman was uncoachable in the best sense: he would tell Kendall how he wanted the defence to line up at set-pieces. At first the manager was sceptical, believing that the conversations should have been the other way round, but he was soon won over. It worked. One of Kendall's great strengths as a manager was that he was open to ideas. 'Howard listened,' the goalkeeper said. 'Isn't that what you're supposed to do?'

Southall's approach to training was unusual but there was something else strange about the man nicknamed 'the Binman'. He was a teetotaller in a squad of avid drinkers.

The defence was a mean and effective unit. At right back, Gary Stevens had come through the ranks at Goodison and was schooled in the Everton ethos by Harvey. Because he had started off as a winger and been converted into a defender, Stevens was a potent threat going forward.

The left back was very different. 'Psycho' Pat Van Den Hauwe grew up in south-east London and aspired to be a hard man almost as much as he wanted to be a footballer. His first club was Birmingham City, which was becoming a finishing school for some of the game's wildest characters. Van Den Hauwe was among the worst.

Once, on an Everton foreign trip, a flight attendant caused some consternation by claiming one of the players had exposed himself on the plane. No one would admit to the act. Two decades on, Van Den Hauwe admitted it to Kendall, who retold the story in his autobiography.

It seems the defender had noticed an attractive young woman in a row behind him with a vacant place next to her. Van Den Hauwe popped into the toilet, stripped naked and went and occupied the empty seat. The squad stuck together and denied any knowledge of the incident so Psycho got away with it.

If only the manager had known at the time that Van Den Hauwe had previous. He had been detained by security while waiting for a connecting flight on a Birmingham tour to South America for exposing his penis.

Sober, he was merely aggressive. Drunk, he was uncontrollable. His entire career was pockmarked with tales of brothels, nightclub brawls, fractious relationships and thuggish associates. Nevertheless, Kendall paid £100,000 to Birmingham to bring a bit more menace to his side. Van Den Hauwe replaced John Bailey, a local boy who was considered one of the manager's closest allies.

The centre backs were Derek Mountfield and Kevin Ratcliffe. Mountfield was an underrated, reliable stopper with a knack of scoring goals. In the title-winning year, he got 14, a remarkable tally for a central defender.

Ratcliffe was the captain, another strong character on the pitch and a natural leader. The Welshman was quick and read games superbly.

Ratcliffe was not a smooth, technically gifted player but he had plenty to recommend him. He was left-footed, which was always a bonus, and aggressive. As skipper, he kept the dressing room in order. In a squad full of big personalities, the centre back had a knack of imposing control.

The midfield powered Everton to greatness. Kendall was always looking for versatility, players who could shift around positions. He wanted men who could perform a number of roles. With this in mind, he put together a powerhouse unit.

Peter Reid was central to Kendall's plans. The midfielder cost £60,000 from Bolton Wanderers and Everton had to change their bank to buy him because the Midland would not extend their overdraft for the purchase. The TSB did and Evertonians everywhere were grateful.

Reid had a magnificent passing range, a delicate touch and a terrorizing tackle but initially Kendall thought he'd made a mistake. The man from Huyton was injury-prone and even Harvey wrote him off at one stage.

There were few players around as clever as Reid. He worked out that his crunching tackles had the potential to hurt himself as badly as his opponents, so he restyled his game. The Scouser became more adept at intercepting balls, at closing down rivals and reading the game. He could still leave the opposition battered and bruised but he became cuter and less obvious in his methods. Sliding challenges and block tackles became a thing of the past as he learnt to protect his fragile knees but playing against Reid was never easy.

You had to be tough to compete with the Huytonian. His teammates needed a thick skin, too. The Scouser had a devastating repertoire of quips. When things were going wrong, he was an inspiration.

He hunted in a pair with Paul Bracewell, who came from the Wirral but had cut his teeth at Stoke City and Sunderland. Kendall had been player-coach at Stoke and knew the midfielder had magnificent stamina and a great positional sense.

On his own, Bracewell was good. In combination with Reid,

he was exceptional. They had an instinctive grasp of each other's play and the positions they needed to take up. Reid called the understanding 'telepathic'. There were better individuals playing central midfield in the first division but there was no better pairing in world football.

The wide men were among the division's best. Trevor Steven formed a tremendous partnership with Stevens on the right and could operate as a winger, swinging in crosses, or tuck in to supplement the central midfield. He was creative but disciplined and weighed in with his share of goals. Liverpool had scouted Steven at Burnley and thought him lightweight and prone to injury. Kendall decided he would perform better at a higher level of the game and brought him to Goodison.

On the other side, Kevin Sheedy was a revelation. The Irishman started his career at Anfield but Bob Paisley was frustrated by his tendency to pick up knocks. Kendall didn't fancy him much either. He was talked into the deal by Harvey, who was very impressed by the Liverpool reserve even though his boss thought the midfielder was lazy. After watching a game where Sheedy had idled through the 90 minutes, the Everton manager asked whether the player could put in more effort. The Irishman answered that he would try harder when he was in the first team.

Sheedy crossed Stanley Park for £100,000, a fee decided by a tribunal. Liverpool felt they had been severely short-changed and despite Kendall's misgivings Everton got their man on the cheap. He became the creative hub of the team. His left foot had the Goodison crowd drooling and, though he was never quick nor particularly mobile, Sheedy could turn games.

Up front, Kendall had options to play alongside Lineker. Graeme Sharp was tall and slim and did not look like a bruiser but few attackers have given centre backs such an awkward challenge. The Scot had mastered the art of backing into defenders and drawing fouls. Liverpool's Alan Hansen, the best central defender of the era, frequently got walked backwards by Sharp and was forced to foul the Evertonian. In aerial contests, the Everton striker would jump early and disrupt his opponent, either winning the ball or earning a free kick. He was a handful. As well as scoring goals, he was useful as an outlet ball with his ability to hold on to possession when his defenders punted the ball upfield.

Adrian Heath was the shorter option. Inchy was clever, mobile and adept at opening up space for his teammates. The midfielders loved to play with Heath because he cleared out channels around the box for them to run into and shoot.

Kendall had made him Everton's record signing when the manager failed to get Robson. He endured a difficult settling-in period but became one of the most important factors in the Goodison revival.

There were other members of the squad who could contribute effectively. Alan Harper was a reliable defender who could play in midfield if necessary and Neil Pointon was an option at left back if Psycho picked up too many suspensions or missed too many training sessions. Kevin Richardson was unfortunate that the centre of the park was policed so well by Reid and Bracewell.

Bobby Mimms, Southall's backup, would have been first choice in many other top-flight sides, even if his lackadaisical attitude to training and laid-back attitude irritated some. The 22-year-old was sent out on loan to Notts County to get some playing time. No one expected him to replace Southall any time soon.

This was the group Lineker joined. They were tight-knit and, with the exception of Southall, drank heavily together, which Kendall encouraged. Even though they were disappointed when Andy Gray left they recognized the statement the club were making when they signed English football's hottest property.

Everton were no longer second best, second choice on Merseyside or anywhere else. They were the champions and their swagger showed it. 'Everyone trusted each other,' Southall said. 'Everyone knew what they had to do. If you didn't, you got told very quickly. The standards were high. If yours slipped, people would let you know about it.'

Their start had been less impressive than expected but there was no sense of panic in the dressing room. Kendall's players had the resilience to put a slow opening to the season behind them.

Howard Kendall had big appetites. He liked to socialize and hold court. In a first division where drinking credentials were almost as important as footballing ones, Kendall was top class.

He had been one of the best players in Everton's history, a Gwladys Street hero. He was a key component of the 1970 title-winning side and part of the club's fabled 'Holy Trinity' midfield along with Alan Ball, the England World Cup winner, and Harvey.

His drinking habits were old school. Neville Southall was stunned when the first question his new manager asked him after the goalkeeper signed for Everton was what he wanted to drink.

'We got on famously,' Ron Atkinson said. 'There was great camaraderie between managers. You'd spend 90 minutes cursing each other and then go for a drink together.'

Atkinson recalls one particular night out with Kendall in the summer of 1985. 'We'd won the FA Cup, beating them,' the Manchester United manager recalls, 'and Everton won the league and the Cup-Winners' Cup. A mate of both mine and Howard's was opening a clothes shop near Bury. He asked if we'd go down.'

So the managers of two of Europe's biggest clubs made the trip to small-town Lancashire to attend the opening of a boutique. If they were not a big enough attraction, they took some props with them.

'We went and took all the trophies,' Atkinson said.

'At the end of the night, we were going for a drink and wondered what to do with the cups.' No plans had been made to transport the precious prizes home, so the two managers improvised. 'A young Man United fan we knew was there and he said he'd take them home and keep them safe,' Atkinson said. 'So we said OK.' The welfare of the trophies was placed in the hands of a supporter while the managers headed off to get themselves a drink. 'He put them in the back of a Hillman Avenger.' Atkinson chuckles at the memory of the humble mode of transport. 'Some of Europe's most prestigious silverware was lying in the back of an Avenger. Then we went and had a few. A great night.'

You needed a strong liver to share a session with Kendall but he did not let alcohol get in the way of management. He was ruthless.

'He was an amazing man, an amazing player, an amazing manager,' Derek Hatton, a long-time friend and admirer, said. 'He was at the peak of his powers in the mid 1980s.'

Kendall knew how to hold both his drink and a team together. He was always looking to improve the side and sometimes even his closest friends knew that he was unrelenting in his pursuit of success.

'John Bailey was his best drinking partner in the team,' Hatton said. 'Howard called him in after training one day and said that he'd just bought Pat Van Den Hauwe, who played Bailey's position. Basically, he was telling John that he'd replaced him.'

After imparting the bad news, Kendall moved on to serious business. 'Howard finished things off by saying, "Anyway, where are we drinking tonight?"'

Kendall was not alone in thinking that off-field behaviour did not matter if it did not affect performances on the pitch.

He encouraged the team to have boys' nights out and would frequently lead boozy sessions. 'Howard treated us like men,' Southall said. 'We responded like men.'

Yet the Everton manager was no football relic. His ideas on training were modern. Kendall did not believe in working his players into the ground. Unlike some other clubs, Everton did little stamina training during the season. Kendall had started as a player in 1961 at Preston North End in an age where being able to use a ball in training was considered a luxury and a treat. There were still plenty in English football who put the emphasis on running and fitness. The Everton manager was not one of them. He had only recently hung up his boots after accepting the manager's job at Goodison and his playing career was recent enough for him to understand his squad's workload.

Training was light, focused on skill and tailored to tactics. Playing 50 games a year took care of fitness. The main work was carried out in the 90 minutes that mattered.

'He was very clever,' Graeme Sharp said. 'The first preseason we expected him to run the bollocks off us. We turned up at Bellefield and there were balls everywhere. All our running was done with balls at our feet. It won the players over immediately.'

The Everton manager tried to keep training moving. He felt that stopping sessions to point out errors led to the players getting bored and affected their concentration. At Bellefield, the ball was always rolling and Kendall and Harvey kept up a running commentary – literally – on how the squad were performing.

Kendall developed his psychological approach to players during his own career. When he started at Preston, the stock response to a defeat – not just at Deepdale – was for the coaching staff to make the players suffer the next day. They would run as a punishment. Victory was rewarded by light work and training with a ball.

When he moved to Goodison, Kendall worked with a manager who took the opposite tack. Harry Catterick would put on strenuous sessions after a victory. When the team lost, they would have less arduous training, lunch and a sauna. Kendall took this a stage further.

After defeats, he would take the team into Chinatown for a meal and beer. It was an environment he loved, anyway, and felt it was important for team spirit to respond in this manner. Sharp recalls the first time the manager took the players out for a Chinese meal: 'Howard said, "I want you all in tomorrow, make sure you're smartly dressed. You might want to leave your cars at home."

'We wondered what was going on. We turned up and there was a coach to take us to the restaurant. Howard said, "Eat what you want, drink what you want. All free. The fines will pay for it."'

Sharp, a serial complainer to referees, had been booked a number of times for dissent and had been fined by Kendall for each yellow card. 'I thought, "Hang on, that means it's me that's paying for it!"'

The boozy afternoons and evenings soon became a team staple. Any problems could be broached and dealt with.

'You need honesty,' Southall said. 'We'd go to Chinatown and the players would have a few beers. There'd be open and honest conversations and we'd clear the air if needed. We rarely lost a game after going for a Chinese. It was good management.'

Kendall would let the players sort things out, 'He'd sit back and watch us and listen,' Sharp said. 'As we got more relaxed we'd talk more freely and he just took it all in. He got the players' perspective.'

The Everton manager did have his quirks. Kendall liked to be the centre of attention and regale the company with anecdotes and stories from his career. He had his biases about football, too. He was suspicious of blond players, whom he felt stood out on the pitch and attracted attention when it was unwarranted. Frank McAvennie would never have been Kendall's first choice, though they would have made successful drinking partners. He had the same prejudice against bald players.

The idiosyncrasies did not hold the team back. Kendall's hirsute, dark-haired side were the best in the country. 'We had everything you need,' Southall said. 'We could play, we could fight. You knew you were going to win things with a team like that.'

They were looking like winners once again. The Blues crept closer to the top of the table as 1985 waned.

United were beginning to self-destruct and Liverpool had a calamitous time over the festive period, losing twice and drawing three times. The New Year's Day programme ended with Everton in second place in the table, just five points behind United and level with Liverpool and Chelsea. West Ham were two points further back but both London clubs had two games in hand on their Merseyside rivals.

It had been an impressive spell for Kendall's team. In the space of ten games, they had reduced a 16-point gap with United to a manageable five.

14

With Love From Manchester

Everton were overlooked by the TV schedulers. Their first live appearance in the league was not to be until mid March, against Chelsea. It was one of a number of surprising decisions. Another was that there would be no live coverage of the biggest game of the year so far: Liverpool versus West Ham at Anfield in January.

The London club were full of confidence. They had lost just once in 20 league games and, unusually, headed north without any fear.

They had two games in hand on Kenny Dalglish's men, whom they trailed by two points. This was their chance to knock Liverpool out of the title race.

The Hammers had not won at Anfield since 1964 but they saw an opportunity to break that run. For almost an hour, the game could have gone either way. Ian Rush hit the post, turning a half-chance into a near miss, but the visitors probably just had the edge overall.

Then George Tyson, the referee, became the most hated man in the East End. Liverpool were attacking the Kop but struggling to break down the resistance of Alvin Martin and Tony Gale. Paul Walsh, selected by Dalglish at the player-manager's own expense, was chasing a ball that appeared to be running out of play. Another attack had fizzled out. Martin, the man from Bootle, was covering the Liverpool forward just to ensure that there was no danger. The West Ham defender made the most marginal contact with Walsh, who tumbled over. The striker did not appeal for a foul and started to rise to continue playing.

He was interrupted by the referee's whistle. Tyson was pointing to the spot. The Kop celebrated, Liverpool's players were grateful but bemused and West Ham went ballistic. Martin was booked during a furious mass protest but things got worse when the linesman called the referee over. After a quick word, Tyson sent off Ray Stewart, the full back, for something he had said.

The years have not dimmed West Ham's fury. 'It was the softest penalty ever seen,' Cottee said sourly. 'They got quite a few of them, soft ones, in front of that crowd, in front of the Kop.'

Jan Mølby, calm as ever, slotted home the penalty. The ten men lost their heads and their shape and Liverpool put them away with a clinical lack of sympathy. Rush added a second goal nine minutes later and Walsh killed the game completely with a third shortly after. Alan Dickens pulled one back before the end but it meant little. It was a serious setback. 'We gave them a real fright,' Cottee said. 'They got lucky.'

'You'd be disappointed if the ref gave that penalty against you,' Mark Lawrenson said. 'We weren't complaining.'

Afterwards, Dalglish was conciliatory. 'From where I was sitting, Martin looked a bit unlucky,' he told the press. He could afford to be magnanimous. News had come through that Manchester United had been beaten at Old Trafford by Nottingham Forest. Liverpool were just two points behind the league leaders and the next home game was against United.

Ron Atkinson's pain could not have been greater. He finally got another striker to bolster his squad. United paid Coventry City £650,000 for Terry Gibson and threw in Alan Brazil for good measure. It made the Lineker deal look even more of a bargain.

United were knocked off top spot in the table by Everton on

1 February. The next day they went to Upton Park for a televised game against West Ham. Their title challenge might have survived the 2–1 defeat; it could not exist without Bryan Robson.

The United captain gave his team the lead but then limped off after a challenge by Tony Cottee. The only relief for Atkinson was that Robson was only ruled out for one game. Unfortunately, that match would be at Anfield. Upton Park would have worse in store for the United captain before the season was over.

There are rare occasions that Manchester and Merseyside come together. Over a weekend in February, the best and worst facets of this complex rivalry between the two cities were on show.

On Saturday, 8 February, a concert took place at the Royal Court Theatre in Liverpool's city centre under the banner 'With Love From Manchester'. Tony Wilson, the Granada TV presenter and founder of Factory Records, was a resolute socialist and arranged the gig in support of Liverpool City Council. The proceeds went to the legal fighting fund for Labour councillors who were still under the threat of surcharge from the district auditor for failing to set a legal rate.

Manchester sent its best bands down the East Lancs Road. The Smiths, New Order and the Fall charged only expenses as a show of solidarity with Liverpool's left-wingers. Here were three groups at the peak of their powers. Tickets cost £6 per head.

John Cooper Clarke, the performance poet, compèred one of the most memorable nights of the year. Each band had a 45-minute slot on stage and all produced performances that have gone down in north-west music folklore.

New Order were first up. They were formed from Joy Division after Ian Curtis committed suicide in 1980. Curtis and his bandmates had agreed that if any member left the group they would not work again under the original name.

At this point in their career, New Order rarely performed the songs from their first incarnation. At the Royal Court, they gave Scousers an unexpected treat by playing 'Love Will Tear Us Apart', Joy Division's biggest hit and best-known song. The audience loved it.

The Fall were on next. Mark E. Smith's ever-changing band of troubadours were in the midst of one of their most accessible and commercial periods. They were probably the least attractive of the three groups to the average gig-goer but their adrenaline-fuelled set was considered by many present to be the highlight of the night. Smith's droll vocals were the embodiment of Mancunian attitude.

The main attraction was Morrissey and the Smiths. They arrived on stage to 'Montagues and Capulets', from Prokofiev's *Romeo and Juliet*, and from that overblown opening launched into a set of unfamiliar songs from the forthcoming *The Queen Is Dead* album.

Introducing 'Frankly, Mr Shankly', Morrissey warned the audience that 'this one is nothing to do with anyone you might know', in case the crowd misinterpreted the song as a jibe against Liverpool's legendary manager. Those looking to hear Smiths hits were disappointed. The only nod to the singles was when Johnny Marr teased the crowd by playing the intros to 'What Difference Does It Make?' and 'This Charming Man' before launching into newer songs.

The performance ended with the three bands and a collection of local musicians gathering on stage for communal singing of 'Maggie's Farm', Bob Dylan's counterculture classic restyled for the Thatcher era. The night was a resounding success and a PR triumph for Derek Hatton and the council. Many in Liverpool accepted the love and appreciated the rival city's show of support. 'Tony Wilson came up with the idea and it was a great gesture for the working class of the city,' Peter Hooton said. 'Lots of people were looking at Liverpool and saying "Good on you" for fighting the Tories.'

The act of friendship meant a lot. When the gig organizer died in 2007 – having restyled himself as Anthony H. Wilson – his passing was marked by Scousers. 'We sent a wreath,' Hooton said, 'with the words "With love from Liverpool". We hadn't forgotten.'

Some of us were not in the Royal Court. I was 500 yards away in the American Bar, where a different sort of singalong was taking place. Concertgoers heading along Lime Street towards the gig must have shuddered at the clear rejection of Mancunian love. 'Manchester, wank, wank, wank!' boomed from the pub out into the February air.

A couple of hundred Liverpool 'boys' were gathered in the Yankee (as it was known) and it was not a place for the faint-hearted. Ron Atkinson and United were due at Anfield within 24 hours and hate was in the air.

Most of us wanted nothing from Manchester. The Smiths, in particular, were near the top of my list of despised bands. Two years earlier, The Farm had played the *Oxford Road Show*, a live Friday-night pop-culture programme that rivalled Channel 4's *The Tube*.

The Smiths opened the show, we were on afterwards and Marillion played as the closing credits rolled. During rehearsals – we were miming, so practising seemed a bit surreal – we crossed paths with the Smiths. Morrissey looked us up and down in a condescending manner and said something I didn't catch. 'What was that?' I asked, following up the question with a mouthful of Scouse invective.

The Smiths' singer sneered and gave a snort, so I took an angry step or two towards him. He scuttled away down a corridor at speed and disappeared until it was time for him to go on stage.

By then we were already in our starting positions 30 yards away. There was no sign of him in the Green Room afterwards. I was still keen to hear what he had said. Someone suggested that he had a headache. That was convenient. The rest of the band were pleasant enough. For Mancs.

I found it hard to get over my antipathy towards Morrissey for a decade. It wasn't until the mid 1990s that I was willing to accept how great the Smiths were. It was an awful time to make that recognition, with Manchester dominant in football and the pop charts. In 1986, they were playing catch-up in both areas and as far as I was concerned Steven Morrissey was just another self-obsessed tosspot who could keep his support.

Manchester had sent love, whether it was appreciated or not. Some of the Yankee's patrons had something entirely different from love in mind for the next day.

Tension was still running high between the two sets of fans. The comparative lack of trouble at the Milk Cup game raised hopes that this Sunday televised clash would pass off peacefully. Merseyside Police were on a high state of alert but they were anticipating the flashpoints to be Lime Street Station, Stanley Park and the streets around the Anfield Road End. The problem came where they least expected it.

The United team always ran the gauntlet when they arrived at Anfield. They knew they were in for a difficult day. Ron Atkinson had his men primed. 'I'd say to the players, "Don't moan about them kicking you. Kick them first!" It was war in a positive sense.

'You'd look at Kevin Moran and Paul McGrath and think, "Thank God we've got these fellas."'

United always expected to have a hard time on the pitch. On that February day, the conflict took a more sinister turn. The critical moment came before the match.

'The coach used to pull right up to the players' entrance,' Atkinson said. 'You'd be right up against the door, down the steps and into the ground.

'We had a standard line coming off the bus. It was typical Scouse stereotyping: "Hands on your wallets and run!" And we'd pile into the stadium.'

Anfield had been refurbished, though. 'They'd changed things in '85,' the United manager said. 'There was now an overhanging shelter above the players' entrance. You couldn't get the coach as close to the door because of it. We were parked about 25 yards away. We had to go through the crowd.'

The players expected jeering and perhaps even jostling from the hostile Scouse reception committee. They were not anticipating being gassed.

'I felt something wet on my hand,' Atkinson said. 'I thought for some reason it was wet paint. It wasn't. It was some kind of gas spray.'

Panic broke out in the crowd. As well as the snarling abusers, there were a number of young autograph hunters waiting for the team. They took the brunt of the spray. Against a backdrop of 'Mu-nich, Mu-nich' chants, chaos reigned.

The burly Atkinson barrelled towards the safety of the dressing room, blindly scattering anyone in his way. Looking back, he can laugh about the very serious incident and his response. 'I ran inside and don't remember much about it,' he said. 'My eyes were stinging. Mick Brown, one of my assistants, said I was throwing people out of the way. I didn't see who it was. Mick said I hurled Kenny and Hansen aside.'

Liverpool's manager and his captain were appalled but not by Atkinson's behaviour. A stream of tearful children and their panicky parents were heading towards the United dressing room, where the injured Bryan Robson helped reassure the victims as they rinsed out their eyes. Most of his teammates went directly

(**Left**) Poverty beside the Mersey: the 'second city of the Empire' was swamped with Irish immigrants after the Great Famine, turning Liverpool into the most squalid city in Britain. This is Emily Place, 1897, a typically grim inner-city area.

(**Above**) Taken almost 40 years later, a court dwelling in Ben Johnson Street, off Scotland Road, shows little had changed in this poverty-stricken neighbourhood where the city's identity developed. The word Scouse was initially used as an insult, but it soon became a badge of pride to be called a Scouser.

(**Right**) The luxury liner *Aquitania* on the landing stage at Liverpool's Pier Head. Wealth and power flowed through 'Torytown' but within a mile there were scenes of unimaginable deprivation.

(Right) Everton FC, 1891. The original occupants of Anfield display the League Championship trophy in their final year at the ground before departing to Goodison Park after an acrimonious squabble over the ground's ownership.

(Above) John Houlding, an Everton director, was left with an empty stadium and no team after buying Anfield against the wishes of the rest of the board. The brewer formed his own club, Liverpool FC, in 1892.

(Left) Striking back: the city developed a reputation for industrial militancy. In 1970, Liverpool was at the forefront of the national dockworkers' strike. Here dockers throng the Pier Head.

(**Left**) In the eye of the storm: Labour councillors Tony Mulhearn (*left*) and Derek Hatton address the media at the height of Liverpool City Council's battle against the Thatcher government in 1984.

(**Below**) In the mid-1980s, youngsters protest on the streets to demand jobs and show their contempt for Thatcher. The boy resting his chin on the 'Giz a job' sign is wearing a ski hat in club colours, reflecting the twin obsessions of the city: politics and football.

(**Left**) The enemy within: March 1989 and Margaret Thatcher visits the region that put up most resistance to her brutal Conservative government policies. She remains one of the most hated figures in history for many Merseysiders.

(Left) Riotous behaviour: 1985 was a violent year in football. In March, Millwall rioted at Kenilworth Road during an FA Cup tie away to Luton Town. Police lost control. Hooliganism became a political issue.

(Below) Liverpool fans battle with police at Heysel Stadium in May 1985. On a dark day for the game and the city, 39 mainly Italian fans were killed before the European Cup final against Juventus. Following this disaster, English clubs were banned from continental competition for five years.

(Right) May 1985: not all the horror was caused by violence. At Valley Parade a stand caught fire during a match between Bradford City and Lincoln City. The fire killed 56 people in the dilapidated ground. In this era, conditions for spectators across the country were unpleasant and dangerous.

(**Left**) Howard Kendall shows off his new striker. Gary Lineker, England's goal-scoring sensation, joined Everton in the summer of 1985, adding extra firepower to the champions. The signing showed that Goodison Park was the most attractive destination in the game.

(**Right**) Lineker celebrates another goal, while Adrian Heath rushes up to congratulate his teammate. The Everton striker's eventual haul would be 40 goals for the season, but he was unable to bring his team any silverware.

(**Below**) The changing face of the game: Laurie Cunningham, Cyrille Regis and Brendon Batson were part of the first wave of black players in English football at West Bromwich Albion. They were nicknamed, rather insultingly, 'the Three Degrees' after the American female soul group at a time when black players had their manhood and fortitude questioned on a regular basis.

(**Above and left**) Frank McAvennie celebrates after scoring for West Ham. The Scot was sensational in the first half of the 1985–86 season when the television blackout was in force. That he was unrecognizable added to his glamour. Everyone knew his name, but not his face. McAvennie was a hit off the pitch, too, becoming a tabloid darling with his taste for nightlife. Wags claimed that Stringfellows was 'as much his club as West Ham'.

(**Below**) Craig Johnston blocks a cross from Kevin Sheedy in the FA Cup final. The midfielder had struggled to break into the Liverpool team, but his performances in the 1985–86 season – and his goal at Wembley – gave the Australian some vindication.

(**Below**) Jan Mølby: 'Corpulent enough to be playing darts for Denmark,' said Brian Glanville, marvelling at the midfielder's unathletic physique. No one doubted the Dane's ability with the ball at his feet, and Mølby's brilliance turned the cup final.

(**Left**) Ken Bates: Chelsea's chairman rallied the smaller clubs in their battle against the 'Big Five'. Eccentric, opinionated and forthright, he installed electric fences at Stamford Bridge to combat hooliganism. The council would not let Bates turn on the current, much to his regret.

(**Below**) Kenny Dalglish turns away to celebrate the goal that sealed the title for Liverpool in the 1–0 victory over Chelsea at Stamford Bridge. In his first year as a manager, the Scot guided the club through the aftermath of Heysel and on to the Double.

(**Left**) Fans went to extreme lengths to attend the 1985–86 cup final. Young men were willing to face a 30-foot drop and risk their lives to gain entry to Wembley for the biggest game in Merseyside's history.

(**Below**) Liverpool celebrate after their 3–1 victory over Everton at Wembley. Just a year earlier, the club were the pariahs of Europe. Now they had completed the most glorious season in Anfield's history.

(**Above**) A disappointed Gary Lineker (*centre*), applauds the crowd. The striker had played his last game for Everton. He would move to Barcelona during the summer and win the Golden Boot in the Mexico World Cup.

(**Below**) The open-top bus tour was another humiliation for Everton. Liverpool, the winners, were in the first vehicle, taking the plaudits of the crowd. The press came behind in another bus. The defeated team trailed the convoy, almost an afterthought. Howard Kendall's side deserved better treatment.

on to the pitch where they could clear their heads in the fresh air. The crowd, not knowing what the players had just experienced, serenaded them with catcalls and abuse.

It was a disruption United did not need. They had enough problems with an injury crisis. Atkinson was so low on players that he was being forced to give a 24-year-old named John Sivebaek his debut in the cauldron of Anfield. The manager was also asking the Dane to perform an unfamiliar role. And Sivebaek, who had signed for the club only days earlier, had the misfortune to be in his manager's path on the route to the dressing room.

'I threw Johnny Sivebaek out of the way,' Atkinson laughs. 'The kid was making his debut at Anfield, I was playing him out of position and he couldn't speak a word of English . . . and I was manhandling him out of my way.'

No one was sure whether the spray was ammonia or CS gas. A 12-year-old was taken to hospital and 22 supporters, many of them children, were affected. The attack had little impact on the United players. 'We just got on with it,' Atkinson said.

In a flat game, United took the lead. The newly acquired Colin Gibson opened the scoring after Bruce Grobbelaar spilt a shot at the Kop end. John Wark equalized for Liverpool. The 1–1 draw meant Everton stayed top but little of the talk afterwards concerned football.

Martin Edwards, the United chairman, was scathing about the behaviour of Liverpool supporters as the team bus arrived. 'I have never known such abuse,' Edwards said. 'It was frightening. A brick was thrown at the coach but luckily it hit a stanchion, otherwise it would have hit Mark Hughes. If you think about it, he could have been killed.'

Peter Robinson, Liverpool's chief executive, was normally sure-footed in public but he made a serious misstep when he tried to deflect some of the blame towards Norman Whiteside.

The United forward had inherited the captain's armband from the injured Robson and had given a pre-match interview where he spoke about refusing to be cowed by Anfield's hostile environment. Robinson alluded to the article. 'It certainly doesn't help when the United captain gives an interview the day before the game in which he talks about refusing to be intimidated.'

As blame-throwing goes, it was nowhere near as bad as Liverpool chairman John Smith's attempts to pin the problems of Heysel on Chelsea fans. Yet it did suggest an unpleasant myopia and naivety in the Anfield boardroom. Any fan could have told Robinson how poisonous this rivalry had become. A letter to the next Saturday's *Football Echo* spelt it out for the Liverpool hierarchy.

A correspondent who signed off as 'Worried Red' wrote: 'On Sunday, the abuse directed at Manchester United officials in the Main Stand was very frightening and the venom and hatred was unbelievable. The guilty ones were not teenage thugs, but older people, many middle-aged or retired.'

Atkinson remains bemused by the hatred in the stands and terraces. Behind the scenes, the relationship between the clubs was good. 'We always had a great rapport,' he said. 'After the match, it was back to my office for a drink or the Boot Room for a beer.'

The United manager and his team were not averse to drinking on enemy territory, either. 'My first Christmas party at United was held at a pub owned by Ian Callaghan and Geoff Strong [former players], who were Liverpool through and through. The players got on great, too.'

Atkinson enjoyed the company of his rivals whenever he got the chance. 'I remember going to Israel and Liverpool were on a trip there. We went to Eilat. Hansen, Rush and all the Liverpool boys were there. We went for a kickabout in the local park and the parkie chased us off. He pointed to a sign that said "No ball games", so we went for a beer. We had a great time.'

Big Ron was a convivial character and good company. On the terraces and in the stands at Anfield he was despised and lampooned. There were a number of banners made for him. The esoteric 'Atkinson's Long Leather', mocking his dress sense, is memorable. Less witty was the obnoxious and pathetic, 'Atkinson's tart is a slut'. More than anyone, Big Ron became the lightning rod for hate directed towards United from the Kop.

The next time United came to Anfield, ten months later on Boxing Day, Bob Paisley, Liverpool's most successful manager, would travel on the front seat of the visiting team's coach as a show of solidarity and to forestall any attacks on the bus. Atkinson would no longer be United manager by then. A Scot called Alex Ferguson would be in charge at Old Trafford. The clubs would never be quite so friendly again after Ferguson's appointment.

15

The gap

Everton were on a roll. Their last defeat had come in December and they were beginning to look unstoppable. Peter Reid returned from his long-term injury against Tottenham in the league on the last day of January and scored the only goal. They warmed up for the second derby of the season with a 4–0 victory over Manchester City. Gary Lineker bagged another three, taking his total to 29 goals in all competitions. They went to Anfield in good heart, five points clear of Liverpool.

Everton had still not been on live television. Their FA Cup tie against Spurs was scheduled to be broadcast but had been called off twice. The postponements gave the Blues an unexpected 11-day break. Dalglish's side had a more rigorous schedule. They played Queens Park Rangers in the first leg of the Milk Cup semi-final and a fifth-round FA Cup tie and replay against York City during the same period.

The derby was Liverpool's first all-ticket sell-out of the season. Most Everton fans were crowded into the Anfield Road End but a substantial number of Blues – perhaps three or four thousand – always congregated on the Main Stand side of the Kop. It made for a rowdy atmosphere but one that did not have the venom of the United game.

When Dalglish accepted his Manager of the Month award for January before the game – a gallon bottle of Bell's Whisky – the majority of people on the Kop groaned. The Scot walked out to collect his prize wearing a suit. Kick-off was a mere 15 minutes away. Liverpool's talisman was injured and with Paul Walsh sidelined with ligament problems the home team were short-handed up front.

There were difficulties on the Kop, too. Before the match, people started scrambling through the gates in the fences as the crowd surged forward. They sat down alongside the pitch to watch the game and the police took a while to regain control of the situation. They began to funnel the pitchside supporters back on to the Kop in the less crowded areas near the Kemlyn Road. Anfield was working itself up into a frenzy.

The game was completely different to the Goodison derby, where the scoring started early and the chances flowed. At Anfield, most of the action was in midfield, where the tackling verged on maniacal. Reid and Steve McMahon tore into each other, two Scousers with an axe to grind. It was compelling: football as a blood sport.

There were casualties. Jan Mølby limped off at half-time with a gash in his shin and Kevin MacDonald joined the fray. There was no space for the league's premier goalscorers. Ian Rush and Gary Lineker barely got a sniff.

It became increasingly clear that a mistake would decide the game. Cue Bruce Grobbelaar.

With little more than a quarter of an hour left, Kevin Ratcliffe got the ball 30 yards out. Liverpool were slow to close him down. They were happy to let a centre half shoot from that distance. The notion appeared justified when the Everton captain scuffed his left-foot shot and the ball bobbled goalwards. It took a slight deflection off Lineker and wobbled on its way to Grobbelaar. The goalkeeper was behind the ball and everyone in the ground expected a routine save. Instead, the shot squirmed through the Zimbabwean and crept into the net. Jim Beglin looked on in astonishment. No one was more stunned than Ratcliffe, who turned to his teammates with a shocked and delighted grin. Large sections of the Kop erupted in celebration. 'Brucie, Brucie, you're a clown,' rang out around Anfield. Even some Kopites joined in.

Liverpool pressed for the equalizer and Neville Southall was forced to make a scrambling clearance at Rush's feet for a corner. The Welsh striker then rounded the goalkeeper and shot from an angle but Pat Van Den Hauwe cleared off the line.

The home side were always likely to be caught on the break and Lineker was the perfect man for the situation. He looked suspiciously offside when he latched on to a long clearance but the ease with which he clipped the ball past the onrushing goalkeeper showed his class. Evertonians – always serial pitch invaders – poured out of the left side of the Kop to join the huddle of celebrations. It was a killer blow.

In the dressing room, Liverpool tried to put a brave face on things. 'I came off at half-time,' Mølby said. 'The last 15 minutes were awful. It was a bad result. Afterwards, we said, "Twelve games left. All we can do is get 36 points and see what happens." We didn't get those 36.'

Grobbelaar was always an accident waiting to happen. The Zimbabwean was prodigiously athletic and talented but prone to mistakes.

He was a character, a showman, in a way few goalkeepers have ever been. His circuitous journey to Anfield took in three continents.

He was born in South Africa but grew up in Rhodesia (now Zimbabwe). There, he served a two-year period of national service in the army during the Zimbabwe war of liberation. He liked to style himself as a 'freedom fighter' in that bush war, despite belonging to the armed forces that were propping up the racist regime of Ian Smith.

In the right-on left-wing atmosphere of 1980s Merseyside, he was happy to let the media and public misunderstand the politics of southern Africa and his role in the struggle. He made his stance clear in a 1986 autobiography. 'Footballers are supposed to be apolitical,' he wrote. 'But you just have to live in Liverpool to feel the atmosphere and realize how the city has declined. Even my mother sensed it. She was appalled that, having risked life and limb in the fight against Marxism, I was now living in a city seemingly controlled by it.' The goalkeeper's world view was madder than Thatcher's.

After leaving the army, he had trials in England for the Vancouver Whitecaps of the North American Soccer League and his ability, agility and confidence earned him a contract in Canada. He was loaned to Crewe Alexandra in the off season and Bob Paisley noticed him.

'I will never forget going to see Bruce Grobbelaar play for the first time,' Paisley said later. 'Before the game, he had three of his teammates lined up on the edge of the penalty area firing in shots at him. Bruce was dancing about like a cartoon character, stopping every attempt. I turned to Tom Saunders, who was sitting next to me, and said, "We can go, I've seen enough."'

Ray Clemence was Liverpool's goalkeeper and Paisley thought Grobbelaar would have years to develop as an understudy. Within 12 months, that changed. Clemence left unexpectedly and the Zimbabwean was No. 1.

Grobbelaar courted the crowd. He warmed up by walking on his hands or swinging from the bar. He bantered with fans, whether it was the friendly faces on the Kop or the snarling inhabitants of the Stretford End. He would make saves that drew comparisons with the very best goalkeepers and then, minutes later, let an innocuous shot slip between his hands into the net.

It is dangerous when a goalkeeper trusts his own ability too much. Grobbelaar would chase crosses through a forest of players in an attempt to claim a catch. When it worked, it was brilliant. When it went wrong, disaster loomed. His nickname became 'the clown'. It was a role he performed off the pitch, too. He was often the butt of vicious dressing-room humour because he was a walking faux pas. 'Bruce couldn't help himself with the ricks,' Craig Johnston, his room-mate, said. 'But he was happy to make himself look stupid for the benefit of others. He sacrificed his own integrity for team spirit.'

Across the league, Grobbelaar was perceived as one of Liverpool's weak links. Alan Brazil, the Manchester United forward, summed him up. 'Great talent and agility,' he said. 'But Bruce always gave you a chance. Put in a deep cross, get off a shot, and there was always a feeling he might get it wrong.'

On the pitch and in the dressing room, Grobbelaar had a thick skin. Off it, he was stung by criticism. A regular correspondent to the *Football Echo*'s letters page slated the goalkeeper repeatedly. The anonymous writer signed off his address as 'the Yankee Bar'.

The pub on Lime Street was rough. Liverpool's away support departed and regrouped there. When trouble broke out – relatively rarely – the staff retreated behind a door at the end of the bar and set off a deafening air-raid siren that paralysed the combatants. A support column in the middle of the narrow bar area was greased heavily to prevent customers climbing up it. They stripped down to their underpants to keep their clothes from being stained and climbed it anyway.

Grobbelaar came in on a number of occasions looking for the anonymous letter writer. He was invariably drunk and unsteady on his feet. It was not a place where the patrons were star-struck. It was not a place to take liberties.

Liverpool's goalkeeper would go from group to group of drinkers demanding, 'Did you write to the *Echo* about me?' He was met mostly with cold indifference or, if he had made a gaffe in recent weeks, raw hostility. But the boys from the Yankee respected him for coming down to try and front up to his antagonist.

Dalglish absolved him for the mistake in the derby by admitting that Grobbelaar had been injured going into the game and should not have played. No one bought it. The goalkeeper had the good sense not to show his face in the American Bar that night. The mood on that part of Lime Street was angry. Less than a hundred yards down the road in the Crown, Evertonians were bouncing. Outside the Yankee you could hear the singing: 'We're gonna win the league, AGAIN!'

There was no Scouse unity in town that night. The Black Marias were loading up outside the Yates Wine Lodge on Great Charlotte Street by 10 p.m. The Bridewell always filled up rapidly after the 'friendly' derby.

Many of the young men who followed Liverpool and Everton were interested in politics. The standard image of football hooligans was of right-wing racists. The National Front had seen the game as a recruitment opportunity and had started canvassing outside grounds in the late 1970s. They achieved some success across the country. Clubs like Chelsea had mobs that gloried in racist attitudes. In Liverpool, the right-wingers were discouraged from operating outside Anfield and Goodison in the most brutal manner.

A good proportion of Liverpool and Everton's more aggressive supporters were left wing – although it did not mean that black players got an easier time of it from Merseyside crowds. Overt racism was not as obvious as at Chelsea and some other clubs but jeers and monkey noises could still be heard either side of Stanley Park.

Some Everton and Liverpool fans were vehemently political but even those with the loosest convictions generally associated themselves with socialism. This was obvious during the industrial action in Warrington in 1983, when Eddie Shah sacked workers at the Messenger newspaper group using the Thatcher government's anti-union legislation.

Young football fans from both clubs joined the mass picket lines every Monday night and fought with police support groups in full riot gear. They later lent their support to miners across the north of England, as well as turning out in massive numbers to back Liverpool City Council marches and rallies.

The Eddie Shah dispute was a forerunner of a bigger media crisis. In Warrington, Shah had used workforce deregulation to bring in non-unionized labour. 'It was a testing ground for Wapping,' Peter Hooton said.

In east London, Rupert Murdoch was planning to change the nature of British newspapers. The print unions were strong and tied to antiquated and expensive practices. With the government's support, Murdoch came up with a plan to break the unions.

When the printers refused a Murdoch proposal that would have put 90 per cent of typesetters out of work and called a strike, the Australian proprietor moved his newspapers from Fleet Street to a new plant in Wapping and a year-long dispute began.

Newspapers, and the print trade in particular, needed an overhaul. Technology was transforming the business and the unions jealously protected methods that were becoming increasingly anachronistic. But the switch to Wapping was conducted with ideological nastiness.

In February 1986, the first big confrontation took place outside News International's new complex half a mile east of the Tower of London. More than five thousand pickets crowded the Highway, one of the main routes to the docklands, and 58 people were arrested. Eight policemen were injured.

A year of confrontation had begun. The last major trouble

in this area had been the Battle of Cable Street in 1936, some 400 yards away, when East Enders galvanized to keep Oswald Mosley's Blackshirts out of their district. It was a victory for decency and community, driven by the people who had grown up in the area.

Fifty years later, there was anarchy on the streets on a nightly basis as Murdoch fought off the pickets to keep the plant – known as 'the Fortress' – pumping out his newspapers. There was very little local about this dispute. The strike-breakers were bused in under police escort. The media was changing out of all recognition. What did this have to do with football? Nothing for the moment but Murdoch's empire was on the march. The wind of change in Wapping was blowing football's way, even if no one knew it.

Most people in the game still saw television as a destructive force. When Queens Park Rangers played Liverpool in the first leg of the Milk Cup semi-final, the London club's programme notes detailed their opposition to the small screen:

> Rangers welcome the BBC here this evening. The Milk Cup semi-final will be televised live to the whole country.
>
> We have mixed feelings about our selection for this honour. On the one hand, it is a pleasure for us to know that our good-looking stadium will be the stage for such a magnificent occasion and will be seen by millions of viewers who will never be here in the flesh.

The objections came next.

> While we could have expected a capacity crowd for this fixture, we shall now be lucky if we see 20,000 persons in the ground. We are not grumbling about the financial aspect of the situation

– the Football League Compensation Committee give us a very fair reimbursement in such circumstances. But the volume of noise and spectator vocal support will not be as great as it should be and that may detract just a little from the glamour of the occasion.

A mere 15,051 people turned up to see Rangers' 1–0 victory. It seemed to prove the point.

QPR were a middling club, nervous of their future in a world where the Big Five were throwing their weight about. The same week as Rangers beat Liverpool, Martin Edwards of Manchester United sent a warning to the less affluent teams.

The Football League Annual General Meeting was looming in April. Edwards delivered a stark threat and his language was instructive. 'Make no mistake,' he said. 'The big bang will happen unless the rest of the league give us their backing.'

The phrase 'big bang' consciously referred to the deregulation of the City and the financial markets. Edwards inferred that the age of collectivism and mutual support in football was over. The old, established bodies like the FA and Football League would be circumvented if it suited the highest earners. It was now survival of the biggest and the rest would have to live off the scraps left to them by the wealthiest clubs.

The sweetener offered for the first division clubs – and a tactic designed to break the Ken Bates–Ron Noades axis – was that the entire top flight would share 50 per cent of revenue. The problem was getting the clubs to agree the deal.

They met at Villa Park in March and the Big Five outlined their strategy. It was enough to get the deal done. Before the ten-point plan, the polling structure of the Football League gave each of the 46 first and second division clubs – the full members – a single vote each. Four associate member votes represented the interests of the third and fourth divisions.

Any rule change required three-quarters – 37 – of the votes.

Bates and Noades could rally enough of the smaller fry to ensure the clubs resisted being financially bullied by the Big Five. The new plan presented by the powerful quintet tried to get round this by suggesting that those in the first division should get two votes each and the determining majority should be reduced to two-thirds.

Two things forced the plan through. The Big Five were not too greedy. The first division clubs were happy to share 50 per cent of the bounty. Secondly, they managed to change the balloting system.

Bates and Noades rejected giving the first division clubs two votes – both ran teams who bounced up and down and could not be secure about their top-flight status. Jimmy Hill, the Coventry City chairman and *Match of the Day* presenter, proposed a compromise. Each of English football's top 22 clubs would be granted one and a half votes. The deal was agreed.

The AGM took place at Heathrow in April. The ten-point plan was ratified. A breakaway had been averted – for the moment. The pace of change quickened even though Bates and Noades were mollified in the short term.

16

Clowning around

Everton started March in an apparently unassailable position. On the first day of the month, they were six points clear of Manchester United, 11 points ahead of Liverpool. Chelsea and West Ham were 14 adrift. The London clubs had games in hand but the champions had dropped just two points since before Christmas.

Steve Nicol went up to Glasgow to tape a World Cup song with the Scotland squad. They had qualified for the tournament in Mexico after a two-legged play-off with Australia and were keen to put out a record. Nicol travelled with Graeme Sharp and the conversation between the friends was not always amicable.

'I came back on the train with Sharpy,' Nicol said. 'We looked at the games left and I told him we had no chance of catching them.'

The Everton striker had experienced enough of the Merseyside rivalry to dismiss Nicol's words. 'He said, "You're sandbagging me,"' the Liverpool defender recalled. 'He still thinks I was. I wasn't.'

With their season hanging by a thread, many Kopites had already come to a verdict on Dalglish's team. They were the worst Liverpool side since the early 1970s.

The criticism was harsh but not entirely undeserved. It was a team in transition with an inexperienced manager. By contrast,

Everton looked a much more coherent, well-developed unit. Many of their rivals thought so, too.

'Everton were consistently the best team of the mid eighties,' Tony Cottee said. The West Ham striker was impressed by the way Howard Kendall's side put pressure on the opposition. 'They were relentless. They never gave you a second to settle.'

Ron Atkinson agreed. 'They were very good, very efficient, very hard to play against,' the Manchester United manager said. 'Howard was very methodical. They hit balls up to the big men and got the runners moving off them. They had a group of terriers in midfield. Everyone knew their job. They were direct and beautifully balanced.'

Dalglish was struggling to get his balance right. To many observers, Liverpool's problems started in goal. Grobbelaar was a liability. The Zimbabwean had now been first choice for five years and shown little sign of throwing off the mental lapses that had characterized his career. The position that should be the most reliable in any team was the most erratic.

The back four were the best in the division. Steve Nicol had taken over at right back from Phil Neal, who had been the mainstay of the defence for 11 years. Nicol was the best in that position in football. The Scot had superb fitness, which amazed his teammates because Nicol's diet was appalling. He was known to eat six or seven packets of crisps at a sitting. The 24-year-old smoked, too, aggravating Dalglish by sneakily lighting up on the team coach. He could drink with the best of them but never stopped running for 90 minutes. Nicol's versatility was such that his manager shifted him around almost every position on the pitch. Had he spent his career in the right-back role rather than filling in the gaps in the team, Nicol might be regarded as the greatest in that position in the history of the game.

At left back, Jim Beglin was beginning to make an impression. The 22-year-old Irishman had replaced another old stager, Alan

Kennedy, who had been shipped out to Sunderland early in the season. The newcomer was inexperienced but was a good tackler and a fine user of the ball. Both full backs were keen to get forward.

The centre-back partnership was one of the finest in football. Alan Hansen and Mark Lawrenson were quick, good tacklers, magnificent readers of the game and both were brilliant with the ball at their feet. They sometimes found physical centre forwards a challenge but few got the better of them.

Gary Gillespie, their back-up, was of the same mould but no-where near as talented. He was a good defender, though, and would have been an automatic first choice for most first division teams. Hansen and Lawrenson set the bar so high that even top-class centre backs looked a notch below their level. 'Hansen and Lawrenson were the best central defence pairing I've seen,' Ron Atkinson said. 'Individually they were not the best in their positions but together they were brilliant.'

Steve McMahon was a growing influence in midfield. The Scouser injected a dose of nastiness into the side and his combative nature gave Liverpool the bite that had been missing since Graeme Souness departed in 1984.

Jan Mølby was developing as the creative focus of the side. The big Dane was not the fittest but his touch and vision were sublime. Someone had to do his running, though.

Craig Johnston was the man for that job. The Australian had come a long way from New South Wales and taken his talent further than anyone had a right to expect. He talked about himself as 'the worst player in the best team in the world'. He undersold his own contribution.

Ronnie Whelan played on the left and was in the throes of transition from a free-scoring attacking youngster to a more disciplined midfielder. Few Liverpool players have ever used space better when the opposition had the ball. He could shut down a player's options by getting into a position that would make the passer think twice before attempting to find a teammate.

Sammy Lee was another of the old guard who was struggling to find a place in Liverpool's new era. The little Scouser had been the engine room of the midfield for most of the decade. Now injuries were catching up with him. When fit, no one was more reliable or put in more effort.

Kevin MacDonald was another option in midfield. The rangy Scot perhaps lacked a little class and pace but he had a clever approach to the game and fine defensive qualities. John Wark gave Dalglish a very different alternative. The former Ipswich Town man had the knack of arriving in the opposition area at the right time and scored vital goals. His influence elsewhere on the pitch was limited.

Paul Walsh was the player meant to fill the void left as Dalglish's career wound down. He won the PFA's Young Player of the Year award in 1984 and there was competition between Liverpool and Manchester United to sign him. He had just begun to show his worth – scoring 18 goals in 25 matches in all competitions – when he ruptured his ligaments against United.

With Walsh gone for the foreseeable future, Liverpool had few options up front but the two players available were the envy of Europe. Ian Rush had consistently been the best striker on the Continent for the first half of the decade. The Welshman was a superb forward but also Liverpool's first line of defence. He pressed opposition defenders and was responsible for many hurried passes that allowed the Reds to regain possession. Lineker was now pretender to his goalscoring crown but Rush was never going to give up his reputation as the best striker in the first division lightly.

Rush was one of the great predators and derby matches were where he shone brightest. He signed from Chester City in 1980 for £300,000, a record price for a teenager. Geoff Twentyman,

Liverpool's legendary scout, put his reputation on the line to sign the kid from St Asaph. Twentyman later said, 'I watched him six times and, finally, at an away game at Rotherham, I decided that despite his youth we had to strike quickly.' It was a huge gamble. 'A lot of other clubs were holding back, waiting for further proof,' Twentyman said. 'Liverpool took some criticism at first when people said it was too much for a teenager.'

It was certainly too big a move for the youngster to handle. He did not want to go to Anfield. He thought his wage demands might force the transfer to break down. Rush demanded £100 per week. He was shocked to find his new club were offering £300.

Twentyman believed in the teenager but few others at Anfield had such conviction. One afternoon the scout was walking down a corridor at the ground when a director passed him and hissed, 'That's a lot of money you've spent on a dud.'

The striker struggled to fit in. He was lazy in training – something he had in common with Lineker – and naturally shy. He found it hard to cope in the brutal Liverpool dressing room where any weakness was seized upon and exploited. He was nicknamed 'ET' because he was always phoning home. When he got into the first team, everything changed.

In 1981, he broke into the starting XI after forcing Bob Paisley's hand by threatening to move. In his first season, he scored 30 goals in all competitions. He repeated the trick in the next campaign and in 1983–84 he racked up 47. He had a disappointing, injury-prone season when Everton won the title but now he was back to somewhere near his best.

He loved playing against Howard Kendall's side. He opened his account against Everton in 1981 but his goals in a Goodison derby a year later catapulted him into Anfield folklore. Liverpool routed their neighbours 5–0 and Rush scored four. Even if he had retired then, the Kop would still be singing songs about him.

'Everton were the team who played with the highest defensive line at the time,' Dalglish said. 'It suited Rushie. Look at his record against them.'

Dalglish and the youngster clicked. It was a fearsome combination. 'We worked so well because he could run and I could pass,' the Scot said. 'I'd just try to put the ball in front of him. Rushie said that he made runs knowing the ball would come to him. That was true but only because his runs were so clever. His run was more important than my pass.

'Rushie was a good passer himself. He could have been a midfielder because his range of passing was great. Rush was easily the best partner I've ever had. We could have been made for each other.'

They were, and Dalglish is keen to give the credit to his fellow attacker. 'He was easy to set up,' the Scot said. 'He took up good positions. He sat on the last defender's shoulder and went into the space behind him. No one could catch him.'

Because of Walsh's injury, Dalglish was forced to pick a man that he would rather use more sparingly: himself. The player-manager was 35 on 4 March and still coming to grips with his first season at the helm. In the first part of the campaign he did not play much. In the run-in, he would have to take to the field more often.

Even at his advanced age Dalglish improved the team. His partnership with Rush was spectacularly fruitful but everyone in the side was lifted by his presence.

Off the pitch, he was clearly the boss. On the field of play, things were more egalitarian. The nature of the Liverpool team was that robust exchanges of views during the game were not only encouraged but regarded as crucial to maintaining the side's high standards. Make a mistake or the wrong choice of pass and your teammates would let you know how they felt about it. Even the manager got an earful.

'When he put himself in the team, he made it clear he was just another player,' Lawrenson said. 'We used to have massive rows with him on the pitch when we tried to play the ball to him out of defence. We'd play from the back. If the pass wasn't perfect – a foot to one side or another – he'd bollock us. Then, at half-time he'd switch from player to manager. No grudges, no hard feelings, just professionalism.'

Liverpool's biggest strength was their winning mentality, created by Bill Shankly in the 1960s and honed to a cold-blooded sharpness under Bob Paisley. 'We expected to win,' Steve Nicol said. 'Losing was a no-no. If you got caught laughing on the coach home after a defeat, you'd get your lungs ripped out.'

Ronnie Moran was the keeper of the flame at Anfield. He joined the club as a youth player in 1948 and became part of the coaching staff in the mid 1960s, graduating to the fabled Boot Room brains trust. He was known as Bugsy and one of his functions was to keep the players grounded. He would patrol the pitches of Melwood during training, picking up on any slackness, goading the 'big-headed bastards' of the team into greater efforts. If Liverpool won a match 4–0, Bugsy would want to know why it wasn't 5–0. If they kept a clean sheet, he would be furious that the defence had even allowed the opposition a chance to score. He wanted perfection. He demanded victory. Losing was unthinkable.

Excellence was treated as the normal state. When Liverpool won trophies, the management and staff acted as if it was expected and played down the achievement. The next trophy was the important one. Once silverware was won, it ceased to matter. Bugsy would go round the dressing room and collect the medals. They would be returned, singly and without ceremony, at the training ground when the players returned after summer.

'We thought every club behaved like this,' Nicol said. 'We were like the fucking Moonies. You got programmed into thinking a certain way with Liverpool. I thought it was normal in football until I went elsewhere. We would still be in the dressing room after winning the league and Bugsy would be telling us not to be late for preseason training. You were thinking about getting there on time all through your holidays.'

At the lowest point in the season, this mentality would serve Liverpool well.

Grobbelaar was the weak link. Games were running out and Dalglish's team could not afford any mistakes. The next match after Everton was a crucial moment in the season. Lose and all Liverpool could do was concentrate on the cups. Win and the faint hope of regaining the title could linger awhile.

On an icy Sunday in north London, the Reds went to White Hart Lane to play Tottenham. The BBC's *Football Focus* preview programme claimed before the game that the Zimbabwean had cost the team 15 points so far in the season. He needed a good performance. Within four minutes, Grobbelaar blundered again.

The goalkeeper hurt himself barging into Chris Waddle and gave away a corner. He then misjudged the set-piece, pushing the ball into Waddle's path and the Spurs winger could not miss from a yard out.

Temperatures dipped below freezing and football was difficult on the frigid pitch but Liverpool plugged away. Jan Mølby equalized after 66 minutes but as the seconds ticked down it looked like Dalglish's team had dropped another two points. Ray Clemence, Grobbelaar's reliable predecessor, was having a fine match for Spurs. With 30 seconds remaining, the season was on the line.

Enter Ian Rush. Ronnie Whelan controlled the ball in midfield and released a pass between the Tottenham centre backs. Rush ran on to the ball and, as Clemence moved to narrow the angle, the Welshman curved a shot into the bottom corner of the net. Liverpool fans among the 16,436 people present went wild. The gap was down to eight points.

'It was a really important day,' Mølby said. 'The pitch was frozen and we were thinking it might get called off. It was a tough match but we won it. It made all the difference in the league. If you're looking for a turning point, then it was at White Hart Lane.'

Pivotal moments rarely arrive alone. A considerable number of Liverpool supporters in north London went down to the picket lines in Wapping that night to express support. A real political and social watershed was occurring in front of their eyes.

Back on the pitch, another critical game was around the corner. Three days after the win at Spurs, Queens Park Rangers came to Anfield for the second leg of the Milk Cup semi-final. The London club were protecting a 1–0 lead from Loftus Road but were massive underdogs.

The home side put in an error-strewn performance. Mølby missed a first-half penalty. Although Steve McMahon gave Liverpool the lead just before half-time, Dalglish's team would live to regret the missed chance.

In the second half, Jim Beglin blasted a panicky clearance into Ronnie Whelan's shins and the rebound went into the net to put QPR in the lead on aggregate. Craig Johnston restored Liverpool's parity in the tie but they still had a mistake in them. Rangers did not need to score. Their opponents would do it for them.

Gary Gillespie was covering a Wayne Fereday cross but his interception only succeeded in wrong-footing Grobbelaar and sending the ball into the corner of the net. It was 2–2 on the night but the tie was gone. Two own goals sent QPR to a Wembley final against Oxford United and left Liverpool shattered. The season was going wrong again.

'We were very disappointed at getting knocked out,' Mølby said. 'We weren't thinking in terms of winning the treble, just getting to the Milk Cup final. Would the season have turned out the way it did if we had gone through to play Oxford at Wembley? Maybe not. But who cares? It turned out all right.'

It did not feel that way at the time.

If Liverpool were having a bad night, Bryan Robson had a worse one. The Manchester United captain was back at Upton Park for a postponed FA Cup fifth-round tie against West Ham. Frank McAvennie scored another goal but all the headlines after the 1–1 draw were about Robson.

United's talisman badly dislocated his shoulder. Jim McGregor, the physio, popped it back in and Robson felt well enough to play cards on the coach going home. It was the second time it had happened. When the doctors examined the injury, they told the patient he needed an operation that would rule him out for the rest of the season and the upcoming World Cup. England's captain refused to go under the knife.

He was back in the United side within the month and played six more times before the end of the season. It was too late to help his team's title challenge. With their inspirational captain struggling to get through matches, Ron Atkinson's team were on the slide. United, for so long the league leaders, were no longer in contention. The campaign that started so optimistically ended in anger at Old Trafford with the fans calling for the manager's head.

Robson only had the World Cup to look forward to in the summer. In a quest to get fit for Mexico, he took advice from John Francome and Peter Scudamore, the National Hunt jockeys who regarded dislocations as an occupational hazard. Robson started a rigorous regime of exercise, doing up to a thousand press-ups a day. He was prepared to suffer any discomfort for the chance to lead England in the summer.

*

Injuries affected other teams, too. The most crucial one in the title race was probably the most pointless. Neville Southall was on international duty with Wales for a friendly with Ireland at Lansdowne Road in Dublin. The Irish team shared the stadium with the international rugby side and, even by the standards of the mid 1980s, the pitch was a difficult one to play on. In the midst of an Irish spring, it was a mudbath. In the 66th minute, Southall jumped for a routine challenge with John Aldridge. The goalkeeper landed in a divot on the floor and could not get up. There was little pain but it was clear from the reaction of the other players and medical staff that the injury was severe. Southall, in shock and unable to comprehend how bad his ankle was, asked to take a shower.

The Welshman had dislocated his ankle and torn all the ligaments. With nine league games remaining and the FA Cup heading towards its climax, Everton had lost the best goalkeeper in the league in a meaningless match. Bobby Mimms was recalled from his loan at Notts County.

It was not only Ireland who enraged Howard Kendall. Bobby Robson took Gary Lineker to Tbilisi in Georgia for an England friendly against the Soviet Union. The games were coming thick and fast and the striker was suffering from a groin problem. Long-distance travel to a destination behind the Iron Curtain was tough enough for Lineker. The Everton manager asked for him to be rested. Robson decided he needed the player. To make it worse, the England boss played the striker for the entire 90 minutes in Dinamo Stadium. It was an unhappy international week at Goodison.

Across Stanley Park the players on national service had a much more upbeat experience. Kenny Dalglish was awarded his 100th cap for Scotland in a 3–0 victory over Romania at Hampden Park and Alan Hansen played just 45 minutes. Dalglish returned to

Anfield from the relatively short trip to find that Paul Walsh was nearing full fitness and would be available for the run-in. Things were getting better for Liverpool.

17

Cold comfort

It was a cold winter. In the early months of 1986, London, especially, was hit by the weather and rescheduling postponed games caused fixture congestion for West Ham and Chelsea.

Frank McAvennie was no longer anonymous. He was recognized from the Phoenix to Stringfellows and all points in between. Defenders had begun to take note of him.

Since the turn of the year, he had only scored one goal in 11 games – seven of them FA Cup ties. In the second half of March, he began to hit the net again. The Hammers were still in touch in the title race, although the table was deceptive. At one point they dropped down to seventh place. If they won their four games in hand they would be neck-and-neck with Everton.

Across London, Kerry Dixon was also suffering a goal drought. His lean spell would last from 28 December until early April, although David Speedie and Pat Nevin were prolific enough to keep Chelsea in the title race.

On 22 March, Chelsea beat Southampton 1–0 at the Dell and sat in fourth place in the table, four points behind Everton. The west London club had two games in hand. It was a promising position for a side with title ambitions.

On their way back from the south coast, Chelsea were not looking forward to a relaxing Sunday off, as most teams would have been. They had an appointment with Manchester City at Wembley the next day in the final of Ken Bates's brainchild, the Full Members' Cup. It was part of a run of six matches in 15 days that started off with a 1–1 draw with Everton. By the time it finished, the idea of matching the champions had disappeared completely.

The weekend of the Full Members' Cup final was a triumph for Chelsea and their chairman. Bates, as the leading voice on the Football League's management committee, had railroaded the competition into existence. It had been the subject of mockery and poor attendances had characterized the tournament. Yet at Wembley, in front of more than 67,000 paying customers, the Full Members' Cup finally caught fire.

Chelsea charged into a 5–1 lead but City stormed back, scoring three goals in the last five minutes in a frantic finale. The game ended 5–4; Bates had brought a trophy to Stamford Bridge and was doubly proud of his team and his tournament. 'If football's dying, I hope it dies like this,' John Hollins, the Chelsea manager, said afterwards. The only thing about to expire was his team's title challenge.

Board a District line train at Upton Park and 24 stops and 48 minutes later you get off at Fulham Broadway. At one end was West Ham, the other Chelsea. The Tube is about the only thing that connects the two clubs – apart from the supporters' mutual dislike. When these teams meet, London pride is important, on and off the pitch. Police went on full alert when the ICF headed west. Chelsea's hooligan gang, the Headhunters, were eager to cause their rivals pain. More calling cards were flashed around when these teams met than at a chamber of commerce networking breakfast.

Six days after Chelsea's Wembley victory and two days from the end of March, the two sides seeking to bring the title to the capital met at Stamford Bridge. West Ham had never been close to winning the league; Chelsea had not brought the title back to west London since 1955.

The pitch at the Bridge was like a bog. It was always awkward at the best of times but a thunderstorm soaked the grassy area so badly that the game was in danger of being called off. These were the sort of conditions that lightweight West Ham sides of the past did not relish. Alvin Martin, their rugged centre back, was injured, which did not bode well against a physical Chelsea side.

The game turned into a rout but not in the way most expected. The Hammers led 1–0 at half-time and Tony Cottee grabbed two more in the second period before Frank McAvennie made it 4–0. 'It really was a day to remember,' Cottee said. 'One of our best performances. The fans will never forget it. We could play but we proved we could battle that day, too.'

The *People* newspaper gushed about the display. 'There was a time,' it said, 'when everyone knew West Ham would blow any sort of title chance when winter rains arrived. A fair-weather team. But they floated around in the mud as happy as pigs in fertilizer and, with three home matches in hand on the leaders, must still be in with a Championship shout.'

Chelsea were coming apart. Their next match was another London derby, this time against Queens Park Rangers, and the Blues were on the receiving end of a 6–0 trouncing.

West Ham were trying to turn up the pressure on the Merseyside clubs. They won two of the next three games – losing disappointingly to Nottingham Forest – before Chelsea made the reverse journey down the District line on 15 April. 'We were confident,' Cottee said. 'We'd played them off the park less than three weeks before.' The East End team were even more buoyant after Cottee gave them the lead shortly after half-time. Within minutes, things began to go wrong. Nigel Spackman equalized after a defensive mistake before Pat Nevin scored the winner for the visiting side. 'We played well,' Cottee said. 'They hit us with two good finishes.'

West Ham had effectively ended Chelsea's title challenge and now the west London team returned the compliment. Everton ended the day ten points clear of the Hammers, who only had two games in hand. John Lyall had an air of resignation afterwards. 'Everton have obviously got an advantage,' the manager said. 'We must carry on and hope they slip up. We've had a great season and it is up to us to maintain it.'

Lyall was focused on the wrong team. Liverpool had whittled away at their neighbours' lead over the previous month. The next day, remarkably, Kenny Dalglish's team went back to the top of the table on goal difference with four games left. Everton had five to play. It was turning into a Merseyside shootout.

How had Everton let their 11-point lead evaporate over the course of six weeks? Injuries were taking a toll but Gary Lineker had picked the wrong time to stop scoring. In the ten league matches in March and April, Lineker scored just twice. That run of games included three draws and two defeats, enough to let Liverpool back into contention in the title race.

Lineker was playing through injuries to his groin and hamstring during this period and could not be blamed for Everton's failure to push home their advantage. Matches like the away game against Luton Town, where Kendall's team threw away a 1–0 lead in the final ten minutes and lost 2–1, could not be held against Lineker. The plastic pitch at Kenilworth Road was notoriously difficult to play on. Luton also held a grudge against Everton. The teams had met in the previous year's FA Cup semi-final, a game the Blues had won in extra time. 'Luton thought they owed us one,' Sharp said. 'It was always a fight when we played them.' It was especially galling for Everton to drop three points in the final minutes after being in front.

Yet Everton were playing to a different pattern from the title-winning side of the previous season. Then, Andy Gray and

Sharp had held the ball up and waited for the midfield raiders to arrive in the danger areas. Now Peter Reid and co. were sitting deeper to take advantage of Lineker's pace behind opposition back fours.

In 1984–85, Sharp led the scoring with 21 league goals but Adrian Heath, Kevin Sheedy, Trevor Steven and Derek Mountfield all got into double figures. Only Sharp and Heath hit ten or more alongside Lineker.

Derek Hatton, who saw Everton frequently, suggests that the side's approach was different when Howard Kendall brought in his star striker. 'Lineker changed the style of the team,' the Evertonian said. 'The season he was there was the only one where we didn't win a trophy.

'But I understand why Howard signed him. It sent out a message that Everton could get the best players.'

Neville Southall, who watched the striker's exploits from the other end of the pitch, accepts that there was a difference in the team's style but believes it was largely a positive development. 'He did change the way we played,' the Everton goalkeeper said. 'It was easier to hit the ball longer earlier. It was better in some respects because he'd be in behind them. He was as quick as lightning.'

The man who was most frequently twinned with Lineker dismisses suggestions that the England striker had a negative impact on the team. Graeme Sharp was impressed by his partner's finishing ability. No one could doubt his predatory instincts. 'Links was unbelievable,' the Scot said. 'He was the best finisher one-on-one.'

The main difference from the other strikers that Sharp played alongside – Andy Gray and Adrian Heath – is that Lineker was only interested in getting the ball in danger areas. 'He didn't get involved in the build-up,' Sharp said. 'We went a bit more direct with him so he could use his pace.'

At Anfield, Lineker was regarded as a very dangerous addition to Kendall's side. 'I've heard people say he changed the way they played and they were better before him but we didn't see it that way,' Mølby said. 'He gave them pace in behind. Sharpie was a proper No. 9 who'd give you physical problems to deal with but Lineker was like Ian Rush. He'd be into any space behind the defence. He was their most dangerous player. You could never rest when he was on the pitch.'

Mark Lawrenson, who was often directly matched against the England striker, concurs. 'He was hard to play against because he didn't get involved,' the centre half said. 'He didn't drop off to get the ball. He was always looking to get in behind you and if he did, he was clever and you were in trouble.'

Lineker was always probing for weaknesses. 'He said to me later that early in every game he'd run offside deliberately to see what the defenders would do,' Lawrenson said. 'If they kept a high line, he'd think, "I'm in."'

The Liverpool player believes Lineker was a defenders' nightmare. 'He was a very dangerous attacker,' Lawrenson said. 'If you switched off for a moment, he was gone.'

Steve Nicol did not see any visible change to Everton's tactics when Lineker was in the team. 'I don't think there was a conscious effort to sit deeper for him. Howard wasn't like that. Reidy and the rest wanted to get forward,' the full back said. 'But you had to be aware of where he was all the time. We didn't do anything special for anyone but you couldn't relax when he was on the pitch.'

Now, at the business end of the season, Everton needed their superstar's goals more than ever. Both the league and FA Cup were turning into a straight fight between the Merseyside clubs.

Wembley was ready to host another big game. Oxford United faced Queens Park Rangers, who had knocked out Liverpool, in the Milk Cup final, the Football League's showpiece match.

Life had changed significantly at the Manor Ground since Robert Maxwell had attempted to subsume Oxford and Reading into a new entity, the Thames Valley Royals, and move them to Didcot. Under the management of Jim Smith – known as the 'Bald Eagle' – Oxford had climbed the divisions and reached the top flight. They claimed a place in the first division a mere 23 years after joining the Football League.

Maxwell was now in the big time. Like Ken Bates and Ron Noades, the Oxford chairman was a man on the make and he relished the publicity football brought him.

Smith led Oxford to back-to-back promotions. In the summer of 1985, after the club had secured promotion to the first division, the manager thought he deserved a pay rise. He went to see his chairman and asked for a salary of £50,000 per year. Maxwell offered £45,000 and a stand-off ensued. The two men planned to get together in London to discuss the situation but the meeting was scheduled for the night of Heysel. The disaster ended the negotiations abruptly. It was a month before the talks resumed.

Taking advantage of the situation, QPR's chairman Jim Gregory came in and offered the Bald Eagle the sort of contract he wanted. Smith took the vacant job at Loftus Road.

Most people around the Manor Ground thought the problem between Smith and Maxwell was less about money than ego. The manager, with his memorable nickname and big media presence, was taking the attention away from the chairman. Maxwell wanted the credit for Oxford's growth. He bade fare-well to the man who had overseen two promotions with the words: 'If you want to go, you go.'

Smith was replaced by one of his coaches, Maurice Evans. The new manager had played for and managed Reading during the course of a 25-year career at Elm Park until he was sacked abruptly in 1984 even though the team were third in the second division. Evans took charge of Smith's team and began a dogged fight to stay in the top flight.

Oxford were third from bottom of the table when the final was played and had four league games left. Unnervingly, one was against Everton. They had not won for seven matches, while QPR were on an eight-game unbeaten run. Before meeting Rangers at Wembley, the notoriously self-effacing Evans suggested that Smith deserved to lead both teams on to the pitch in the ceremonial walk from the tunnel to the halfway line. The Oxford manager even said that it did not matter whether his team won or lost. 'There's too much emphasis on being a winner nowadays,' he said. 'I am one of those strange people who likes to put entertainment first and winning second.' It was not an attempt to play mind games.

Smith's new team froze on the day. QPR barely landed a blow on Oxford, who went in 1–0 up at half-time and had extended the lead to 3–0 by the final whistle.

Evans sent the club's 72-year-old trainer to collect his medal afterwards. Ken Fish had been involved at Oxford for more than two decades and Evans, who had served a similar stint with Reading, explained his rationale. 'Everybody will say I'm strange but going to get that medal did not mean anything to me,' the manager said. 'Mr Fish has been at the club so long he deserves it.'

Maxwell, meanwhile, was basking in glory. Oxford still had a relegation battle to fight, though.

It had been a manic March. The freezing weather created a backlog of fixtures and the season needed to end on 10 May because of the proximity of the World Cup finals. The workload was as heavy as the pitches.

Everton played nine games in the month, including FA Cup and Super Cup ties; Liverpool had the same number of matches.

West Ham took to the pitch eight times but faced a logjam of fixtures in April. Manchester United also played eight. Chelsea had the fewest games in the period, seven, but also looked forward to an exhausting run-in.

Injuries were piling up. United were down to third as Ron Atkinson's walking wounded limped out of the title race. 'We played Everton on Easter Monday,' the United manager said. 'All our centre halves were injured. Mark Higgins played with a broken arm. We suffered with injuries. Robbo was out, McGrath out. Strachan injured. It was difficult.'

Ominously for Everton, United held on for a 0–0 draw at Old Trafford, meaning that the month ended with Liverpool going top of the league on goal difference. It had been a wild 31 days for the Blues. They ended the first day of March 11 points clear of their neighbours. The draw with United meant they had dropped seven points since then. But the league had to take a back seat as April began. The FA Cup semi-finals were round the corner.

18

Up for the cup

The FA Cup was important for both Liverpool and Everton. Until the mid 1960s, it was a symbol of Everton's superiority in the city.

The Blues first won the oldest knockout competition in the world in 1906, beating Newcastle United 1–0 at Crystal Palace. They triumphed again at Wembley in 1933, cruising to a 3–0 victory over Manchester City with the great Dixie Dean on the scoresheet. Liverpool, meanwhile, were unable to get their hands on the venerable old trophy.

Liverpool's first two finals ended in disappointment. They played in the last final before the First World War, a 1–0 loss to Burnley in 1914, and their first visit to Wembley in 1950 ended with a 2–0 defeat by Arsenal.

By the time the sixties arrived, Liverpool's inability to win the cup was a standing joke. Evertonians sniped that the Liver Birds would spread their wings and fly when the Reds won the trophy. It underlined Liverpool's status as second-class football citizens against the prestige of the Mersey Millionaires of Goodison.

The crucial tipping point in the balance of power between the two clubs came in 1965. Bill Shankly's first great side reached the final in an eventful campaign. In the third round, Shankly's team won away at West Brom before making hard work of Stockport County, who would go on to finish bottom of the fourth division, drawing 1–1 at Anfield before sealing the tie with a 2–0 win at Edgeley Park in the replay.

In the fifth round, Shankly's team were drawn away to Bolton Wanderers. The 1–0 win was straightforward enough but a surge of away supporters after the goal caused a wooden barrier to collapse at Burnden Park. There were no serious injuries but it was a worrying incident that again highlighted how precarious safety was for football fans. Few lessons ever seemed to be learnt: 33 supporters had died in a crush in the Railway End at Burnden in 1946 at a cup quarter-final against Stoke City. This day in 1965, all the Liverpool fans were able to walk away from an FA Cup tie.

It took two attempts for Shankly's side to beat Leicester City in the last eight, a single goal in the Anfield replay deciding the tie after a 0–0 draw at Filbert Street. That set up a semi against Chelsea – the glamorous west London media darlings – at Villa Park.

Somehow, Shankly got his hands on a Chelsea brochure prepared for the eventuality that the London club were successful in the semi. The Scot exaggerated the significance of the document and raged against the arrogance of Liverpool's opponents. The team were instructed to 'stuff those wee cocky southern buggers'. They duly did and a 2–0 victory put them on the road to Wembley.

The scramble for tickets was even more frenzied than usual. The cup was the holy grail to Liverpool fans. They flocked south displaying the usual fanaticism but it was mixed with fear and craving. They were desperate to kill off the sense of superiority the cup wins had brought to Goodison. They were terrified defeat would reinforce the myth and inferiority complex.

Evertonians looked nervously at the Liver Buildings but they could take heart because Liverpool's opponents in the final were Don Revie's Leeds United. The Yorkshire side were emerging as one of the first division's powerhouses. For the next decade, they would be one of England's best sides. They were talented, brutal and their cynical nature reflected the personality of their manager.

The final was attritional. Gerry Byrne broke his collarbone in the first minutes of the game. There were no substitutes, so Liverpool were faced with a choice: go down to ten men or let Byrne play on. The defender continued. For 90 vicious minutes, the teams battled it out in difficult, rainy conditions with neither side able to score. Byrne would face another 30 minutes of agony.

Extra time burst into life. Roger Hunt gave Liverpool the lead three minutes into the additional period, heading home a cross from the magnificent invalid Byrne.

Billy Bremner, the Leeds midfielder, equalized eight minutes later but Shankly's team would not be denied.

With three minutes left, Ian St John scored a diving header. Liverpool had at last won the cup. The Liver Birds stayed put, despite the Everton propaganda. Nothing changed . . . except now Anfield had no reason to feel inferior to Goodison. The balance of power was shifting. Now Kopites could sneer at their neighbours. After all, Everton had not won the cup since before the war.

That did not last long. A year later, Scouse fanaticism was on display at Wembley again. Everton reached the final against another Yorkshire club, Sheffield Wednesday. If film of the Kop singing on the BBC's *Panorama* documentary series in 1964 had cemented the passion of Anfield's disciples in popular consciousness, then this May Saturday two years later let the nation see that the Blues were just as ardent, excitable and manic as their Red friends and relatives.

Before the match, young Evertonians stripped the local touts of their tickets. After 1966, the black-market profiteers had an extra expense on cup final day – bodyguards. The 'liberation' of tickets became part of football underground folklore. Inside the stadium, the ardour of the Gwladys Street took centre stage. Eddie Kavanagh was its personification.

It looked as if it was going to be a disappointing final when Wednesday went 2–0 up just before the hour mark. The showpiece event seemed to be subsiding without the late drama of the previous year.

Then Everton hit back. Mike Trebilcock, a Cornishman who would only play 11 games for the club in three years, scored twice in five minutes to level the scores. Kavanagh, who had once been on the books at Goodison as an aspiring player, chose this moment to earn infamy.

Balding and dressed in a suit, Kavanagh stepped from the terraces to join the celebration. 'As soon as that ball hit the net, I was on me bike,' Eddie later said. 'That's how quick it was. I think the crowd got to you more than anything. They were all screaming. You'd have to see it to believe it. I couldn't explain that.'

The players – and the television viewers – were struggling to explain or believe what they were seeing. First, Kavanagh ran to the goalscorer. Many of the players would have known the interloper from his time on the staff. The Cornishman was not one of them.

'I'd seen Trebilcock and I went for him first,' Kavanagh explained. 'I grabbed him, pulled him on the ground. He shit himself because he didn't know me. We all played in blue and white, didn't we? Sheffield were in blue and white, and we're in blue and white, so he didn't know who I was.'

His plan was to head next to the goalkeeper, Gordon West, to offer some advice. 'I was coming across then to Westy. I was going to say, "Gordon, for God's sake don't let no more in."'

The next few moments would turn Kavanagh into an Everton

legend who will be talked about long after Trebilcock is forgotten. The police were at hand to eject the pitch invader. The first officer grabbed at his quarry but, like his team, Kavanagh was not going down so easily. As he ran away, the constable grabbed a handful of jacket. Eddie wriggled out of his coat as if shedding a skin and the policeman landed flat on his face having arrested the top half of Kavanagh's suit.

'I'd seen this busie [policeman] come after me,' the Evertonian said. 'He caught up with me and got me by the coat. But I just took it off.'

Shirt hanging out and braces askew, Kavanagh set off for the goal area but his mazy run was ended when another policeman came from nowhere and performed one of the few rugby tackles seen on cup final day. The Scouser remained disappointed and resentful about it until the day he died in Cantril Farm in 1999.

'I didn't see the other fella come around me,' Kavanagh said. 'He wasn't even a busie, he was only a special [constable], but I didn't see him coming because he wouldn't have caught me. Six of them had me pinned down like I was one of those [great] train robbers.'

Kavanagh was escorted from the pitch and thrown out of the ground. By the time Derek Temple scored the goal that won the cup for Everton, Eddie was back in the stadium having bunked in. He was able to sum up what winning the cup meant to him – and many others, Blue and Red, across Merseyside.

'I was hysterical,' he said. 'After all the years we'd waited. There's never been a build-up like that. If you love your side like I do, you're not worried about your kids, or your ma or your da, you're just wanting to win the cup.'

For his efforts, Kavanagh won the nickname 'the first hooligan'. It was unfair. But his sense of overwhelming excitement was not so unusual at Goodison or Anfield. The FA Cup always brought out the fanaticism of the city. Those two Wembley finals in 1965 and '66 put the madness on a national stage at a time when the world's attention was on Merseyside.

Since then, each team had won the cup once: Liverpool in 1974 and Everton a decade later.

Most of Kendall's squad owned a cup-winners' medal from the victory over Watford two years earlier. At Anfield, only John Wark had won the trophy, with Ipswich Town. Throughout the most glorious years in Liverpool's history, a time when they had won seven titles, four League Cups, four European Cups and a UEFA Cup they were unable to win the FA Cup. They wanted it badly. But there was an extra incentive.

Kendall and Dalglish had their sights set on another Wembley visit but also on something much more special: the league and cup Double. That feat had only been achieved twice in the twentieth century and four times overall. Everton had come close the previous season but Manchester United stopped them. They now aimed to go one step better.

The Merseyside clubs were neck and neck in the league. They hoped to be kept apart in the FA Cup draw.

The FA Cup began for top-flight teams on 4 January. It was cold and snowy on Merseyside. Both clubs were drawn at home, so their ties were played simultaneously, two 3 p.m. kick-offs on Saturday. Everton made hard work of lowly Exeter City, winning 1–0, while Liverpool dispatched Norwich City with five unopposed goals.

The Blues had an easier time of it in the fourth round. Drawn at home to Blackburn Rovers they advanced 3–1. It looked trickier for Dalglish's men. They were handed a trip to high-flying Chelsea but the Reds negotiated a difficult tie by winning 2–1.

The fifth round took nearly a month to complete because of bad weather. Liverpool drew 1–1 away to York City, brought the third division side back to Anfield and eased to a 3–1 victory. Everton's tie with Tottenham Hotspur – planned to be their first live televised match since the blackout – was postponed and when the game was eventually played Kendall's team secured a 2–1 victory.

Both teams took two attempts in the quarter-finals. Everton survived an awkward encounter on the plastic pitch at Luton Town. After a 2–2 draw they went back to Goodison Park and beat the team they had defeated in the previous year's semifinals 1–0. Liverpool drew 0–0 with Watford at home and, on a Monday night at Vicarage Road, took until the second period of extra time to edge ahead 2–1.

The draw was kind and kept the Merseyside giants apart. Liverpool would face Southampton at White Hart Lane – their fifth meeting of the season because of both teams' involvement in the Super Cup. Sheffield Wednesday came out of the bag to face Everton. Their semi-final was slated for Villa Park. The dream of a first Merseyside FA Cup final was alive and well.

Merseyside was desperate for an FA Cup final derby. Liverpool and Everton had never reached the Wembley showpiece together.

Two years earlier, the teams had contested a Milk Cup final. Huge numbers of Scousers had decamped to London and used the event as an expression of local pride. Chants of 'Merseyside' resounded across the capital.

That final, in March 1984, was in a different political climate. The miners' strike had just got under way and the city council were on the offensive and making progress in their battle against Thatcherism. There was optimism and defiance among the legions of young Scousers heading to Wembley. 'Maggie, Maggie, Maggie! Out! Out! Out!' was chanted almost as much as Liverpool and Everton songs. There was still hope that the National Union of Mineworkers would force the Thatcher government into retreating on its more extreme policies. Things had changed significantly since then.

The left-wingers were on the run. Not just on Merseyside. In March, 80 Labour councillors from Liverpool and the London borough of Lambeth lost their case against their removal from office and the imposition of personal fines levied for refusing to set a legal rate. They were facing disqualification for five years. There was a feeling that the left's defeat was inevitable. The only victories were coming on the pitch.

19

Fighting talk

FA Cup semi-finals used to be one of the great experiences for football supporters. They kicked off at 3 p.m. on Saturday, took place at a neutral venue and generally had a more or less even split of fans in the stadium. The final at Wembley always had too many neutrals present because the FA rewards its functionaries and county associations with tickets for the big day. Many sell them on at exorbitant prices but enough are keen to see the game to give the atmosphere a different feel. At the semis, there were very few non-partisans in the ground.

White Hart Lane was the venue for Liverpool's last-four tie with Southampton. Tottenham Hotspur's ground was an atmospheric, claustrophobic stadium with the main standing terrace running the length of the touchline. Usually, the most fanatical supporters stood behind the goal – like on the Kop or in the Gwladys Street End – but at the Lane they occupied the Shelf, a two-tiered standing section with a level of seats perched above. It was a fearsome sight for rival supporters. There was plenty to be concerned about on a visit to Tottenham.

The 30-minute walk from Seven Sisters underground station was legendary. In the 1970s and '80s, it became regarded as a sort of sniper's alley for away fans. Before and after the match, travelling supporters would run the gauntlet on their journey up the High Road. Groups of Tottenham hooligans would pop out from side streets and pubs in ambush parties. West Ham's Green

Street had a worse reputation and the walk up the Fulham Road to Chelsea was always a nervous one but many seasoned match-goers regarded a trip to Spurs as the most hostile and dangerous day of the season.

Liverpool fans of my generation had been on the receiving end of one of the worst beatings of the era at Tottenham. In 1980, the Reds were drawn against Spurs in the sixth round of the FA Cup. Terry McDermott scored a magnificent goal to give Liverpool a 1–0 win and the Scousers in the Park Lane End went wild. The Tottenham fans reserved their craziness for after-wards.

There was anarchy outside. Running battles took place down the High Road. Liverpool might have won on the pitch but the local boys ensured that we would remember the day not for McDermott's goal but the terror and beatings that followed. Even now if a middle-aged man claims to have 'followed Liverpool everywhere in the seventies and eighties', reply with the simple phrase 'Tottenham in the Cup'. If they don't visibly wince at the memory, they're lying.

Personally, it was not a lucky ground. In 1984, Liverpool were drawn at the Lane in a Milk Cup game. For midweek matches in London, we had a familiar routine. Meet between 11 a.m. opening and noon in the Wine Lodge, move to the Yankee around 1 p.m. and then leave there at 2.55 and nip to platform seven at Lime Street to get the 15.05 to Euston.

It was a good system. The licensing laws forced pubs to shut in Liverpool at 3 p.m. but in those pre-Heysel days you could drink at the buffet of the ordinary timetabled trains. Drink had long been outlawed on football specials, so taking normal services was desirable because it meant access to more beer.

There was still time in London to get a couple of pints before the match, so we took the Victoria line to Finsbury Park and drank in the pubs near Highbury. The logic was simple: Arsenal territory was the least likely place in north London to run into trouble when you were playing Tottenham.

When we got back to the Tube, the ticket office was shut, so we jumped on, expecting to pay at Seven Sisters. When we got there, we joined the queue to pay at the excess-fares window inside the barrier.

The rest of our group got their tickets and were waved through. I was the last. The policeman who grabbed me had let the others go. Why he picked on me I'll never know.

He asked where I'd come from. I said Finsbury Park. He asked why I'd been to that station. I explained the rationale. It was a safer place to drink. Then the officer said he did not believe me. He thought I'd come from Euston and tried to bunk the Tube.

I denied it but then he played his trump card. He smelt my breath and said, 'Drunk, are we? And disorderly? You're heading for a night in the cells.'

I folded immediately and said I'd come from Euston. With a smirk of triumph, he led me into a room concealed in the Tube station. He clearly wanted to nick a Scouser and I was the unlucky victim.

Initially, I planned to give a false name and address. Few people carried any form of ID and the ruse had worked before for plenty of people I knew. Unfortunately, I had a student rail card in my shirt pocket. It was concealed under a crew-neck jumper but if he did decide to search me and I'd given a false name it would definitely mean an overnight stay in the cells.

It was just as well I gave the correct details. There was a knock on the door and the policeman opened it. One of my mates was standing there and asked, 'Can Tony come out to play?' To say I was unimpressed is an understatement.

Anyway, the constable took my details, issued me with a caution for underpaying the fare and kicked me out. I was at least able to get to the match. I shouldn't have bothered. Less than five minutes after kick-off, Bruce Grobbelaar spilt a routine shot into the path of Clive Allen and Tottenham scored the only goal of the game. It was a night to forget all round.

It had been wiped from my memory until I arrived back from work one day to an angry household. A policeman had turned up earlier with the message that I'd been charged with the offence because it was 'football-related'. There was a letter from Horseferry Road Magistrates Court.

After asking around, I was expecting a £10 fine, so pleaded guilty by post. The case came up the day after Millwall rioted at Luton. The next letter told me I'd have to pay a £50 fine and £50 costs.

That was what it was like to be a football fan in the mid 1980s. Even when you did your best to avoid trouble it might seek you out. And on semi-final day it found me again on Tottenham High Road.

Everyone was expecting a quiet afternoon. There was no history of trouble between Liverpool and Southampton and with the numbers on each side more or less similar, few Scousers expected any disorder. The mood in north London was relaxed. Our guard was down.

Halfway to the ground, a big crew of Southampton appeared from a narrow street on the other side of the road, moving fast and radiating hostility. They passed us but crossed over further on to chase a car that had honked its horn at them. The driver and passenger were wearing Liverpool scarves and they accelerated through a red light to escape the mob kicking the car.

Now the Southampton lot were on our side of the street and scanning the crowds for anyone they suspected of being Liverpool fans. We were still pretty blasé about the situation. They were not very experienced. Our band of 11 mates was spread out over 50 or so yards in three groups. The first two passed them without incident. A London mob would have spotted us as Scouse in seconds because of the way we dressed.

The last of our friends approached them. Big Al, the man who had knocked on the police-room door two years before, was among them. He was 6 ft 4 in. and stood out. A Southampton fan shouted at him, 'You're a Scouse bastard, aren't you?'

Al replied quietly but from 30 yards away I could read his lips: 'So what if I am, dickhead?'

Then it was pandemonium. Al disappeared and everyone started shouting. As a group we had observed a lot of trouble over the years and talked about how we should handle it when our turn inevitably came to get done. We agreed that if we were split up, as now, and could not save the person getting the beating, that it was better to stay out of it. There was no point in another of us getting a kicking if we couldn't help. It did not work like that.

One of the lads with me was younger than us and down from Scotland for the game. I told him to go into a newsagents' shop, gave him a shove to get him started and headed for the melee shouting at the top of my voice. It was a mistake.

About thirty of them were still across the road and homed in on me. Within seconds, I felt the first concussive blow to my head. For a few moments it all went blank.

When the thought processes started again, I was pretty comfortable. About a dozen of them were trying to punch me and it was too many. I'd ducked into a boxer-style crouch and as they tried to pound my head they were hitting each other's hands. I was thinking of staying put because it was only a matter of time before the police arrived until I heard a Hampshire voice say the dreaded words, 'Stanley him!'

I'd seen the damage a Stanley knife could do. Outside the Anfield Road End I'd watched a fella get his back striped with two blades in one sweep. His shirt was soaked in blood before he even realized he'd been slashed. I could live with a sliced back but this Southampton mob struck me as a bit clueless. One idiot trying to scar my face and missing slightly could slice into the neck. So I decided to bolt.

There was a little gap in the circle around me and I slipped out of it, crossing my legs as I emerged back into the light. Unfortunately, I tripped myself up. They were still punching each other's fists when they realized I was out and down on the floor. I'd always been taught that the important thing was staying on your feet. Once you were prone, they could kick your head. Now they advanced grinning.

Defenceless, I began shouting at them. 'Go 'ed, shitbags, kick me when I'm down. There's only about twenty of you and I'm on my own. Go 'ed. Go 'ed.' The rant froze them for a second. It allowed me to scramble up against a wall and get back on my feet. I bounced up and down, bunched my fists and said, 'Right, now I'm ready for you.'

Then they descended on me. This time a different voice said, 'Throw him through the window.'

It was another development I didn't like. They dragged me down the wall and I grabbed at the corner of the brickwork with one hand and cupped the other around the part of my neck that was susceptible to a slash. One of them hit my clutching hand with something hard – a piece of stone or concrete chunk – and three or four dragged me towards the window while the rest pummelled me as I went. Then, as I was beginning to brace myself for impact against the plate-glass shopfront, they were all gone. A punch caused me to shut my eyes and when they opened I was on my own with the match-day crowd walking past looking at me with curiosity. Some of them, middle-aged Southampton fans, were laughing and goading me.

If the entire incident took a minute, I'd be surprised. A more sensible estimate would be 30 seconds. Maybe less.

A hand touched my shoulder and it was a policeman. 'Come with me,' he said gently.

He walked me to a van across the street and said, 'Get in and sit down.' I thought he was worried about me because of the beating and said, 'No, no, I'm all right. I'm fine. I don't need to go to hospital or anything. I'll be OK.' I must have had a blow to the head or something to be thinking that way.

'No, you won't, you Scouse bastard,' he said. 'You're nicked.'

I exploded. 'You've just watched them beat the shit out of me for doing nothing and now you're arresting me? Arrest them, you shithouse.'

He had hold of me and was dragging me towards the van but I was pulling away. A sergeant at the front of the vehicle was laughing. 'You got a kicking there, Scouse. They did you good and proper. Get on your way.'

The constable released me, gave me a shove towards White Hart Lane and then toe-ended me up the backside as hard as he could. That was the blow that hurt most.

Big Al wandered up beside me looking dazed. He said, 'My watch is gone. I've lost my watch.' A third policeman overheard him. This copper was chuckling, too. He pointed back down the road to the corner where Al had been attacked. 'They got you at the lights, kicked you across the road to the other side and booted you all the way up to that shop,' he said, tracing the 50-yard journey with his finger. 'Your watch will be there – or in someone's pocket.'

They had observed the whole incident unfolding. They knew who started it and who were the victims. Still, we knew we were lucky not to be locked up.

One of the other lads came across the road shaking his head. 'They were a very unprofessional mob,' he said. 'You both got away with one.' He turned to me. 'They hit each other more than they hit you.'

We did a head count. There were five of us together, six missing. Three were lost in the fracas, two were heading for the cells and the other bumped into us in the ground. 'We weren't expecting that,' Al said once he'd got himself together. 'We will be after the match, though.' And we were.

The legends of football hooliganism talk about equally matched mobs of 'lads' facing off against each other. The books about the subject are written in a pathetic, mock-heroic style that elevates the protagonists into knights of the streets. It's all rubbish.

Most incidents of violence occurred when one side had significantly bigger numbers than the other. It wasn't some kind of mano-a-mano showdown. It was bullying on a grand scale. The victims of choice were almost always those not in a position to fight back.

Across the Shelf, there were similar tales of surprise attacks, outnumbered groups being chased by mobs of Southampton and individuals being picked off. It turned out Everton were to blame.

Two years previously, the Blues had played Southampton in that year's semi, again in north London but this time at Highbury. The game was tense, tight and went to extra time. With just three minutes of the 120 left, Adrian Heath scored the winner for Howard Kendall's side.

After nearly a decade and a half of misery, the Evertonians at Highbury exploded with joy. Arsenal's ground was the only significant stadium in England that did not have pitchside fences to prevent supporters encroaching on the field of play. At the final whistle, Blues surged on to the pitch and, irked by the celebrations, Southampton fans confronted them. There were riotous scenes as the fans clashed. Everton moved on to Wembley, won the cup and soon forgot about the incident. Southampton supporters had no final to go to. They harboured a festering resentment against Scousers and expressed their anger on another semi-final day.

Even though hooliganism had dropped off after Heysel, it still sporadically re-emerged. The trouble before and after the semi-final at White Hart Lane barely made an impact in the media, despite the hysteria around fighting at matches.

The threat of violence was a fact of life for fans. However, in 15 years of going to away games – mostly travelling independently, eschewing police escorts and frequently encountering confrontational situations – this was the only real beating I received. Counting that day, I probably threw five punches in a decade and a half. Two of them were at Liverpool fans. Despite the mythology and incidents like the one on the Tottenham High Road, the game was not quite as dangerous to watch as people believed.

Both semis were anxious affairs. Everton faced Sheffield Wednesday. It was 20 years since Eddie Kavanagh's moment of glory at Wembley on the last occasion that these two sides met in the FA Cup. The happier, innocent days of 'the first hooligan' were long gone but the semi at Villa Park was as tense as the final two decades earlier.

Everton were without Gary Lineker and Neville Southall but were too strong for the Yorkshire side. Alan Harper put Howard Kendall's team into the lead but Carl Shutt equalized within two minutes. The game went to extra time but Everton's class showed in the additional 30 minutes. Graeme Sharp scored the winning goal and Everton were back in the final for the third year running.

At White Hart Lane, Liverpool were having a similar grind. It was 0–0 after 90 minutes and the most notable incident occurred ten minutes before half-time when Mark Wright, the Southampton centre back, suffered a dreadful injury. Wright collided with Craig Johnston and his own goalkeeper, Peter Shilton, and broke his leg.

The game remained scoreless until Ian Rush struck twice in extra time against a tiring Saints side. The Shelf bounced up and down and, amid the joy of victory, there was only one thing anyone connected with Liverpool needed to know: who would they face in the final. As Johnston left the pitch, he looked at Ronnie Moran and asked a simple question: 'Them?'

Bugsy nodded slowly and deliberately, the victory over Southampton already forgotten. Moran's mean-eyed focus was already on 'them'. The first Merseyside FA Cup final was on. The next month would define heroes or create a lifetime's bitter memories for Everton and Liverpool.

20

Showdown

With less than three weeks left in the season, the maths was simple. Everton and Liverpool were level on points but the Blues had a game in hand – against West Ham at Goodison. If Kendall's team won all their matches, they would win the title.

West Ham had moved into third place in the table and had one more game to play than Everton. They still had a chance if the Merseyside teams made any mistakes. It would be difficult for the Hammers. Their last five games were concertinaed into nine days. Winter, as much as anything else, had made things awkward for Frank McAvennie and co.

They were still dangerous. In late April they thrashed Newcastle United 8–1 at Upton Park. McAvennie got on the scoresheet but the most remarkable scoring feat of the game came from Alvin Martin, the centre half. The man from Bootle scored a hat-trick – rare enough for a defender – but what made this particular trio of goals unusual was that a different goalkeeper was between the posts for each of Martin's strikes.

Newcastle were suffering a goalkeeping injury crisis. Martin Thomas, who started the game, was barely fit and conceded four goals, one of them to the West Ham defender, before failing to reappear at the start of the second half. Thomas was replaced by Chris Hedworth, a reserve defender, who let in a header from Martin 19 minutes into the second period before swapping the goalkeeper's jersey with Peter Beardsley. The England striker saw out the rest of the game but when West Ham were awarded a penalty, the Hammers urged Martin to take it to complete the unprecedented hat-trick. The defender dispatched the spot-kick and Upton Park rose to give acclaim to one of its heroes.

The fixture list had given the East End club too much to do. They kept winning but something had to give.

Liverpool were the team of the spring. They had suffered injuries, too, but even without Mark Lawrenson at the centre of defence they were not conceding. After the Everton defeat in February, they leaked only four goals in 12 games. They steamrollered themselves back into contention. But games were running out.

Kendall's team had not exactly hit poor form. Since the derby, they lost just once in eight matches. As April turned to May, eight days determined the direction of the title.

On Saturday, 26 April, Liverpool hosted Birmingham City at Anfield. It was a mismatch. Kenny Dalglish's team romped to a 5–0 victory while the packed crowd on the Kop waited to hear how Everton had fared at Nottingham Forest.

Dotted across the vast terrace were a number of supporters clutching tiny radios to their ears. They provided updates on other games across the country on a weekly basis. They often appeared to be alone – the groups of mates who attended the match together talked among themselves and had no need to spend the 90 minutes listening to the radio. On days like this, though, the loners and their transistors provided a vital service for the eager hordes behind the goal. In the days before smart-phones and mobile technology, fans were almost incommunicado inside grounds for the duration of the game. There were updates of scores at half-time but otherwise it was a case of waiting five minutes or more after the final whistle to hear results read over the tannoy. Live updates had one source: fans with radios.

By the time Liverpool were three goals to the good, the

majority of people inside Anfield had lost interest in the match they were watching. All they cared about was what was occurring at the City Ground in Nottingham. It was 0–0. That scoreline kept the title race alive but things were still in Everton's hands. Kendall's team could afford one more draw and still maintain pole position.

In this environment, any news – even if it was fake – was eagerly embraced. With about ten minutes left, a rumour spread across the Kop that Forest had scored. Premature celebrations broke out, while the more cautious waited, fingers crossed, for the full-time results to hopefully confirm Everton's demise. There was only disappointment. There was no goal.

In the East Midlands, it was equally tense. Bad feeling was in the air. The Everton fans taunted the home supporters all afternoon with chants of 'Scab', a legacy of the miners' strike when Nottinghamshire's pitmen crossed the picket lines. At the final whistle, they sang 'We're gonna win the league' as their team left the pitch. The draw was not the ideal result but it was good enough. A much more damaging blow than losing points had occurred, though. Peter Reid had picked up another knock and left the stadium on crutches.

Everton were still on course to win the title – and therefore the Double. Liverpool had two games left, Everton three. The most crucial week of the season started with Goodison looking the likeliest place for the championship trophy to reside for another year.

Both teams were away next. On the last day of April, a warm Wednesday, an armada of coaches and cars left the city heading south, Reds in the direction of Leicester City and Blues on their way to Oxford United. Both teams were in a battle against relegation.

United were in the drop zone with City just three points above them in the last safe position. All four teams were desperate for points.

Liverpool went to Filbert Street to play the only team that had beaten Everton twice in the league. Leicester were awkward opposition at this stage of the season but Dalglish's team had won nine out of their last ten games.

Everton travelled to Oxford to face the winners of the Milk Cup. United had lost their only game since the final and were hanging on to their first division status by their fingertips. It turned into a momentous night.

It was hard to have fond memories of the Manor Ground but it was the scene of one of Kendall's great escapes. Two years earlier Adrian Heath had scored the late equalizer against Oxford that was widely believed to have kept the Everton manager in his job. On this night, it would be the scene of another turning point.

Winning would not be easy. 'It was a horrible place to play,' Peter Reid said. 'And we had loads of injuries. I failed a fitness test.'

The kick-off was 7.30 p.m. Liverpool would start their game 15 minutes later. Everton had the chance to go back on top before their rivals finished playing but there were problems before the match. Gary Lineker's hamstring was sore and he had scored only once in eight league games. Everton badly needed him to hit the target against Oxford. Instead, the striker was thrown further out of kilter. The England forward had a lucky pair of boots that he had worn all season. They were battered, patched up and looked wrecked but Lineker was comfortable in them. The kit staff left them at Goodison.

The league's leading goalscorer was forced to wear a new pair of shoes. There were better moments to break in fresh footwear.

★

Back in Lineker's home town, everyone had the right boots at Filbert Street. Mark Lawrenson was fretting on the bench because he was concerned that, with two league games left, he might not break into the team in time for the FA Cup final. Otherwise Liverpool were relaxed. Kenny Dalglish named an unchanged side. The Reds were confident.

Their supporters did not share that bullishness. Many were concerned they would get locked out. Everton's match at the tiny Manor Ground was all-ticket. Leicester decided to make their game pay-on-the-gate. Many thousands more Liverpool fans arrived in the East Midlands town than Filbert Street could handle. Fleets of coaches left Merseyside – it was impossible to get a train home after the match – and the Nottinghamshire and Leicestershire police forces made life difficult by stopping numerous buses to check for alcohol. Their tactics, honed to perfection intercepting flying pickets during the miners' strike, were aggressive and unsympathetic to the travelling Scousers.

We were on one such coach that left from outside the Liverpool Supporters' Club on Lower Breck Road, near Anfield. With the exception of my 14-year-old brother, it was a rugged crew – the Yankee on the move. The restrictions on alcohol appeared to have encouraged the widespread use of cannabis.

There was an empty seat next to my brother and we found out who would fill it when the driver foolishly drove straight on to the M62, bypassing the Rocket pub, a well-known pick-up spot for passing coaches. We had to turn back because an infamous Red named Scrat was waiting for us. He had achieved celebrity in our circles in 1981 before the European Cup semi-final against Bayern Munich. Scrat was part of a group of Liverpool fans rounded up by police in the Bavarian city during an over-exuberant night out. He was at the back of a line being loaded into the German equivalent of a Black Maria when a scuffle ensued further up the queue. Scrat took his opportunity and

escaped – still wearing handcuffs. Soon, groups of young Scousers were scouring Munich for hardware stores. Hacksaw blade
sales soared. According to the stories, it took all night to cut the
escapee out of the restrictive bracelets. The incident was even
mentioned on the BBC's nine o'clock news. Thuggery drew little
respect in our circles. Quick wits and comic escapes from the
authorities were admired.

The journey was dogged by police stops and heavy traffic.
Once we reached the region that had failed to support Arthur
Scargill and the miners' union, passing pedestrians were abused
as scabs. We were hyped up for a massive night.

At the ground, the queues were huge and growing but we got
into the south terracing, where it was difficult to get a good view
of the pitch. It felt too full and in the minutes before kick-off
there was a swarm of young men climbing the fence to get into
the squat East Stand seats. The official attendance was 25,799 but
we suspected there were many more inside the stadium. There
were constant rumours that the clubs allowed in more paying
customers than they declared. For high-demand matches, they
could make a tax-free killing and avoid some of the Football
League's shared revenue levy. In the days before computerized
turnstiles, it was possible. Perhaps it was just cynicism but we
frequently laughed out loud at the attendance announcements.
This was another occasion when it seemed the crowd had been
underestimated.

The radios were out again, in much greater numbers. It was
not just the anoraks and loners looking for information. Everyone wanted to hear what was happening at Oxford. They had
kicked off and were playing at the Manor Ground when the
teams came out to warm up in Leicester.

Everton were on top. Chance after chance came to Gary Lineker.
Whether it was his hamstring or the stiff boots, his fluid running

style looked stilted and his almost inexplicable anticipation was off beam. Normally, he hit the ball early, so that the opposition goalkeeper could not get his feet set and get balanced for the save. Alan Judge, in the Oxford goal, was able to get into position. On a couple of occasions it looked like the Everton striker was aiming for Judge rather than the net. He was clearly out of sorts. 'Links missed about five chances,' Sharp said. 'It was shocking because he was such a great goalscorer. No one could blame him because he was such a great striker but some of them were chances you'd bet on him taking.'

As half-time loomed, Kendall's team were level. That would not be good enough if Liverpool won. It would take the advantage away from Everton and hand it to their neighbours.

In the East Midlands, another striker was having a better night. Ian Rush, the boyhood Evertonian whose every move in football seemed designed to heap misery on the team he supported as a child, was on the prowl.

Until Lineker's emergence, few questioned the Welshman's pre-eminence in front of goal. By the time he ran on to the pitch at Leicester, Rush had scored nine career goals against Everton. Now he was in a position to break blue hearts again. Not only that, but Liverpool had never lost a game in which Rush had scored.

With 20 minutes gone, Dalglish picked up the ball in midfield, looked up and saw his strike partner run across the box. The player-manager sent the ball into Rush's path. With two defenders closing in on him, the Welshman shifted the ball from left to right foot. He showed none of the tentativeness that Lineker was displaying at Oxford and snapped in a shot. He got lucky when the ball took a big deflection off Russell Osman, leaving the goalkeeper Ian Andrews with no chance. Dalglish's side were one up. While Lineker had dried up as the season hurtled towards a climax, Rush began to show his best form. He would score 11 goals in the league and cup during Liverpool's unbeaten run.

Others chipped in. Eight minutes later it was two. Steve Nicol released Ronnie Whelan and the Irishman lobbed the ball over Andrews to double the lead. Liverpool fans behind the goal celebrated wildly and spilt over the fences on to the sidelines of the pitch. Some needed treatment from St John Ambulance personnel but the causes were mainly excitement. Most quickly recovered and returned to the crowd – generally to the East Stand with its much better view. Everyone seemed to accept that the game was over at Filbert Street. Attention was now switched to the Manor Ground.

The pressure was on Everton and as Liverpool enjoyed their lead at half-time, Kendall's side were emerging for the second period. They had 45 minutes to save their title challenge.

The Evertonians were packed into a ramshackle terrace at the Cuckoo Lane End behind 15 feet of fencing with their team attacking the goal directly in front of them. Their radios cackled with bad news: Liverpool were winning. They became more frantic as the game started to open up and Everton hurled everything at the Oxford goal. Lineker twice tested goalkeeper Judge but the more Kendall's team pressed forward, the more spaces opened up in front of Bobby Mimms. Billy Hamilton, the big Northern Irish striker, skimmed the Everton bar and John Aldridge patrolled the halfway line looking for any chance to break towards goal.

Aldridge, a Liverpool fan, was desperate to score. Not only would it give Oxford a chance of staying up, it would be his contribution to Anfield's title challenge.

Kendall sent on Adrian Heath for Kevin Richardson in the hope that Inchy would replicate his heroics of two years earlier but the switch left Everton a man short in midfield. It was all or nothing for the champions. Their grip on the title was loosening.

Aldridge got the ball wide in the box and was chased by Mimms. The Scouser chipped back cleverly across goal and Hamilton was in the perfect position. It looked impossible for the striker to miss but Gary Stevens came flying back and swung his left foot at the ball. It appeared the full back had only helped Hamilton's effort into the back of the net but the ball rapped on to the bar and out of play for a corner. The Cuckoo Lane End swooned with relief as Hamilton sat eight yards from goal shaking his head.

Oxford were on top. Ray Houghton thought he had scored with a downward header but Mimms produced a miracle save. The young goalkeeper had not conceded in the league since replacing Neville Southall. Most people expected the Welshman's absence to undermine Everton's season. Mimms had proved a more than satisfactory replacement.

Kendall, in his customary suit, barked out orders from the bench. He checked his watch. The seconds were ticking away.

All 'School of Science' pretensions went out the window for Everton. They pumped long balls into the box, causing havoc. Heath finished a bout of head tennis with an effort that Judge collected with relief. They were no longer playing to Lineker's strengths. The fans behind the goal were twitching with nerves.

The home side were desperate, too. They were lofting high balls into the Everton area. With two minutes left, one found Hamilton. Uncharacteristically, Kevin Ratcliffe allowed the Northern Irishman to hook away from goal with the ball. It was surprising because Hamilton, one of football's battering rams, had the turning circle of a truck. The striker rolled the ball back to Les Phillips, who was advancing from midfield. Phillips reached the inside-left channel on the edge of the area, steadied himself and shot.

★

At Filbert Street the match was meandering along. There was little of interest happening on the pitch. Even the Leicester fans were more concerned with events elsewhere. Ipswich Town, another of their relegation rivals, were losing to West Ham at Upton Park. The home supporters were praying for an Everton goal. Top and bottom of the league were intimately entwined.

Suddenly, behind Bruce Grobbelaar's goal, there was a commotion. It started as a hubbub and then erupted into frenzied celebrations. Oxford had scored. At least that was the rumour. Those of us who were not close to a radio fretted about whether the reports were true.

All along the East Stand, supporters charged to the front and shook triumphant fists towards the pitch and hugged each other. Both sets of players appeared bewildered.

'I lost concentration,' Steve Nicol said. 'The cry went up from the crowd. It was one of the few times I stopped thinking about a game during the match. I was thinking, "Let them be right."'

Jan Mølby got the message right away. 'You knew something big had happened,' the midfielder said. 'People say, "Did you know Everton had got beat?" You could tell by the commotion in the stands.'

Les Phillips's shot had beaten Mimms at the Manor Ground. Everton were 1–0 down and had barely any time to rescue themselves. Dalglish and his men had their fate in their own hands for the first time since August.

At the final whistle, Liverpool fans poured on to the pitch. The celebrations lasted all night.

On the way home, with less harassment from the police, Freddie, the coach organizer, arranged for us to stop at a pub in Stoke-on-Trent. Just after midnight, the landlord opened the back door and fifty or so thirsty Scousers filed in and drank until gone 4 a.m. The publican's wife provided us with free sandwiches and a healthy whip-round was the reward for the couple's troubles. It was a far cry from the previous summer and the appalled stares of travellers on the platform at Preston. We were not quite the outcasts we had been in the weeks after Heysel. It was good to be welcomed.

We got home late. The shift workers were travelling to work. It would not be a pleasant day for Evertonians. We were happy, even though my brother had to go to school and I was due in work in three hours. There had never been a moment during this epic campaign that realistic Liverpool supporters believed that Dalglish would lead this team to the title. First Manchester United and then Everton looked like they had run away with the league. Even when Liverpool were chipping at Everton's lead, few thought Kendall's team would slip up. They seemed too good to surrender their advantage.

In the course of two hours, with one game left for Liverpool, an entire season had been turned on its head. Who wanted to sleep? Nights like this did not come along very often.

It was a much tougher few hours for Everton and their fans. Their defeat was a shocker. Oxford had not won at the Manor Ground since Boxing Day. The first league goal that Mimms conceded – although it was not the goalkeeper's fault – was catastrophic. Neville Southall hated being on the sidelines but he had every sympathy with his understudy. 'It was difficult to watch but Bob came in and did really well. No one could blame him for anything.'

Lineker gave an uncharacteristically whingy interview to ITV's *The Midweek Match* where he talked about the problem with his boots. Some of his teammates thought he was throwing the blame at the backroom staff. Pat Van Den Hauwe articulated this in his autobiography. 'If a certain pair of boots are so precious, you should pack them yourself. Gary was obviously disappointed with the defeat and the chances he missed, but sometimes you have to hold your hands up and admit defeat.'

Kendall hid his emotions and remained upbeat. 'I have suddenly become a Chelsea fan,' he said. Later, in his autobiography, he took a sideswipe at Lineker, saying, 'We lacked killer instinct.'

There was nothing for it but to have a drink. The team got back to the city and immediately headed for Chinatown and the nightspots. They were soon joined by the Liverpool players.

'After the Leicester and Oxford games, me and Rushie went on the ale with Ratcliffe and some of the others,' Mølby said. 'We were out until after 2 a.m. We had a great time.'

Little of the competition and aggression on the pitch was carried over to the pubs and nightclubs. 'They were great lads,' Peter Reid said. 'We'd try to kill each other on the pitch and then have a pint. We'd drink in the same places, so we were always bumping into each other.'

It was still in the back of both sets of players' minds that the next time they would bump into each other on the pitch would be at Wembley.

21

Bridge of sighs

Chelsea's season had petered out but winning at Stamford Bridge was no foregone conclusion for Kenny Dalglish's team. Everton were not the only ones wanting the Reds to slip up.

'The romantics among us would love to see Liverpool falter and open the door for West Ham to clinch the title for the first time in their history by winning at Everton on Monday,' wrote the *Daily Express*'s Steve Curry on the morning of the final Saturday of the league season. It was wishful thinking and it would not have gone down well in the Shed, either.

The pressure was on but Liverpool were well used to dealing with this sort of situation. 'It sounds trite,' Lawrenson said, 'but every game was massive. I was more worried because I'd been injured. I was thinking I may not start.'

The centre back's experience helped. He'd been in big games throughout his Liverpool career. The newer players like Mølby had not been in this position before and were less certain. 'I was nervous,' the Dane said. 'We weren't quite convinced. It was a difficult place to play.'

It was forbidding for supporters, too. There was always a hostile atmosphere at the Bridge. It was an ugly, open stadium with a greyhound track between the crowd and the pitch. Behind each goal there were semicircular terraces. The away section was at the north end of the ground. It was vast, roofless, open to the elements and could accommodate 11,000 people. It would need all that space for the Liverpool fans arriving in anticipation of winning the title. The match was pay-at-the-gate and there were concerns that the away support would exceed that number.

Opposite was the Shed, which was named for its strange roof that covered only a small part of the sprawling terrace. The East Stand was an incongruous three-tiered 1970s construction that looked like it had been transplanted from a different century on to the rest of the stadium. Between the East Stand and the Shed were strange kiosks that faced out on to the playing area.

Across the pitch the West Stand had wooden tip-up seats at the back but trackside the seating was on concrete in a section known as 'the benches'. This part of the ground was occupied by a particularly nasty set of Londoners.

The strangest thing about Stamford Bridge? There were always cars parked on the greyhound track behind the goals. It was not advertising, just a group of motors sitting idle for the duration of the game.

The potential for trouble was always high at the Bridge. Because the away end backed on to railway lines, opposition supporters had to enter on the Fulham Road, close to the home fans' turnstiles. At most stadiums, the groups looking for aggravation could be directed towards opposite ends of the ground. Here they all converged on a couple of hundred yards of west London street.

Scousers and Chelsea fans had some history together. In August 1977, after a League Cup game at Anfield, a paltry number of travelling supporters were being bused back to Lime Street for the football special. They were attacked on Scotland Road with a barrage of bricks. The windows of the Londoners' transport were smashed in the ambush.

Chelsea's mob wanted revenge and anyone from Merseyside would do. The next year, a west London crew jumped Everton supporters in the Tube station at Kensington High Street. It became a famous incident in both cities. London Underground were in the process of installing strip fluorescent lighting on the platforms. Combatants on both sides claimed to have picked up the long, tubular bulbs and squared up to each other like Jedi knights with lightsabers. The Scousers came out worse on this occasion and soon graffiti appeared at Lime Street Station with a simple rallying cry: 'Ordinary to Chelsea'. A new chant was born to let the London boys know that Liverpool fans were a different proposition. 'We won't be like Ever-ton,' we sang, 'we won't die at High Street Ken.' In Scouse, it sort of rhymes.

When Liverpool drew Chelsea in the FA Cup in 1982, there were plenty who took up the graffiti challenge and passed up the special trains to get to the capital early on the ordinaries. There was skirmishing all day but the worst violence took place in the ground in front of the cameras. The no man's land divide of terrace isolating the away fans was breached and vicious fighting took place over the railings separating the two sets of supporters.

By the mid 1980s, Combat 18 and other right-wing groups had a solid tochold in Chelsea's Headhunters hooligan mob. Merseyside's reputation for left-wing politics added an extra dimension to encounters between the two sets of fans. Violence was never ideological but there is no doubt that the political differences played a small part in the contempt in which both sides held each other.

The authorities had been nervous enough to move Chelsea's game at Anfield earlier in the season to a noon kick-off to reduce the possibility of trouble. With Liverpool needing three points to win the league at the Bridge, a huge number of Liverpudlians travelled south for the game. It was another security nightmare for the capital's police – for more than one reason.

Liverpool's 'worst' fans rarely tried to seek out trouble. They were thieves. They would shoplift and opportunistically dismantle cigarette and fruit machines. Their speciality, though, was jewellery shops. 'Big crowds were used as a front for professional criminals,' Peter Hooton said. 'It wasn't unusual for shops to get done at away games.' These career thieves had found a way to combine their business with their favourite form of recreation: football.

The majority of supporters arriving at Euston were ushered on to the Tube and headed for Fulham Broadway, where a strong police presence aimed to get them into the ground and off the streets as quickly as possible. A few small crews headed off into the West End. Most wanted nothing more than a beer or two. Others had different plans. There were easy pickings on this busy May Saturday.

One mob went to the Edgware Road. In those innocent times, some jewellers' shops still had unbarred windows and the age of unbreakable glass had not yet arrived. The Scousers' plan was to practise some smash-and-grab and soon glass and empty ring trays were scattered around the streets. Rings were always a favoured item for the robbers. They were small, would be over-looked at the perfunctory turnstile frisks by police and had good resale value. They generated funds for the return trip to London the following week for the cup final. While the Headhunters were prowling around the Tube system looking for Scousers and picking off strays, Liverpool's boys were chalking up an early victory on the Edgware Road.

At the ground there was confusion and frustration. The weight of visiting fans soon overwhelmed the small number of turnstiles and queues backed up. The police response to the situation was to bring in a mounted unit, which only served to crank up the tension and anger. Like most forces around the country, the officers on duty were less concerned with the safety of individuals than with stopping fighting between fans. That mindset, combined with the foolhardy decision not to make the game all-ticket, set up a dangerously crowded and panicky situation.

Legend has it that a well-known supporter named Bobby Wilcox came across a closed and unused turnstile. Wilcox levered the door ajar, clambered inside and took a seat before opening for business. He began clicking countless supporters through, demanding a 15p entry fee for comic purposes.

Expecting there would be chaos at the ground, our little group severely curtailed our normal pre-match drinking. Instead of leaving the pub at 2.30 and rushing to the stadium, we were at the ground more than an hour earlier. It was relatively civilized when we entered – apart from running the gauntlet of abuse as we walked the length of the West Stand. It was worth giving up beer for an occasion like this.

The excitement mounted as kick-off neared, although most of the conversation centred on the purpose of the eight cars parked between the far goal and the Shed and the small hillock of sand that sat on the track at our end. The Bridge always felt surreal: part building site, part car park, part battlefield. At least the electric fences were turned off.

At Goodison the mood was reversed. Belief had been strong since Christmas that Everton would defend their title. Even Peter Reid and Derek Mountfield's long absences had not affected the team's performance or the sense of inevitability that grew throughout the winter and spring. One night in Oxford had destroyed that conviction.

The Blues were playing Southampton and gathered more in hope and loyalty than anticipation. The supporters were rewarded with a dominant performance against opponents who were suffering an injury crisis. Five regular outfield players were missing for Southampton and the goalkeeper was a 17-year-old fresh from the youth team.

Both matches kicked off at 3 p.m. Up on Merseyside the game was dead as a competition early. Mountfield opened the scoring with ten minutes gone and then Gary Stevens doubled the lead after 29 minutes. As Southampton restarted the game, a buzz began to sweep Goodison. In the Gwladys Street End, groups of people began to celebrate. The word spread that Liverpool were one down in west London.

This was the moment Gary Lineker got his shooting boots back – literally. The battered, patched-up footwear had been found in a skip on return from Oxford and Lineker made it 3–0 while the crowd fizzed with excitement. The Double was back on for Kendall's men.

At Stamford Bridge, Dalglish pulled one of his tactical surprises. He reverted to a back three but instead of using Jan Mølby as a ball-playing sweeper, he was keeping things tighter against Chelsea. Mølby was not quite right after picking up a knock at Leicester and the player-manager switched to three centre backs.

Mark Lawrenson's fear of being left out was unwarranted. 'Kenny wouldn't tell you the team until about an hour before the game,' the centre back said. 'He probably thought we'd run off and tell the opposition.'

The information would certainly have caused raised eyebrows in the Chelsea dressing room. It was not what anyone expected.

'Anyway, he said we'd play three at the back: Jocky, Dizzy and me,' Lawrenson said. 'We'd never worked on it in training, it was just, "This is what we're going to do" in the team talk.'

It looked an unduly negative selection for a team that needed to win. A draw would probably suffice to stay ahead of Everton, who in those circumstances could finish on the same points total, but Liverpool's goal difference was significantly better.

The problem was that a tie at the Bridge would give West Ham a late and unexpected opportunity. If Dalglish's team drew and the Hammers won their remaining two games, the East End club could end up a point ahead of Liverpool. Victory was imperative.

The home team started well. Liverpool's system looked as if it lacked adventure and Chelsea had lots of possession without seriously threatening Bruce Grobbelaar's goal. Then the method behind the player-manager's logic started to emerge. Steve Nicol and Jim Beglin, the full backs, were pushing on to join the attack. The first real chance of the game came halfway through the first period. Beglin surged forward, found room in the area and shot only to see his effort cleared off the line. The ball went out for a throw-in.

It came back into the penalty box and was scrambled clear to Ronnie Whelan 25 yards out. The Irishman shot but the ball was blocked and looped into the air. Whelan leapt and headed goalwards. Beglin, who had stayed up to support the attack, chipped the ball forward. It spun downwards just inside the Chelsea area. Dalglish, stepping in front of his marker, cushioned the ball on his chest, waited for it to drop and then calmly dispatched his shot into the far corner of the net from 16 yards. It was a remarkable, stunning piece of skill – and just about the last moment of flair the crowd at the Bridge would see that day. The player-manager wheeled away in celebration, the joy apparent on his face. Now it was time to take the sting out of the game. Just 24 minutes had gone. More than an hour was left.

Why it took so long for the real scoreline to reach Goodison has never been explained. The harsh truth had begun to dawn in the Gwladys Street End before half-time arrived. The goals continued to fly into the Southampton net – the game would end 6–1 – but the last, faint vestige of hope ended with the news that Liverpool were in front at Stamford Bridge. Lineker bagged another hat-trick but it was too little, too late.

At Upton Park, there had been similar misleading speculation about the result at the other end of the District line. West Ham had beaten West Bromwich Albion 3–2 with a late penalty and were ecstatic until they reached the dressing room. 'We got told Liverpool had drawn at Chelsea,' Frank McAvennie said. 'I've never seen so many grown men cry when we heard the true result.'

The Scot had mixed feelings when he was told who had scored at the Bridge. Dalglish was McAvennie's idol. The West Ham striker had fulfilled a dream when appearing alongside the Liverpool player-manager on Scotland duty. He said, 'How hard was it for me when I heard who'd scored? Kenny was my hero. It was one of the greatest moments of my career when I played with him. I was delighted for him but sick for myself.'

McAvennie's frustration was palpable. 'They won it because they'd won it before,' he said. 'They ground out results and knew how to win. But we were the best team in the league.'

On the north terrace we were ecstatic. It was tense but it was impossible to imagine the team getting to this situation and throwing it away. We had seen Liverpool squeeze the life out of matches many times before. We were not interested in being entertained. We were interested in winning. The team had the same attitude.

'Has there ever been a more professional performance?' Nicol asked. 'We made the game crap. We killed that game. We were never not going to win it.'

Few teams were better at taking the excitement out of a match. 'If we scored after 20 minutes, everyone could stop watching,' Nicol said. 'The game was over. We played the same in the league as we did in Europe. The first job was to keep the ball.'

Watching from the sidelines, Mølby was able to confirm the Scot's verdict. 'It wasn't a great game on a rock-hard pitch,' the Dane said. 'We did what we did well. Got ahead and held on.

'We may not have been the best team ever but we knew how to win games.' Mølby echoes McAvennie's view. 'We ground out results. We got into a relentless stride. After the Everton game, we knew there were 36 points left. We only got 34 of them.'

Lawrenson credits Dalglish's acumen in team selection. 'Kenny got it right,' the defender said. 'We didn't concede. But not only that, Jim Beglin supplied the pass for the goal. If we'd have been playing 4–4–2 he probably wouldn't have been so far up the pitch.'

The team gathered afterwards to salute the supporters. 'Hand it over, Ever-ton,' rang out from the visiting fans. Then the players trooped off the pitch to the dressing room to celebrate with champagne and beer. There was no trophy presentation, no fireworks or booming music, just the sound of Scouse voices from the north terrace and a team that still had a mission to fulfil: winning the cup. Everyone in the squad was conscious that this was one competition that Liverpool had struggled in for more than a decade.

'There was an element of joy and happiness in the dressing room but there was a big shadow over us – the FA Cup,' Mølby said. 'You looked around at Hansen and Dalglish and they'd won the league plenty of times before. They'd won European Cups. But they'd never won an FA Cup. They'd never done that before.'

Psychologically, Liverpool were on top after nearly two years of playing catch-up with Everton. They had taken the title back. And they had one last indignity to inflict on their neighbours on this final day of the league season.

'We hit the ale in the dressing room and carried on drinking on the bus home. We were in a pretty happy state,' Lawrenson said. 'We were all hammered and then the coach broke down.

They had to call Liverpool – Ellison's, the bus company – for a replacement.'

While they waited, the players continued their knees-up. It took a couple of hours to get a substitute vehicle out to the new champions. When it arrived, it was a surprise.

'They sent the Everton team bus,' Lawrenson said. 'The irony of it. We'd just beat them to the title and the last part of our journey home was on their coach. We thought it was hysterical.

'Anyway, we made sure we trashed it.'

They had destroyed Everton's title dream, wrecked their transport and Liverpool's next mission was to ruin the entire season for the Blues by beating them at Wembley.

By the time they reached the city limits, the army of Liverpool fans had a new ditty for their songbook. It would not go down well with their Evertonian friends.

> The Blue-nosed bastards aren't the champions any more,
> Cos they went to Forest and they only got a draw,
> Then they went to Oxford and the bastards couldn't score,
> So the Blue-nosed bastards aren't the champions any more.

Liverpool fans poured off the trains and coaches and headed to town, where Everton supporters had been drowning their sorrows since just after 5 p.m. The last thing they needed was a late influx of thirsty, overexcited Liverpudlians flooding into the pubs. It was a combustible place.

Derby nights in the city centre can be fractious. This was even worse than when the two teams played each other. An exchange of views in the Great Charlotte Street Wine Lodge escalated and a glass was thrown as the Everton contingent left. At first the mood was to let it go but the insult festered among the Liverpool boys as the drink went down. Everyone knew where the Blues were headed: Daley's Dandelion on Dale Street.

The name belies the sort of place Daley's was. There were plenty of Scally hangouts around town but this was one of the worst. Reds and Blues drank there and frequently came together during Groundpig's residency in the place. The main characters in both mobs knew each other well. Liverpool's boys decided to go down to Daley's. The lobbed glass was an affront too far on a night like this.

The brawl that followed was massive, vicious and uncharacteristic. Both sides launched themselves at each other with a gruesome fury. Bouncers converged from across town but it took the arrival of the police to stop the mini riot.

Both sides went home to nurse their bruises. The feud could not continue. They had to live with each other, after all, and share the same city. They would have laughed through broken teeth about the notion of the 'friendly derby'. And another one was only a week away.

22

Echoes of Europe

The most surprising headline the day after Liverpool won the title did not concern Dalglish's team. The future of Everton's superstar striker was the subject for discussion.

The story was in all the papers and the *Sunday Express*'s version was about as succinct and representative as any: 'Barcelona will have to offer a massive £3 million to persuade Everton to part with English shooting star Gary Lineker.'

The price was huge but the message from Goodison was clear. The man who had scored 37 goals so far in his first season on Merseyside was on the trading block. It was all a matter of price. It needed to be exorbitant because Leicester were due a third of any profit.

Lineker was not the only one pondering what life would be like in Catalonia. Kendall had already been approached about taking over the reins at the Nou Camp.

Terry Venables was widely believed to be leaving Barcelona. The Englishman suggested the Everton boss as his successor. Barca representatives approached the Goodison board and asked for permission to speak to their manager. Kendall met the Catalan delegation in a London hotel during the run-in and verbally agreed a deal to step into his fellow Englishman's shoes.

Unexpectedly, Venables signed a new contract to stay in Spain. He had, after all, taken Barcelona to the European Cup final.

This was the big stage Kendall had expected to be on when Everton won the title a year earlier. Heysel had ended that dream. Venables' extended contract blocked another avenue for the Everton manager.

While the Liverpool players continued with their party, Everton had another game to prepare for. West Ham United were at Goodison on the Monday of cup-final week in a play-off for second place in the table. It was the match nobody wanted.

For the Hammers, it was their fifth game in ten days. They were exhausted. Everton won 3–1 and Lineker got another two goals. After scoring only once in 11 league games when his team were neck and neck with Liverpool on the run-in, he notched five in the two final league matches, all of them after Kenny Dalglish had effectively brought the title to Anfield with his goal at Stamford Bridge.

West Ham kept up the pressure right to the end, winning six of their final seven matches before the defeat at Goodison. It was the highest position the East End club had achieved in the league.

'If we could have won the title, we would have beat Everton that last day,' Cottee said.

His strike partner agrees. 'If Liverpool had lost at Chelsea, we'd have certainly won the league,' McAvennie said. 'No one wanted to play at Goodison that day. Second or third made no difference to me. I wanted to be first. Nothing else mattered. We should have beat them for the fans but it was hard to get motivated.'

The Scot believes West Ham's mistake was chasing the FA Cup as well as the title. 'We should have concentrated on the league. We played seven FA Cup ties getting to the quarter finals. It was just too many games.'

McAvennie's brilliant season was over. He never quite re-captured his pre-Christmas form but his final haul was still impressive. He finished with 26 goals in the league. Cottee was not far behind with 20.

'For one season we competed,' Cottee said. 'We genuinely had a chance of winning the top prize. Two West Ham players got more than 20 goals each. It's pretty rare to get one player who does that in a team.'

Their overall total was even more eye-catching: 54, with Cottee knocking in six of the extra eight. He gives the credit to his partner. 'People don't talk as much about Frank as they should,' he said. 'It's a shame. He was exceptional. A hard worker, great instinct and an unbelievable eye for goal.'

McAvennie would be spoken about a lot but increasingly for the wrong reasons. He began to cause more carnage in his personal life than in penalty areas. On the pitch at least, this was the time of his life.

Manchester United finished fourth and ended the campaign with Bryan Robson sidelined with injury. He was in a race to be fit for the World Cup. The ten-game winning start seemed an age ago. The impression was beginning to form that Ron Atkinson's forward motion had stalled and United were a club in reverse. A joke spread round Merseyside, based on the constant speculation about first division managers being poached by Spanish clubs. 'See Big Ron's off to Spain,' it went. 'Last week in July, first week in August.' A package holiday seemed the likeliest route to Iberia for the United manager.

At the bottom, Oxford and Leicester survived. On the final day of the season, Oxford beat Arsenal 3–0 to ensure safety. The six points Leicester took off Everton made all the difference for the East Midlands side.

Liverpool had a game left, too, although they were not taking it wholly seriously. Three days after winning the title, they were at home to Norwich City in the second leg of the ScreenSport

Super Cup semi-final. The first leg was a distant memory. It had been played at Carrow Road back in February before the big freeze disrupted the fixtures. It ended in a 1–1 draw. The return was shoehorned in to get it out of the way before the season ended.

The Football League had originally planned a one-off final at Wembley for its new competition but the attendances quickly convinced the ruling body that it would be a mistake. As gates for league games climbed throughout the season, the Super Cup failed to capture the public's imagination. The decision was made to make the final a two-leg affair.

Still, events conspired to ensure that Kenny Dalglish and his team could not completely dismiss the match. Everton had advanced to the final in the other bracket. Even in a derided tournament like the Super Cup a double header of derbies would generate significant revenue for both clubs. It was a balancing act for Dalglish. He left himself, Alan Hansen, Jan Mølby and Ian Rush out against Norwich. They, at least, could be secure about their places at Wembley.

Before the football, there was the celebration. The trophy for winning the title was presented before kick-off.

The Football League appeared to have a conveyor belt of bad ideas at its Lytham St Annes headquarters. In the period between the Leicester and Chelsea games, the organization had been in touch with Anfield to suggest presenting the trophy at Wembley. It was a startling presumption and Peter Robinson shot it down immediately. He had also seen an opportunity to bolster the crowd against Norwich. The chief executive said, in an interview with the *Echo*:

> 'We told them that if we did win the league – and it is far from settled yet – we would prefer the trophy to be handed over at the Super Cup tie at Anfield next Tuesday.

'It will be a more personal occasion and would give the team a perfect Wembley send-off. However, I must stress again that nobody here is taking anything for granted.'

The League's thought process was surreal. When would the presentation at Wembley have taken place? Before the cup final? Or after – in which case, what if Everton won? It made more sense to do it at Anfield, even if it did not inspire anywhere near a full house. Fewer than 27,000 turned up to see the ceremony.

The traditional League Championship trophy was in mothballs. Canon, the photography company, sponsored the competition and had their own prize – a futuristic 22-inch gold construction that the more dirty-minded likened to an erect penis. It was not as attractive as the ornate, intricately decorated trophy that had become a familiar resident at Anfield, and exuded no sense of history. It was the sort of prize worthy of a Sunday league team rather than the champions of England.

Jack Dunnett, the League president, handed the trophy to Dalglish rather than Hansen, the captain. The player-manager raised it to the Kop and then passed it down a line of players. At the back of the queue, looking embarrassed and shuffling around, was Bob Paisley, the most successful Liverpool manager and Dalglish's mentor during this first, tumultuous season. Paisley had won nothing in his inaugural campaign in charge and remembered well the lonely experience and the pressure. It was a touching moment when he was handed the trophy, and the nearest thing to sentimentality at Anfield.

Norwich took advantage of the little lapse in cold-bloodedness and took the lead after two minutes. The Kop responded to the goal, and the relatively meaningless nature of the game, by supporting the East Anglian side throughout the first half, cheering their touches, chanting their name and jeering Liverpool players.

By half-time they had bored of this pantomime and reverted to normal service, roaring on their team. Sanity was restored and the home team scored three in the second period.

At the final whistle Dalglish was interviewed on the pitch by the BBC. He was asked about the possibility of winning the Double. He was typically awkward. 'Well, we're the only team in with a chance of doing it, aren't we?' When the reporter suggested that Liverpool teams had been to Wembley before and failed to achieve the feat – against Manchester United in 1977 – the player-manager was equally curt: 'Not this season, we haven't.'

There were four days to the cup final. All the focus turned to Wembley.

The next night, the European Cup final took place in Seville. It was a very different atmosphere from Heysel.

Two of Europe's biggest clubs had faced off in Brussels, each bringing massive support to the ramshackle stadium in the Belgian capital. A year on, it was a predominantly Catalonian affair. Barcelona were playing Steaua Bucharest in the Ramón Sánchez Pizjuán stadium, an arena that had undergone an overhaul for the 1982 World Cup.

Few Romanians travelled to Spain. Andalusia's biggest city was swamped by Barca fans. Most considered the result a foregone conclusion.

The game could not pass without a nod to the memory of Heysel. Delegations from Liverpool and Juventus, including club officials and fans, gathered to pay their respects and pledge friendship at Seville City Hall.

British interest in the final centred on Terry Venables and Steve Archibald, the Scottish striker that El Tel brought to the Nou Camp. They were upstaged by the unfancied Romanians.

The game went to extra time and penalties. Venables' team

then proceeded to miss all four spot-kicks they attempted in the shootout. It was a crushing blow for Barcelona. Real Madrid, their greatest rivals, had won the competition six times. This was the Catalan team's second final and they had lost both games.

In contrast to the previous year, there were no arrests. The Seville authorities had their hands full, though: 17 Romanians defected and claimed political asylum.

The result heaped more misery on Howard Kendall and his squad. 'Watching two ordinary sides battle out a war of attrition brought home to me how much we had lost because of the Heysel disaster,' he wrote in his autobiography. 'I would have backed us to beat either of these two teams.'

This was the final they had imagined themselves winning a year earlier. Like Barcelona, Everton were completely over-shadowed by their main rivals' European Cup record. After winning the Cup-Winners' Cup so easily, the next step to cap-turing the continent's major trophy seemed a natural one.

Would they have won it in 1986? It is a leap of faith to claim Everton would definitely have dominated the tournament. Although Steaua and Barca were poor in Seville, they were good teams. The Romanians had a relatively easy route to the final but it is wrong to think Steaua were a bad side. They scored 13 goals and conceded two on their way to Seville. They were no pushovers. Teams from behind the Iron Curtain often came from nowhere and surprised Western European clubs with seemingly greater pedigrees. Ask Liverpool, who were knocked out by Dinamo Tbilisi, CSKA Sofia and Widzew Lodz over the previous eight years.

Barcelona had a much tougher time on their way to the final, edging past Sparta Prague and Porto on aggregate and beat-ing Gothenburg on penalties in the semis. Venables' team also beat Juventus in the quarters. Some of those teams would have presented robust opposition to Kendall's men. Playing Juventus would have been unthinkable. If Everton had been allowed to enter the tournament, drawing the Turin side would have caused a multitude of problems.

A year on from Heysel there was an element of forgiveness in the air. In the wake of the dull final, Francesco Morini, the Juventus director of sport, called for the immediate reinstatement of English teams in Continental competition. That included Liverpool.

Graeme Sharp is realistic. 'It was sad we couldn't go in,' he said. 'But there were no guarantees we would have won it. There were more important issues at stake. I'm not bitter. We could have drawn Juventus in the first round.'

This was Everton's big chance, though. No wonder Kendall brooded on it for the rest of his life.

23

Preparation

While Everton wondered about what might have been, Liverpool focused on the future. There was little interest in events in Seville. 'It didn't concern us,' Steve Nicol said, his one-track mind firmly in a groove.

'Everything we did was the same,' the Scot said. 'At the start of the week the staff were on us: "Don't get caught up in all this cup final nonsense."'

This was where Ronnie Moran proved his worth. He enforced the Boot Room philosophy. 'Bugsy would be all over you,' Nicol said. 'We were programmed. It was drummed into you.'

Even in the insulated worlds of Melwood and Bellefield it was impossible to escape the sense that something huge was happening in the city. No one could be immune to the madness of cup-final week. By Thursday, decorations were going up on houses across the region. Windows were adorned with scarves, banners and pictures of footballing heroes. Some households that were split down the middle had both sets of favours on display, often in the same window.

In the block where we lived, the line of bollards were painted first as red men, then overnight daubed over to make them blue. By the morning of the final, there was a peace of sorts: two were red, two blue.

The ticket allocation was 25,000 for each club. That was never going to be enough. Face value was £25 for the most expensive seats, £9 for the cheap benches down by the dog track and £6 on the terraces. There were tales of the least expensive tickets fetching more than £150. Prices spiralled as the days slipped by. It was hyper-inflation on a grand scale but for those of us who had them, the tickets were priceless. While Liverpool and Everton fans scrambled to find a way of paying for an expensive jaunt to London, the FA announced record gate receipts of £1.1 million.

Liverpool released a cup-final song, a tradition that had evolved in the early 1970s. Like much of that era's fashions it was decidedly tacky. It was a forgettable ditty called 'Running Like The Wind'. The production sounded prehistoric. It must have cost next to nothing to record.

Against a background of a tinny synthesizer, the team's voices barely broke through a fog of reverb. When you heard the lyrics, you wished you hadn't.

> We're gonna run like the wind,
> We're gonna fight and give everything.

The city that spawned the Beatles should have hung its head in shame. Instead the chorus blasted out from jukeboxes in pubs across town.

> We are running fast and free,
> We're gonna go down in history,
> And show them what we can win,
> Running like the wind.

Gary Lineker and Ian Rush adorned the cover of the *Radio Times*. It was clear proof that this was bigger than the usual cup final.

Dalglish and Kendall had to keep their men grounded amid all this craziness. They also had to deal with the awards season and the announcement of World Cup squads.

Lineker was named the Football Writers' Footballer of the Year and accepted the honour from Bobby Moore at the journalists' annual dinner in London on the Thursday night. It was the Everton striker's second personal trophy in the season. He had been voted Professional Footballers' Association Player of the Year earlier in the campaign by his fellow pros. He did not miss too much preparation. The striker was notorious for spending more time in the bath than on the training pitch.

Dalglish was honoured with the Bell's Manager of the Year award. Feted and lionized, these men were preparing for the game of their lives.

Others had their egos wounded. Alex Ferguson, who had taken over Scotland after Jock Stein's death, omitted Alan Hansen from the Scottish squad while selecting Dalglish and Steve Nicol. It was a strange decision but Ferguson plumped for his Aberdeen centre-back pairing of Willie Miller and Alex McLeish. They were fine defenders but leaving Hansen out looked like an act of madness – or vindictiveness. The Liverpool defender had made a gruesome mistake against the Soviet Union at the 1982 World Cup in Spain and had never been forgiven for it.

Kendall was also concerned about a central defender. Derek Mountfield was struggling with a knee injury that had required an operation earlier in the season. The moment of truth was close at hand.

The exodus south started on Friday. The advance guard loaded on to trains at Lime Street and headed for London. The afternoon commuters at Euston were startled by hundreds of red and blue sun-hatted youths streaming up the platforms chanting 'Merseyside, na, na, na'. Every penny was precious on this adventure. Some planned to sleep rough; others like me headed for King's Cross. The dosshouse bed and breakfasts around Argyle Square charged £6 per head and crammed people in, sometimes six to a room. It was worth it.

All across London, small mixed groups of Scousers wandered about. As the afternoon and night went on, the tales of high jinks became more exaggerated. A rumour from the early afternoon claimed that a number of Scousers had managed to get into the public viewing area of the House of Commons and unveil a hammer and sickle flag. Any act of resistance to Thatcherism, no matter how inconsequential, was considered a victory. The mood was not as overtly political as at the Milk Cup final two years earlier but at the local elections two days before Wembley the Conservative Party was virtually wiped out in Liverpool. The Tories were left with one councillor. It was clear that the Labour council would soon be thrown out of office and some expelled from the party but they still had plenty of support from the young bucks roaming around Britain's centre of power.

Others were putting Proudhon's dictum into practice. If all property is theft, there were a lot of goods liberated by Scouse crews that night. Most, though, were well behaved if raucous. The trouble of the previous Saturday in Daley's was largely forgotten and the sight of mixed groups of Evertonians and Liverpudlians clearly confounded some Londoners. The most common greeting throughout the long night was a simple plea: 'Any spares, mate?'

At Liverpool's hotel, Mark Lawrenson was still nervous. Even though he had played in a back three at Chelsea he was concerned that his manager would revert to a flat four. Gary Gillespie's displays during Lawrenson's absence had made the Scot the apparent first choice.

'I was worried I wouldn't be in the side,' Lawrenson said. 'All players are selfish and want to play. Roy Evans said to me, "Don't fret, you'll play." But Dizzy was in great form and I didn't think we'd go three at the back. As it happened, Dizzy took ill on Friday night before the game, so I was playing anyway.' With his long experience of big games, Lawrenson slept easily.

Jan Mølby was more excited. 'The cup was bigger than the league,' he said. 'It meant more. It was the two best teams in England – and probably Europe. I couldn't wait.'

Merseyside emptied on the morning of Saturday, 10 May. As well as the scheduled rail services, 19 football special trains left Lime Street. A convoy of 400 coaches clogged the motorways and thousands of cars, scarves streaming from their windows, dodged in and out of the traffic.

Their destination was Wembley. The 'home of football' was about to be occupied by Scouse squatters.

The old stadium was a strange place. It was situated on the fringes of London in an area with little to recommend it to fans. The grandiose twin towers gave a false impression. Even in 1986 it was beginning to crumble.

It was not a great place to watch football. Like Stamford Bridge it had a wide dog track. At the back of the terrace behind the goal, supporters were a long way from the action. The far goal was nearly 200 yards distant. It did have a sense of theatre, though. It was used rarely enough to make a visit an event.

Liverpool and Everton had been there so often in recent years that they claimed a proprietary right to the place. Local newspapers often referred to it as 'Anfield South' or 'Goodison South'. The teams had only faced each other there twice before, both times in 1984 and never for an FA Cup final.

The standing ends of the ground were sweeping arcs. The lower sections, closer to the track, were shallow terraces that quickly became crowded. The view was awful but people piled into them because they were nearer to the pitch.

The upper terraces were the place to go. The camber was

steeper and the steps higher. They gave a better depth of field. Clear sightlines made up for the long-distance view. And it was roomy at the back of the section. When Wembley was at its 100,000 capacity, there was space for, maybe, 20,000 more people. A full house was not the shoulder-to-shoulder jam experienced on the Kop or in the Street End. The bunkers knew this. Those without tickets were aware that there was lots of empty space for them to occupy.

The best way to get into Wembley without a ticket was straight-forward: go up to a turnstile without a policeman or steward on the other side and slip the gateman a tenner. The premium for a really big game might force the price up to £20. This had to be timed correctly. Go too early when it was quiet and the police were less busy. They could survey and monitor more than one entry point. The busier the turnstiles the less chance there was of prying eyes observing the transaction.

Getting into the ground was only half the problem for the ticketless. There was a second gate into each individual section. To pass, you needed the ticket stub. There were always lost souls wandering round the concrete bowels of Wembley pleading for spare stubs. If they were left on the concourses after kick-off, the police and stewards would pick them off and demand to see their stubs. If they could not produce one, they were ejected.

The touts stayed away. Scousers made them nervous. They could cope with one Merseyside team with the help of a couple of hefty minders but two sides from the city made it a danger-ous day for black-market operators. Ever since the Everton boys turned stripping touts of tickets and cash into a sport 20 years earl-ier, gangs of Scousers targeted the London spivs. The touts made sure most of their transactions were done in the days before the match. One was quoted in the press as saying: 'I have only a hand-ful of tickets left but there's no way I'm going to Wembley with all those Scousers outside.' For once, the stereotype was spot-on.

There were forgeries knocking about but they were pallid imitations of the real thing. The gatemen could see them coming. They were only useful with a £10 note slid underneath, so it was pointless buying any.

Those with real tickets had to be wary. The snatchers were out. The most venal Scallies would wait at the top of the steps leading to the turnstiles and look for the most vulnerable – the elderly, children, the innocent – and if they produced their ticket too early would grab it out of their hands and run. The wise kept the precious piece of paper in their pockets until they were actually in the turnstile. The same logic applied inside the concourse with the stub.

There were just too many people outside the ground. We were in by 2 p.m. and went up into the top section. Before we went on to the terraces, we leant out of the window in the staircases to the upper section and looked at the melee 30 feet below. There were thousands besieging the gate and still legions of people streaming up Wembley Way and circling the ground.

Even against Manchester United in the League Cup final of 1983 the crowd was slack in the upper section and the gangways were free. This day they were packed. Movement was difficult and you needed to squirm through the bodies to engineer a spec.

Outside, desperation was kicking in. Young lads started climbing the aluminium fences, initially to try to shin over them and lower themselves to the other side. The 20-foot drop made it impossible.

Then men looking out of the windows began beckoning to them, reaching out their arms. One or two weighed it up and slid back down the railings, deciding that this was not a matter of life or death. Others hung on, leant across and made the fateful decision to go for it. The iconic image of the day was of the young lad making a fingertip lunge towards a group of three men in a window, grabbing a hand, swinging for a moment and then securing his grip before being pulled into the stadium. Had he missed the grasping fingers or slipped he faced a 40-foot drop.

Inside, we could see nothing of this. What we could see were people, fans wearing ski hats and sun hats, walking about on the roof. How they got there was anyone's guess. They were getting to see the game, though, which was good enough.

Even if you couldn't make it to London this was a big day. The television cameras went to Lord Street in Liverpool's main shopping area and it was like a ghost town. Saturday afternoons were normally bustling. Not now.

The BBC and ITV started their coverage early. The season began with blank screens and ended with the usual cup-final overkill. The BBC's programming began at noon and – interspersed with racing from Newbury – had all the usual set-pieces of the era: a 'road to Wembley' review, a visit to the team hotels and a camera on board the coaches. They also added some quirks. Gary Lineker played Mark Lawrenson at snooker in a match modelled on the massively popular *Pot Black* show. 'It was best of three and he beat me 2–1,' Lawrenson said. 'He'd had breaks of over 100 and I was Liverpool's best player on 22. He won the first frame, I bored him to death in the second and he sneaked the third frame.'

Roger McGough, the Evertonian poet, did a humorous poem about divided loyalties – and the togetherness – of the city. Dressed half in red and half in blue, he was the funniest contributor to the show. It was not verse that would win any awards but it brought a smile to the viewers.

> I'm an ordinary fella, six days a week,
> But Saturday turn into a football freak,
> I'm a schizo fanatic,

It's sad but it's true,
One half of me's red,
The other half's blue.
I can't make me mind up,
Which team to support,
Whether to lean to starboard or port.
I'd be bisexual,
If I had time for sex,
But it's Goodison one week,
Anfield the next.
But the worst time of all is derby day,
One half of me's home,
The other's away.
And now we're at Wembley,
Me head's in a spin,
Cos I bet fifty quid on each side to win.
I'm shouting for Liverpool,
The Reds can't lose.
Come on Everton,
Gerrin there Blues!
Give it to Dalglish (what a pudding!)
King of the Kop,
All of a sudden.
Goal! Offside!
And after the match,
It's walk back alone,
Argue, argue,
All the way home.
Some nights when I'm drunk,
I've even let fly,
I've give myself a poke in the eye.
But in front of the fire,
Watching *Match of the Day*,

Tired but happy,
I look at it this way.
Part of me's lost,
Part of me's won.
I've had twice the heartaches,
But I've had twice the fun.

For his finale, McGough hoisted the first half-and-half scarf in recorded history.

Mel Smith and Griff Rhys Jones, the BBC's most prominent comedy duo, were shoehorned in despite neither having any connection with the teams or the city. Their big joke was not knowing where Everton was. They suggested it was just outside Brighton before deciding that it was across the Mersey on the Wirral.

Less appealing was a sketch by Warren Mitchell playing Alf Garnett, the bigoted Cockney character from *Till Death Us Do Part*. In perhaps the most misjudged sketch in BBC history, Mitchell's satire went badly wrong. It was meant to parody the worst sort of Little Englander mentality but its execution showed it was a serious miscalculation. Wearing a West Ham scarf, Garnett launched into a rant that made many viewers wince. He railed at Scousers in London. 'With their empty beer cans and crisp packets, being sick in everyone's garden,' he said. 'It's us who has to clear up and our bloody rates that has to pay for it after they've gone. Not their bloody rates. They don't pay rates in Liverpool, do they? Liverpool town council, the bolshy bastards.'

After the politics, he turned to Heysel. 'Hooligans, ain't they? They got us banned out of Europe.'

Then it got really offensive. And not just for citizens of Merseyside.

It's not a European Cup without us, is it? It's a bloody wogs' cup, innit? And all because of a load of drunken Scouse gits we're banned out of Europe.

They didn't want us banned out of Europe when Adolf Hitler was about. No, it was all 'Voulez-vous, Tommy' and 'Parlez avec moi ce soir, Tommy' and 'Come and liberate us, Tommy'. Now it's all 'Piss off, Tommy', isn't it? Should have left them to Adolf Hitler. He'd have given them soccer hooligans all right. I'll tell you something else, if old Gorbachev starts and the Ruskies start it'll be 'Come back, Tommy. All is forgiven.' And all because of a load of bloody Scouse gits who couldn't hold their duty-free liquor.

The misguided attempt at satire was soon forgotten. Most football fans probably missed the part of BBC's afternoon programming which would have the longest effect on both football and society.

The scheduled news bulletin contained a story about the printers' dispute at Wapping. The report was about a meeting between unions and police trying to defuse the violence on the picket line at Rupert Murdoch's new plant. The clashes a week before were 'the worst since the dispute began'.

The police presence at Wapping the previous weekend had been overwhelming: 1,744 officers were deployed and their tactics drew comparisons with Orgreave. The police charged the crowd 11 times and Brenda Dean, the general secretary of SOGAT, said 'the police conducted a riot'.

Speaking to the BBC, Dean looked an unlikely radical. With a Princess Diana haircut and a Thatcheresque pearl necklace, she articulated her position on the cup-final news bulletin. 'Everyone hopes every demonstration is going to be peaceful,' she said. 'Certainly, we don't want to see a repetition of what happened to decent ordinary men and women. And we believe that's not going to happen.'

Dean would be disappointed, as the picket-line clashes turned increasingly poisonous. The police were again being used as an arm of state policy.

Unusually, the authorities were positive about the conduct of the fans. They were behaving well, the Met said. There were 27 arrests overnight.

ITV's coverage started five minutes later than the BBC's and was interrupted for 20 minutes of wrestling at 2.10 p.m. Jimmy Tarbuck hosted a pre-match 'party' which featured many *Brookside* stars and this caused a row with political overtones. Ricky Tomlinson, one of the soap opera's major characters, was not invited on to the show. Tomlinson was politically active and had been sentenced to two years in prison for conspiracy to intimidate during the national building workers' strike in 1972. He pointed the finger at the Tory comedian.

'Tarbuck has not forgiven me for remarks I made about professional Scousers who make a living out of the city but can't wait to get out of the place,' the *Brookside* actor said. 'It is also a well-known fact that Tarbuck appears on Maggie Thatcher's political platforms and I am a member of the Labour Party. He is operating a Jimmy Tarbuck blacklist and it is not on.'

After all the nonsense it was a relief when the clock ticked down to three o'clock.

24
The clash

It was a relief for the players, too. Cup-final tradition meant the eyes of the world would be on them all day. At their hotels on the fringe of London, both teams prepared for the journey to the stadium. From the moment they boarded the coach until they reached the sanctuary of the dressing room, the cameras would be on the players.

The staff at Liverpool's hotel formed a guard of honour as they walked out to the coach. Bob Paisley went first, to rapturous applause. Dalglish followed a couple of minutes later. The player-manager went to reception, as if to check out. A couple of dozen fans watched him and then a young boy went up and asked for an autograph. The Scot obliged and others rushed up to get a signature.

The applause was more spontaneous at the Everton hotel. A hundred or so people milled around the coach but there was a very businesslike air about Kendall's team. This was the third time they had taken this journey in three years. They knew this route well. Neil Pointon and Neville Southall led the way, both on crutches from their injuries. After the walking wounded boarded, the rest strutted out. They looked confident.

Reid and Bracewell took their seats and scanned the newspapers. They looked at the sports section of the *Daily Star*, ignoring the front page – 'Maggie fights back' was the headline. Everton looked relaxed. Kendall was all smiles. There was no sign of the destruction that Liverpool had wreaked on the coach the previous Saturday.

Dalglish's team got to the stadium first. They were checking out the pitch in their grey double-breasted suits when their opponents arrived. Even then, the Liverpool manager was reluctant to let anyone know his team.

Craig Johnston was interviewed on the pitch. He spoke of the birth of his daughter Cassie two days earlier. His wife was still in hospital. Always an emotional character, the Australian was having a week to remember.

He had real concerns about the pitch. He was asked whether the grass was too long. 'Yeah,' he said. 'On purpose. Me and Stevie Nicol walked down this right-hand side and it's very, very muddy. It's a bit of a disgrace. The other side is quite good but this side's a disgrace.'

Dalglish was on next and was asked the same question. His reply was pragmatic. 'I suppose the team that loses will complain about it and the one that wins will think it's great.'

Bob Wilson, the former Arsenal goalkeeper, suggested the far side was muddy. 'I don't know, Bob, I've got new shoes on,' Dalglish said. 'I didn't fancy going over there.'

No wonder the Scot was relaxed. Like the rest of the Liverpool side he had long been forewarned about the dangers of the pitch at the national stadium. 'Bob Paisley had told us years before about Wembley,' Lawrenson said. 'He told us not to run with the ball. If you did, your legs would go after 70 minutes.'

Everton, in similar suits, inspected the pitch after their rivals retired to the dressing room. Gary Lineker was not concerned about the surface but he had plenty to say about his boots. He was now back in his old favourites. 'I went a spell when I never scored and then I got injured with these [new] boots on,' he said. 'I got back my lucky ones that I'd scored a few goals with and I got the menders – adidas – [who] fixed them all up for me and they've done a tremendous job and I've got playing in them again. The only game I missed unfortunately, because they forgot to put them in the skip, was against Oxford and I didn't score that day and we lost. They'll be on today and that's for sure.'

The pressure was building. 'Getting a bit nervous now,' Sharp said.

The last player to be interviewed on the pitch for the TV audience was Ratcliffe. He sent out a message to the country. 'You look around and there's blue and red everywhere,' he said. 'In every part of the ground. That's just great to see.'

Then it was off to the dressing room. The time for talking was over.

Finally, the tension overwhelmed the phlegmatic Steve Nicol. 'In the tunnel it got to you,' he said. 'Then it was the crowd noise, lining up and shaking hands.'

'It was our third FA Cup final in a row,' Graeme Sharp said. 'We'd been here before. We were ready.'

'Abide With Me' was sung. It is the cup final's traditional hymn. A few people joined in but the Liverpool end countered with 'You'll Never Walk Alone', which roused the Blues into chanting 'Ever-ton, Ever-ton, Ever-ton'.

Then the teams emerged, led by Howard Kendall in a black double-breasted suit and Kenny Dalglish in his tracksuit. They walked out of the tunnel at the Everton end and it was from there the chants of 'Merseyside' began and circled the stadium. They were followed by 'Are you watching, Manchester?'

The national anthem was played and booed by a good proportion of the crowd and the teams were introduced to the Duchess of Kent. Then, at last, the preliminaries were over. It was time to release the tension. 'As soon as you broke for the warm-up it was back to normal,' Nicol said. 'Get your mind right, get a good first touch and you're off.'

While the players got ready for the action, the Liverpool end boomed 'Champions'. Alan Hansen and Kevin Ratcliffe joined the referee, Alan Robinson, for the toss-up. It was another victory for Liverpool. Hansen chose to attack the tunnel end, where the Evertonians were massed.

At last the referee blew his whistle and this most intense of derbies started at a frantic pace. There was plenty of contact but the referee let play go until Paul Bracewell clattered Jan Mølby after four minutes. Everton were clearly aiming to deny the Dane the time and space to show off his passing ability.

'There were plenty of physically demanding games but Everton could play and were tough,' Mølby said. 'You could never get rid of them. They hung around in matches and made life difficult. They were a wonderful side. They played 4–4–2 and had great balance. They'd kick you. They would leave you battered and bruised.'

Graeme Sharp was relishing the combat. 'Hansen and Lawrenson were good footballers but they didn't like the physical side of things,' the Everton striker said. 'Andy Gray always said get the ball up and on top of those centre backs. Rough them up. We learnt that lesson. And we did.' With Sharp's physicality and Lineker's speed, the Liverpool defence had their hands full. They could be drawn into mistakes. 'I could buy fouls by jumping early,' Sharp said. 'They didn't enjoy it.'

Crunching challenges were nothing new in games between these teams. The ferocity was now ratcheted up a notch. 'We were trying to hurt each other,' Craig Johnston said. 'It might come as a shock to people in these politically correct times but it was true. Derbies were different. They were meatier.'

After Bracewell's challenge, Liverpool needed to impose themselves. They were not to be bullied. Ronnie Whelan picked out Peter Reid and chopped the Everton midfielder down. Reid rose from the turf cursing his opponent. This was where the man from Huyton thrived: when conditions were at their rawest. 'They were physical, too,' he said. 'No favours were asked. It was always a battle. We gave them it back.'

The first 15 minutes were bitty, full of niggle with an under-current of spite. The players were nervy and errors common. 'When you're making mistakes, you start not wanting the ball,' Johnston said. 'If it comes your way, Reidy, Sharpy and the rest come piling in, trying to injure you. They want to put fear in your mind. And you want to do the same to them.'

The ideal situation was to leave a boot on the opponent without attracting the referee's attention. 'You meant to do it,' Johnston said. 'You tackle them and catch them and nobody notices except you and them. If you do it right, you get that feeling: "They won't come back."'

Everton always returned for more. Derek Mountfield went through the back of Dalglish and sent the player-manager flying to the floor. At last, 17 minutes in, the referee decided to have a word. The Everton centre back appeared far from contrite.

Kendall's side began to turn up the pressure. Gary Stevens found space out wide and curled an inviting cross towards Sharp. Steve Nicol got his body in the way and strong-armed his friend and fellow Scot away from the ball. Sharp went to the floor and rose aggrieved, demanding a penalty.

'No chance,' Nicol said. 'It wasn't a foul. Well, not much of one.' At the other end, Ian Rush had a chance but shot high over the bar. The millions watching on television were beginning to despair that the game was turning into a dull, tense affair that could only maintain the interest of those with local pride at stake. Then the drama took its first twist.

Around the half-hour mark, Dalglish was unable to take control deep in the Everton half and Reid picked up the loose ball. The midfielder looked up and saw that the Liverpool defence was too square and Lineker was lurking. This was an opportunity but the pass had to be inch perfect. It was. The 50-yard ball went over the top and Lineker and Hansen were in a footrace. The Scot was quick but there was only one winner. The Everton striker reached the ball first and shot with his less deadly left foot. Bruce Grobbelaar blocked the effort but could not push the ball out of the danger area. Lineker was on the rebound in a flash and this time it fell to his right foot and there was no mistake. The scrambling goalkeeper got his hands to the second shot but it was not enough to keep the ball out of the net. It was Lineker's 40th goal of the season.

'He got the better of Jocky,' Lawrenson said. 'At least Hansen couldn't blame me.'

Everton fans went wild. In the horrified silence of the other end, the noise sounded disembodied, as if heard through a radio fogged by static. A few Blues jumped around near us and shouted with joy among the mass of mute Reds.

Reid sprinted upfield with an ecstatic look on his face to join the celebrations. Lineker's name cascaded from the terraces. Everton were on top on and off the pitch. Suddenly, the rigours of the past few weeks seemed to have caught up with Dalglish and his men. They looked tired and were hanging on for the half-time whistle.

At the break, they had to troop down the tunnel surrounded by Evertonians. Blue shirts were met with applause and encouragement and red jerseys with sneers and triumphant abuse. 'At half-time going down the tunnel the Liverpool lads couldn't believe it was only 1–0,' Sharp said.

In the dressing room, Dalglish's team slumped in their seats and awaited the inevitable tongue-lashing. 'Ronnie Moran went mad,' Lawrenson said. 'I'd never seen him so angry and Ronnie was tough. He went ballistic. We just hadn't played. He told us it looked like we'd been on the piss all week. And we had.'

At times like this there was no point in arguing back. 'Bugsy was the most rational man in the world,' Nicol said. It was never merely raw anger from the Boot Room veteran. 'He could dissect any argument and destroy anyone who thought they were clever. It was best to shut up and listen.'

They did not need to be told how poor they had been. They also knew they were still in the game. 'We were terrible,' Nicol agreed. 'But they weren't great, either. We were worse. Big Al still crucifies himself about the goal.'

Dalglish was calmer than Moran. He reminded the team how they had come from behind in the title race and told them that the next 45 minutes could turn a good season into an historic one.

'It's not like we'd been played off the park by a bad team,' Mølby said. 'They were a great side. When they're beating you, you can understand it. All you can do is knuckle down, stay in the match and wait for your chance. Don't let them run away with it. At half-time we were saying, "Don't go 2–0 down. Stay close."'

In the Everton dressing room Kendall was telling his players to keep on doing what they had done in the first half. 'Don't give those Red bastards an inch,' he demanded. 'Howard wasn't a very vocal manager,' Ratcliffe said. 'He didn't need to be. Everybody knew their jobs.'

Everton began the second half by executing their plan perfectly. Dalglish's team were in disarray. Kevin Sheedy went close to scoring twice, once with a free kick that swerved just wide and then with a shot that Grobbelaar pushed out for a corner. The goalkeeper was under siege.

From high up on the terraces it looked like Liverpool were a beaten team. We were desperately trying to generate noise, imploring them to get back into the game, but all the sound was coming from the tunnel end. Everton were in the ascendancy. Liverpool were about to hit rock bottom.

Grobbelaar misjudged a cross from Sheedy and, although no damage was done, it clearly affected the Zimbabwean. The attack petered out when the ball ran to the edge of the area where Jim Beglin was waiting. Grobbelaar signalled to the left back to leave it so that the goalkeeper could collect it but the young Irishman touched the ball by mistake, knocking it away from his teammate. Steven was lurking and Grobbelaar had to scramble to get the ball in his grasp. He was outraged. He screamed at Beglin. That was not unusual. What he did next was shocking: he squared up to the full back and pushed him in the chest.

Liverpool teams did not lose their discipline like this. While the Everton sections laughed and mocked 'the clown', there was a gasp of disbelief at the other end.

It appeared there was no way back for Liverpool. Disgusted, I made to leave. A friend grabbed hold of me and bear-hugged me until calm was restored. 'It's still only 1–0,' he said. It was almost too much to bear: losing the biggest game in the city's history and the team fighting among themselves.

What effect did it have on the players? 'The pushing match between Jim and Bruce helped us, I think,' Lawrenson said. 'After all, we couldn't sink any lower.'

Mølby agrees. 'I can imagine people thinking we were crumbling under pressure,' the Dane said. 'If you were part of it, you'd understand. We'd seen things like that lots of times and knew it wouldn't affect them. Jim would get his mind back on the game; Bruce would put it out of his thoughts. These things happen in teams. It didn't make any difference to us.'

Nicol had a much more simple take on the incident. 'Bruce's not right in the head,' he said. 'We all knew that and shrugged it off after two seconds. If Hansen would have done it, we would have been thinking, "Holy fuck!"'

Grobbelaar did not shrug it off so quickly. Moments later he caught a long throw from Stevens but sent his clearance out of touch to give Everton the ball back. He was struggling to keep his composure and Dalglish's frustration was palpable.

Nearly an hour had gone and Kendall's team were by far the superior side. The margins between these two sides were small, though. A single mistake could turn the game. Stevens made it.

The Everton full back was in his own half when he misplaced a pass and Whelan grabbed possession. The Irishman looked inside and found Mølby in space. The Dane moved towards Mountfield and played the ball through the centre back's legs. On the other side was Rush, stealthily moving through the Everton defence unmarked. The ball rolled beautifully into the Welshman's path.

Bobby Mimms came out but even Neville Southall would have been helpless in this situation. Rush touched the ball around the goalkeeper with his right foot and shot with his left. Johnston came haring through and slid in, attempting to steal the goal from the striker, but the ball was already over the line when the Australian made contact. For all their dominance, Everton were back level. Their nemesis had emerged from the stupor of the first 57 minutes to break blue hearts again.

'We caught them for that first goal,' Mølby said. 'They were going forward and made a mistake and gave the ball away.' In their quest to attack, the Everton midfield lost track of the Dane. 'It was the first time in the match I was on the wrong side of Paul Bracewell and Reidy, and I had time and space on the ball.'

The mood of the entire stadium changed in an instant. 'I knew the moment I scored we would win,' Rush said. He was not the only one.

'We'd never lost when he'd scored,' Nicol said. 'We weren't going to start now.'

Suddenly, Liverpool looked more composed but the game could easily have turned again minutes later. Steven played a long ball into the opposition box and Hansen, with Lineker close by, sliced his clearance across goal. The ball dropped to Sharp 20 yards out. Grobbelaar was left stranded out of his ground by Hansen's mistake. The Everton striker looped a header over the despairing goalkeeper and it dropped towards the net. It looked a certain goal. Wembley held its breath as the ball arced goal-wards. Grobbelaar went into reverse but his position looked hopeless. As the ball dropped below the bar, the Zimbabwean leapt, arched his back and flicked it over the bar milliseconds before it crossed the line. No one could believe it, particularly the Everton striker. 'I thought I'd scored,' Sharp said. 'That was Bruce all over. Everybody knew what he was like. People slated him but then he'd pull off a save like that.'

The goalkeeper had made the journey from erratic to extraor-dinary in a matter of minutes. Suddenly, Everton looked like a beaten team.

'The big turning point was the incident between Bruce and Jim Beglin,' Ratcliffe said. 'It seemed to make a massive change to the game. That and Bruce's save from Graeme Sharp were the turning points. Liverpool seemed to raise their game and surpass us, and our chance had gone.'

The Liverpool end was bouncing now to 'We Shall Not Be Moved' and the team were suddenly a living expression of the song. Mølby was controlling the game. Liverpool's midfield runners were pouring forward. Beglin found Rush on the left with a long ball and the striker fed Mølby inside him. The Dane controlled the ball quickly, spotted Johnston at the far post and sent in a firm, low cross which the Australian side-footed into the net. Johnston did not need to steal a goal. He had his own now. The game had turned on its head.

Kendall now had to take a chance. He replaced Stevens with Adrian Heath in an attempt to get his side back into contention. It made things worse.

Heath was supposed to get up front and support Lineker and

Sharp. The switch had another effect. It forced Everton to go to three at the back and unbalanced the side.

'For 60-odd minutes we were running the show,' Reid said. 'Then Howard took Gary Stevens off because he made a mistake with a pass for the goal and we lost our shape.'

Mølby agreed. 'They had to change the way they were playing,' he said. The chances started to come quickly. 'Things opened up for us. I should have scored. I was clean through.'

Lawrenson thought back to Paisley's advice about not running with the ball at Wembley. 'They gave us a chasing at first but Bob knew his stuff. They ran out of steam.'

The big Dane was now at his imperious best. He found Whelan, who was storming into the vacant area where Stevens might have been. The Irishman advanced to the edge of the area, took stock of the situation and then lobbed the ball over the heads of Pat Van Den Hauwe and Ratcliffe to the back post where Rush was arriving unaccompanied. The striker hammered the final nail in Everton's coffin, taking one touch before powering the ball into the far corner.

'Something happens when you keep on doing the right thing,' Nicol said. 'Even when it wasn't working, we carried on playing our way. It told in the end. It was like someone squashed the life out of them.'

With seven minutes left Liverpool were in full control. Rush had one more chance when he tried to lob Mimms but a third cup-final goal was not to be. 'Rushie should have got his hat-trick,' Mølby said. 'He chipped the ball into Mimms's hands. It was more like a back pass.' A fourth goal would have been cruel, though.

The final whistle sounded and Everton players slumped to the floor, beaten 3–1. Liverpool's team hugged and celebrated. They had done the Double, a feat only achieved in the twentieth century by Tottenham Hotspur in 1961 and Arsenal in 1971.

In his first year as a manager, Dalglish had made history.

This was the point where the supporters of the defeated side normally began to leave. Usually some would remain to see the presentation of the trophy and clap their team but the majority would start to make their way home. Very few Everton supporters left their places. Wembley was still close to full when Hansen led the winners up the steps to the Royal Box to receive the cup from the Duchess of Kent. The Liverpool captain turned, faced the end where the majority of his side's supporters were, and pumped the trophy into the air.

Behind them came Everton. Their climb up the 39 steps appeared to be significantly more difficult. They were dragging exhausted, defeated bodies up the stairs.

Liverpool had started their lap of honour when Ratcliffe and his teammates came back down the stairs. Sheedy and Sharp had reached the end of their tether. They headed straight for the tunnel and the dressing room where they could hide from prying eyes. The rest of Kendall's team took a slow walk around the stadium, acknowledging the supporters who had backed them all the way. Reid wore a rueful, agonized smile. It was almost a grimace.

Then something unprecedented happened. The chant of 'Merseyside, Merseyside' began again and rang around the ground. Evertonians joined in and sang as lustily as their victorious rivals. It was a massive show of unity. Despite the defeat, the Everton supporters recognized that something bigger than the game was happening.

'It was an unusual atmosphere,' Lawrenson said. 'We'd won, beaten our neighbours, our mates, and we did the Royal Box thing and all that. Normally, half the crowd leaves but everyone stayed and were singing. Remarkable.'

When the city needed to present its best face, the Everton fans were there for it. In football terms, the club had been hurt more than any other by Heysel. If Evertonians had left en masse or the neighbourly rivalry had spilt into viciousness, then it would have confirmed all the preconceptions about Merseyside. Instead, the two sets of fans stood together and made a statement of unity.

'There were bigger things at stake,' Derek Hatton said. The politician and strident Evertonian felt sick about the defeat but understood the importance of not souring the occasion. 'A lot of people say the game didn't matter. You almost felt guilty about the banter beforehand and feeling miserable afterwards. You couldn't really have a go at Reds like we did on other occasions.'

Reid, like many of Everton's players and fans, was awed by the experience but endured it through gritted teeth. 'We saw kids together at the final, one with a red scarf, one with a blue. They were all mixed in. In that way, it doesn't get any better for a Scouser. '

The competitor in him had different emotions. Losing the final left him feeling hollow. 'It was horrible,' he said.

Mølby, a recent arrival in the city, was impressed with how the Everton players behaved. 'It must have been hard for them but they deserved to be part of it,' he said. 'They deserved some of the acclaim. They'd been a big part of a great season. It was the perfect antidote to the year before. They'd helped bring a feel-good factor back to the sport. English football had lost sight of what it was supposed to be about. It found itself again that season.'

Neville Southall had to watch from the sidelines and shared his teammates' disappointment. Yet the injured goalkeeper knew implicitly why the Everton fans stayed on the terraces and joined in the applause and chanting afterwards. 'It reflected the city,' he said. 'What happens in the city affects everyone. They cared about each other. If people didn't care, there wouldn't be football clubs. It was a reflection of community.'

25

Homecoming

Not everyone was concerned with the bigger issues. Nicol was verbally sparring with Hansen about the summer. 'The World Cup was coming,' he said. 'Big Al had just been told he wasn't going to Mexico. I was. I was knackered and he was laughing at me and saying, "I'm off on holiday and you're going to Mexico. Unlucky." We were taking the piss out of each other.'

Johnston was at the other end of the emotional scale. It was the greatest moment of his career. It was the culmination of a long journey for the midfielder. He had come to England at the age of 15 to follow his ambition to become a footballer. A trial at Middlesbrough had ended on the first day when Jack Charlton, the manager, told him to 'fuck off back to Australia' and that he was the worst player he had ever seen. Humiliated, and with a return ticket that was not valid until three months later, Johnston hung around the training ground, hiding from Charlton and trying to improve his game. He had given everything for Liverpool but, until this season, had struggled to hold down a regular place. Now he had scored the goal that put the cup in Liverpool's hands.

'I was very emotional,' he said. 'I wanted to fit in, be seen as a great player like all the people around me. To have done the Double, to have achieved something Liverpool had never done before, and to have scored, was moving. I was on a high.'

Using a huge, bricklike early version of the mobile phone, the man nicknamed Skippy phoned New South Wales from the dressing room. He spoke to his parents, who had mortgaged their house to send him to Middlesbrough all those years ago, and had difficulty making himself understood to his mother. When he finally spoke to his father, Johnston asked, 'Had you worried today?' He had come a long way in so many senses.

The winning dressing room was in chaotic uproar. The players and staff tucked into champagne and beer and cameramen milled around. Yet the old Liverpool mindset was already kicking in. 'No one said "Well done" or "Congratulations",' Lawrenson recalled. 'We just had a drink. It didn't sink in that we'd done the Double, not for a couple of years.'

There were some unexpected occupants who did understand the level of the achievement. 'Sammy Lee had some mates who were real Scallies,' Lawrenson said. 'You'd give them two lounge passes for the game and 14 of them would end up in there. They were just like that.'

The team knew they were in the stadium but not their whereabouts. They could not have predicted where they would find Lee's mates.

'Someone said we should get washed and changed and get ready to go into town,' Lawrenson said. 'We stripped off and went to the bath. At the old Wembley, it was about 5 feet deep. We got there and there were three of Sammy's mates there, fully clothed and soaked through, saying, "Come on in, the water's great." It was surreal. That's how happy everyone was.'

Well, not everyone. Out of the public eye some of the Everton players had suffered enough. They went back to the pre-planned banquet at a West End hotel and ate and drank in a very muted atmosphere. Lineker was interviewed for television and expressed the view that 'there was no need to feel down'. The striker was always good in front of the cameras. Reid gave a very different impression: the man from Huyton looked haunted and called Everton's season a 'failure'.

The next morning the two teams were due to fly back to Merseyside on the same plane. It had been arranged before the final without any thought about how the losers might feel. There was no chance that Reid would be on the flight or involved in the open-top bus tour of the city that would follow it. 'I had a drink with the boys and got off,' he said. 'I got my mate to pick me up. I fucked off and didn't do the bus parade. Howard said he'd fine me two weeks' wages. I said, "That'll do me" and pissed off. I watched the parade from a pub in Bolton.'

It was not only the players who were feeling distraught. Cynthia Kendall worried as much for her kids as her husband. 'I think it's all the more difficult because it's Liverpool,' the Everton manager's wife said. 'It's harder. The children have friends at school who are all Liverpool supporters and it's important to them that they go back with their heads held high.'

At that point, Cynthia had not seen her husband yet. She was asked if she was looking forward to that moment. 'Not really, no,' she said. The pain and disappointment of everyone connected with Goodison made their public show of solidarity even more impressive.

At the Liverpool hotel, the post-match feast had a very different atmosphere. On the coach journey from Wembley to their central London base, the sound system was cranked up and the team sang along to Chris Rea's 'I Don't Know What It Is But I Love It', their theme song from the European Cup win in 1984. It was not exactly cutting edge rock 'n' roll but Dalglish looked like a parent having to endure a teenager's record collection. Liverpool had something to sing about. Everton did not. Drink flowed at both hotels but only one team went to bed happy. 'From the moment you wake to the moment you go to sleep, it was perfect,'

Mølby said. 'It was special. The crowd singing "Merseyside" was brilliant. It was all great.'

The Everton players would have argued differently.

Outside Wembley the mood was unusual. Groups of mates met up around the stadium and there were very few spats and little gloating. Most Reds commiserated with their Blue friends. The phrase 'there'll be other years' became the late afternoon's cliché.

There was plenty of humour. An Evertonian mate walking back to Wembley Central Tube station encountered a London bus in the slow-moving traffic on the High Street. He lay down in the road in front of the double decker, covered his eyes with his blue-and-white scarf and waved the driver towards him. 'Come on, you big red bastard, end it for me.' Even his fellow Blues laughed.

The lack of anger from the losing fans was startling. The camera caught John Hurt outside the stadium wearing a replica shirt with a blue scarf dashingly swished around his neck. Surrounded by a growing group of Scallies, he was asked if defeat hurt more because it was Liverpool that had beaten Everton to the Double. 'I suppose, in a sense,' the actor said. 'But at least it's Merseyside.' The boys behind him nodded in agreement. It summed up the mood even if the joke on the Kop for months afterwards was that the Elephant Man was a Blue.

The next morning the teams gathered at the airport for the flight home. It was the last place Kendall and his men wanted to be but they forced themselves to go through with it. 'I couldn't believe what they made us do,' Sharp said. 'It was unbelievable. On the plane, Liverpool were all celebrating and we were sitting there miserable.'

On the runway at Speke it was even more painful. A brass band played 'Here We Go' as the teams disembarked. The body language of the Everton players spoke louder than any words.

They stood around, downcast, as their rivals larked around at the bottom of the stairs.

Kendall and Dalglish did a joint interview in the terminal. No losing manager had ever had to suffer such onerous media duties. The reporter asked if the men were still friends. There was a very telling pause before the Everton boss cracked a joke. 'I want him to retire, now,' Kendall said, nodding at the Scot.

Always one to rise to the challenge Dalglish quipped back, 'Somebody thought I had at half-time.' It was quite a double act, though Kendall might have winced at the word 'double'.

'It's not war,' Dalglish said, 'it's a game of football. You've got to keep it in perspective. Fortunately, we're a lot better off than some other cities.'

The parade through the city piled on the misery for Everton. Unlike in 1984, the losers trailed behind. There was little sympathy on the Liverpool bus. 'They were fuming,' Lawrenson said, amused even now. 'We were on the first bus, the journalists on the second. Everton were on the third.'

The Blues felt like an afterthought, slinking home behind the victors. The majority of people on the streets were decked in red. They climbed atop roofs for a better view, gathered in clusters on road signs like nesting crows and a man dressed in a gorilla suit perched himself on a traffic light. Liverpool were loving it, Everton suffering every moment. 'We had the trophies, all they had was a few cans of ale,' Nicol said.

That beer was going down quickly on the Everton bus. They were drinking to forget. The problem was that the copious amounts of alcohol had to come out. There was no toilet on the bus. 'All the boys were trying to do it in cans,' Sharp said. 'I couldn't do that. I said to the driver to stop for a minute on Queens Drive and got off.' It was a road lined with semi-detached houses. The Scot looked around for a place to pee.

'There was a woman in her doorway waving at us, so I went

over and asked her if I could use her toilet. She sent me upstairs and when I came out there was a queue down the stairs with the rest of the team waiting to use it.'

The parade was being televised but the cameras mainly focused on the Liverpool team. Someone must have noticed the commotion around the Everton bus and the pictures of what was happening were beamed to the watching public. One viewer took offence. 'The woman's husband was sitting in the living room watching it on telly,' Sharp said. 'He saw us going in. He was a Red and the next thing he's running up the stairs kicking us all out. I was the only one who got to use the toilet.' They were used to Liverpudlians taking the piss. Now they weren't even allowed that satisfaction.

There were Evertonians about. A group ran alongside the third vehicle carrying a white bedsheet that was spray-painted with the words: 'Chin up, lads, win or lose we support you.' It was scant consolation.

As a public-relations exercise the bus tour worked. The image of Scouse solidarity was reinforced. But most of the Everton team wished they had followed Reid's example and regretted that they weren't drinking in a pub in Bolton.

The media coverage focused on the difference 12 months had made since Heysel. The *Sunday Times* said:

> A year ago Liverpool was to the world what Chernobyl is now. Yesterday the true spirit of our premier football city was allowed to drift around the globe, bounced by satellite to upwards of 50 countries and between 200 and 500 million people who, we trust, gained a kinder picture of the English at play.

The analogy of the nuclear reactor that had exploded catastrophically in the Soviet Union the previous month was extreme but it rather neatly summed up how toxic the city's reputation had been. And it was not just Heysel. The political, social and cultural climate had all contributed to the poisonous reputation conferred on the region.

Tony Wilson, the man who sent love from Manchester to Liverpool City Council, opened a Granada TV special programme with these words: 'Twelve months ago, after the Heysel Stadium disaster, English football was on its knees. At 4.40 last Saturday afternoon, a whistle blew and it was clear English football was back standing tall. How does it feel to win not just trophies, but respect?'

The game had salvaged its reputation. Well, almost. As the teams were flying back to Speke airport, the FA announced that UEFA had informed it that the ban still stood. English clubs would not be going back into European competition any time soon.

At Anfield, where the mood was so dark after Brussels, the elation faded quickly. 'It was just relief,' Lawrenson said. 'After what had happened the year before at Heysel, it was a great relief.'

The spotlight had been intense throughout the campaign and the young, inexperienced manager had come through the stiffest test of his career. 'We felt it for Kenny,' the centre half continued. 'He had the most pressure. He just appeared to go about the job serenely and not feel the pressure.

'He always made us feel that success was not about him, that it was about the group. It was some achievement from him.'

It was. But in defeat Everton did something more important than winning trophies. They lost with dignity. Despite the crushing disappointment, Kendall and his team managed to maintain that perspective Dalglish talked about. Their sportsmanship and solidarity was as crucial to this feel-good ending as Liverpool bouncing back to win the Double. They might have felt like crap but Everton restored faith in the game. That was a more difficult task than achieving victory on the pitch.

English football had not only been saved but it had started moving in a different direction. The power of television had begun to exert itself, the Big Five were flexing their muscles and the drawing power of star players was becoming more and more apparent.

Hooliganism was on the wane. Towards the end of the season there appeared to be greater numbers of children and women at matches. The tide of history that was dragging the game to destruction before Heysel had turned; now the undertow was pulling, unseen, towards a place called the Premier League.

Everton played a huge role in this life-affirming season. West Ham, Manchester United and Chelsea had all lifted spirits and drawn people back through the turnstiles.

Gary Lineker emerged as the country's hottest property. English teams could not play in Europe but Englishmen could. One way or another the nation would continue exporting football to the Continent.

Frank McAvennie had risen from obscurity, experiencing anonymous fame before becoming a vivid, blond celebrity. His landmark season was unforgettable. Bryan Robson's was worth wiping from the memory. The man who could have turned the campaign was too brave and too injury-prone for his own good. United would have to wait for a new age to dawn before they stamped their authority on the league.

And Liverpool, tainted, triumphant and seemingly indestructible, were girding themselves for the next titanic struggle against Everton. The two sides would remain flagbearers for the beleaguered city. By the end of the summer Derek Hatton and his fellow councillors were stripped of office and facing huge fines. Politics was a sport at which Merseysiders were losing. But who could beat their teams on the football pitch? No one.

Football's most critical season was over. The game was alive and still kicking.

Epilogue

Well, the season was not quite over. There was still a World Cup to come before thoughts turned to the next campaign.

Nothing quite builds excitement for football fans like a World Cup. British teams would be playing foreign opposition. It was an even more exotic treat with the Heysel ban in place.

England, Scotland and Northern Ireland qualified and most of the main figures of the domestic season were in Mexico. Bryan Robson was deemed fit enough to play, offering the Manchester United midfielder another opportunity to consolidate his position as England's hero. Gary Lineker would lead the line for Bobby Robson's men.

The striker had played his last game for Everton. A deal was agreed with Barcelona before the tournament started. Lineker would swap Goodison for the Nou Camp. The price was £2.8 million. In his autobiography, Howard Kendall was ungracious about his 40-goal hitman. 'Although he had scored so many goals I didn't think his departure would cause irreparable damage to our team,' he wrote. 'Indeed, to the contrary, I felt it might heighten the teamwork that had brought us such outstanding success a year earlier. As it happened, that was the case.'

Frank McAvennie was in the Scotland squad. He would not get the chance to play alongside his idol, as Kenny Dalglish withdrew. The Liverpool player-manager said his ageing body needed to recover over the summer. Many suspected that if Alan

Hansen had been on the plane to Mexico then Dalglish would have joined him.

West Ham's superstar did not get much chance to show a global audience what he could do. He came on as substitute for the first two games – defeats by Denmark and Germany – and sat frustrated on the bench as Scotland played out their final group game, a 0–0 draw against Uruguay. McAvennie was back in Stringfellows a little too quickly for even his liking.

Robson, the man who was too courageous for his own good, led England out for the opening game against Portugal. English expectations were high, as they always are at the beginning of big international tournaments. Reality hit home quickly.

Portugal won 1–0. It was a very disappointing performance for the supporters who had travelled to Central America. It was hard to feel too much sympathy for England fans, though. A group in the crowd held up a bedsheet with the words 'West Ham NF' on it. It was not unusual. The National Front preyed on the jingoistic mentality that was rife among England followers and the organization's racist, fascist insignia frequently adorned their flags. There were plenty on display in Mexico.

Worse was to come. Next up were Morocco, the group's supposed whipping boys. England matches do not come uglier than this encounter.

The game was meandering towards half-time in the heat of Monterrey when Robson chased a ball down the inside-left channel in the opposition area. A defender challenged the England captain and Robson went to ground heavily. When he did not get up quickly everyone knew what had happened. Ray Wilkins crouched over his teammate and gestured furiously at the referee to get medical help on to the pitch. The shoulder had dislocated again. When England needed a hero, Robson was the obvious candidate. His body refused to cooperate.

The ball had gone out for a corner. Wilkins went out to take it and stayed wide when the defence cleared. England gained possession and the ball came back to Wilkins but the midfielder was offside. In frustration – and perhaps still annoyed about the referee's slow response to Robson – he threw the ball at the official's feet with venom. The Paraguayan referee produced a red card. With three minutes left to the interval, England were down to ten men. They held on to draw 0–0.

Lineker was having a torrid time. Bobby Robson had deployed him alongside Mark Hateley. The ball was not coming forward quickly enough and when it did England were lofting aerial passes designed to hit the big target man alongside Lineker. The striker who had scored 40 domestic goals was receiving possession with his back to goal. It nullified his strength – raw pace.

After Morocco, the players staged a revolt against Bobby Robson's system. In the general reshape of the team, out went Hateley and in came Peter Beardsley, a clever forward who would drop deep and look to release an early ball for his partner. Peter Reid came into the side, too. He knew exactly how to get the best out of Lineker.

It was like a switch had been flicked. In the final, must-win group game against Poland, the striker ran wild, scoring a hat-trick in the 3–0 win. In the first knockout round, Paraguay could not cope with him. Lineker got two in the 3–0 victory. The world sat up and took notice.

The quarter-final was an epic. England versus Argentina in the Azteca Stadium, Mexico City, in front of 114,580 people and a global audience on television.

It was the first meeting of the nations since the Falklands Conflict in 1982, when Argentina's attempt to occupy what they referred to as the Malvinas led to a British task force being deployed in the South Atlantic. More than 900 were killed as British troops pushed the Argentinian forces out of the Falkland Islands. Two-thirds of the dead were South Americans. Margaret

Thatcher called a general election on the back of the military success. Before the Argentinians invaded the Falklands, the Conservative government was in trouble. Unemployment was rising and the Prime Minister was deeply unpopular. Victory in the South Atlantic changed the public perception of the government and generated huge support. Thatcher won by a landslide at the 1983 election. The huge majority in the House of Commons gave her the authority to embark on a programme of radicalism that would change the nature of British society.

Argentina was still angry, Britain still tub-thumpingly triumphant. The quarter-final was shot through with political undertones.

It is a match remembered for Diego Maradona's performance. Before the game, he said that the Malvinas were not a factor. Later, he admitted he was lying.

There was sporadic fighting in and around the stadium between English and Argentinian fans before, during and after the match. The clashes were not serious enough to overshadow the football. The day will always be recalled for Maradona's four-minute spell that etched itself into football legend. First, he punched the ball into the net in the 'Hand of God' incident to put Argentina 1–0 up. Then he ran with the ball from his own half to score one of the greatest goals in World Cup history. It was Maradona's day. It could easily have been Lineker's signature moment.

Trailing by two goals with time running out, Bobby Robson sent on first Chris Waddle and then John Barnes. With two wingers, England suddenly began to stretch the Argentina defence. Barnes in particular rampaged down the left. With nine minutes left, the Watford winger drove past two defenders to the byline and produce a cross that Lineker headed into the net.

Barnes was in sublime form. The racists with their NF banners must have been conflicted when the man with Jamaican

271

heritage looked like dragging England back into the match. 'I didn't care,' the winger said. 'I had nothing but contempt for them [the racist fans] and they weren't going to stop me playing.' With three minutes left, Barnes was at it again. He sent over a dangerous cross to the back post. It was an awkward ball for Lineker. Few players could have twisted their bodies into a position to make contact. The striker headed the ball from less than a yard out. It seemed a certain equalizer. Instead, Julio Olarticoechea threw himself in the way and the ball stayed out of the net. That, as much as any point in the entire tournament, is the moment when Argentina won the World Cup.

If Lineker had scored and the game had gone to extra time, Barnes, with his fresh legs, would surely have created more chances for England. The South Americans were tiring. History could have been very different had that late header hit the net. Or not. 'If we'd have made it 2–2, then Maradona would have gone up the other end and scored the winner,' Barnes said. 'He was unplayable. The greatest ever.'

Lineker was the highest scorer at the World Cup with six goals. Yet the Olarticoechea block was an allegory for his season. Forty domestic goals and six in the World Cup should have brought more reward than a clutch of personal honours. He won the Golden Boot in Mexico to go with the Football Writers' and Professional Footballers' Association Player of the Year awards but the greatness of his season was undermined slightly by the failure of his teams to win a trophy. It would have been much more satisfying if Lineker had shot his sides to success. For a player who was so often in the right place at the right time, this season he was always in the wrong situation.

The World Cup brought Lineker global attention. It was a different kind of fame from McAvennie's. The Scot's elevation to notoriety suited the Thatcherite narrative: grab success quickly and enjoy its benefits with shameless abandon. The media were predisposed to celebrate quick-hit fame. Vulgarity was a sign of vigour and if McAvennie appeared a little crass, it went with the territory.

The West Ham striker was an unlikely poster-boy for the 'loadsamoney' age. He was just a working-class Glaswegian man who loved scoring goals and the attention it brought. His personality and beliefs were grounded in a west of Scotland culture that the Conservative leadership found alien. But he was one of the symbols of an era when Britain's horizons were narrow. Unknowingly, McAvennie became emblematic of conspicuous consumption. The public enjoyed him for that as much as his goals but the road to excess was a blind alley for such a brilliant footballer.

Lineker never captured the imagination of red-top editors. He was sensible, generally guarded in his comments and articulate in a predictable manner. He was married and avoided the whiff of scandal.

McAvennie's image was colourful but cartoonish. Lineker's was solid, perhaps a little dull. The reality was different. The England striker could carouse with the best of them. The big difference is that McAvennie had little room for growth on and off the pitch. The shelf life of a tabloid tearaway is limited. Lineker would develop as a player and a person. The move to Catalonia would help that journey.

Yet again, a team got Lineker on the cheap. The deal was agreed before the World Cup. If Everton had waited until after the tournament they could have upped their asking price.

At the same time the Lineker transaction was taking place, Liverpool sold Ian Rush to Juventus for £3.2 million and Dalglish was allowed to keep the striker at Anfield for another season on loan. It was not the best bit of business Kendall had ever done.

So, the campaign was finally over. The European ban may not have been lifted but many of the clouds over the game had gone.

English football, with its ability to regenerate itself on an annual basis, had come close to the brink after Heysel but survived. It was time to move on.

There was one, last loose end. The ScreenSport Super Cup final still needed to be settled.

The final would be played in September, a month into the new season. Five games of the 1986–87 campaign had already taken place before Everton went to Anfield for the first leg. Liverpool won 3–1 in front of a crowd of 20,660. Ian Rush scored twice.

Two weeks later, on the last day of September, the second leg was played. This time 26,064 showed at Goodison. Rush, the scourge of Everton, got another hat-trick in a 4–1 victory. Both matches felt like friendlies.

At the end, Liverpool took another lap of honour. This time very few Evertonians stayed. The Gwladys Street End emptied and only the away supporters in the Park End lingered to watch the faintly embarrassed celebrations. There were, incongruously, two trophies handed over to the team, the Football League's version and the sponsor's award. The Liverpool players took them to their fans and, somehow, the silverware disappeared into the seething mass. When Rush and his team got back to the dressing room, there was no sign of the cups. 'They went missing,' the striker said. 'The home fans were gone but we went over to our lot and a few of the fans had got on to the pitch. I handed one of them the cup I had. That went straight inside his coat and was never seen again.'

No one ever asked where the trophies were. No one has ever found them. It summed up the Super Cup's place in football history.

At last, a line could be drawn under 1985–86. A new era had started. The game had changed for ever.

What happened next

The wheels of justice ground slowly over Heysel but a number of people were held responsible. Captain Johan Mahieu, the policeman responsible for Z section, was given a nine-month suspended sentence. Albert Roosens, the general secretary of the Belgian FA, was given six months, also suspended.

It took nearly four years for the criminal court system to reach a conclusion: 24 Liverpool supporters were extradited on involuntary manslaughter charges. Of them, 14 were found guilty. They were sentenced to three years in prison, 18 months of which were suspended. Those convictions were handed down on 28 April 1989. By then, Merseyside was reeling from the Hillsborough disaster which happened 13 days earlier.

In contrast with Hillsborough, officials lost their jobs over Heysel. An official inquiry took place in Brussels. Changes were made to policing and stadium safety. There was no cover-up. Belgium learnt from the disaster.

Liverpool's 47 councillors lost their appeal against the £106,000 surcharge. An extra fee of £242,000 was imposed. Most of the money was raised through collections, donations by the Labour movement and contributions from trade unions but the fightback against Thatcherism was over.

Derek Hatton was expelled from the Labour Party a month after the cup final. He was later accused of corruption and underwent a long trial. In 1993, he was acquitted. 'The whole weight of the British Establishment was against me,' he said. 'They wanted me in jail but there was no evidence. I didn't do it.

'After the trial, the verdict came in. I left the court and walked down the street. I was delighted. Some fella saw me and shouted across the road, "Brilliant, Degsy, you got away with it!" Sometimes you just can't win.'

Hatton is now a businessman and entrepreneur. He remains a committed socialist.

Margaret Thatcher is dead. Her demise, at the age of 87 in 2013, was celebrated wildly in central Liverpool.

The Big Five finally lost patience with the Football League and led a breakaway in 1992. Their creation, the Premier League, changed the nature of the game.

Everton won the league in 1986–87 without Gary Lineker. It was the last time they won the title.

Howard Kendall moved to Athletic Bilbao in 1987. He never got to lead a team in the European Cup. 'If Heysel had not happened, Howard would never have left Goodison,' Neville Southall said. The goalkeeper is probably right. Kendall returned to England and had two more spells in charge at Goodison. He never recaptured the success of the mid 1980s. The greatest manager in Goodison's history died in 2015. Almost to the end he could outdrink the entire company and entertain them with tales of the glory days. Chinatown would never be the same again.

Frank McAvennie went back north to Celtic in 1987 but had been bitten by the London bug. He spent much of his wages on flights south – and fines for being late for training. The scrapes and scandals got more frequent. He came back to Upton Park in 1989 but broke his leg. By then, there were more cocaine than champagne moments.

His lowest point came in 2000 when he was charged with conspiracy to supply ecstasy and amphetamines. He spent a month on remand in Durham prison before he was acquitted by a jury.

He is living in the north east of England, has cleaned up his act and is as vivacious as ever. He will always be a West Ham hero.

Gary Lineker scored 21 goals in his first season at Barcelona. Then Johan Cruyff decided to play him deeper and wider. Sometimes genius is unfathomable. Lineker had spells at Tottenham and in Japan with Nagoya Grampus Eight. He was within one goal of equalling Bobby Charlton's scoring record for England but was substituted by Graham Taylor in the striker's final game for the national side, much to the player's regret.

Lineker was never booked or sent off. He had a reputation for being a little bland. Then his personality began to show. He became the front man advertising Leicester-based Walkers Crisps and the presenter of *Match of the Day*. He has commented increasingly on social issues, often challenging right-wing narratives. He has turned into a national treasure.

Kenny Dalglish did not retire. After a trophy-less season in 1986–87, he retooled Liverpool, buying John Barnes, Peter Beardsley and John Aldridge. They went close to winning the Double again the next season, losing the FA Cup final to Wimbledon.

The Hillsborough disaster changed everything for the Liverpool manager. His role in bringing comfort to the families of the dead elevated his reputation in the city but came at great emotional cost. He resigned as Liverpool manager in 1991, after winning the title the previous season. It is a surprise he lasted that long. The club let him down by not providing enough support. Few people in football understood the depth of the trauma suffered by all those involved at Hillsborough and Dalglish carried out more difficult duties than anyone had a right to expect of a football manager. He took them on willingly.

After a short break, he came back to manage Blackburn Rovers. The Lancashire club won the Premier League in 1994–95. It was a stunning achievement.

He returned as Liverpool manager in 2011 and was the last Anfield incumbent to win a trophy – the League Cup the following year. The American owners of the club sacked him three months later. They thought he was a relic of a different age. He was: one where silverware was important and substance outweighed image.

After a spell when he was treated as an outsider – he did not feel welcome at Anfield – the owners realized his status in Liverpool and made him a non-executive director. They have now named a stand after him.

West Ham went back to being the sort of club that gets relegated, comes back up and then provides easy fodder for the bigger teams. They moved from the Boleyn Ground to the Olympic Stadium in Stratford in 2016. They left their soul behind in Upton Park.

Ken Bates sold Chelsea to Roman Abramovich, changing the English game for ever. The Russian oligarch's money elevated the west London club to one of the sport's richest and most powerful teams. Stamford Bridge is now a compact, atmospheric ground and cars no longer park pitchside. These days the headhunters at the match are from recruitment agencies and have large expense accounts. But the Bridge has enough old-school supporters to remain hostile.

Ron Atkinson went on to win trophies with Sheffield Wednesday and Aston Villa. His success was overshadowed by controversy in 2004. The man who helped break down racial barriers in the game was heard on TV commentary making an offensive racist comment when he thought the microphones were off. It destroyed his career as a pundit. There is no excuse for what he said. It was common language until the 1990s and Atkinson had not moved with the times.

It was a sad ending. Big Ron is no bigot. He remains an excellent talker about the game and a brilliant raconteur.

Television was supposed to kill football. It had the opposite effect. The small-screen deals have spiralled in a manner that no one could have predicted. In 2017, the team that finished bottom of the Premier League received £93.5 million in TV cash. The boom shows no sign of levelling out. The money has turned the game from the cottage industry it was in 1985 into a billion-pound business. The visionaries of the 1980s were thinking in terms of thousands of pounds. They could not have imagined how things would turn out.

Everton were hurt by the consequences of Heysel but a myth has developed that the disaster ended their march to dominance. Kendall won the title in 1986–87 but the momentum began to fade. Everton's recruitment was not as ambitious as in the summer of 1985. Plus, they let their biggest assets go. Kendall went to the Basque Country; he said in his autobiography that the Goodison board did not match Bilbao's financial offer until very late. Had they put the money on the table earlier, he would probably have stayed.

Colin Harvey was a great coach. He was not a great manager. Everyone willed him success but there was something missing – Kendall.

Everton were affected badly by Hillsborough. They felt a fraternal pain at the city's loss and, unfortunately, were facing Liverpool in another Merseyside FA Cup final overshadowed by tragedy. This game was more difficult for the Everton players than in 1986. 'The '86 final was a year on after Heysel and the disaster didn't happen to the city,' Neville Southall said. 'In that sense you were distanced from it. In 1989 it was a month on from the disaster and everyone knew someone affected by it. It was hard to play. I didn't want to play. We couldn't win. If we had won, we still would have lost.'

Southall is right. Liverpool had the backing of the vast majority of families of those killed in the disaster and a reason to play. Everton only had their competitive instinct, which was seriously blunted by events. It was another day when Merseyside came together at Wembley but there was nothing uplifting about it this time. The agony was still too raw for both sides.

The last time Everton won a trophy was 1995, when they beat Manchester United in the FA Cup final. As the millennium arrived, they changed ownership and the finances were so badly managed that in the course of a decade the club went from having assets of about £20 million to being almost £50 million in debt. Evertonians wondering why the club have suffered in the 2000s should look closer to home than Heysel.

Everton are on the way up again. They are looking to move to a new dockside stadium and have some cash at last. Better days should lie ahead.

The relationship between Liverpool and Everton fans – especially the young ones – has grown bitter. It is unseemly that Steaua Bucharest flags are displayed on the Kop to mock Evertonians. It shows a complete misunderstanding of history.

The same can be said of the attempts by some to recast Heysel as Everton's tragedy. There were no chants of 'Murderers' in 1986. The city, the clubs and the supporters have changed. It has not been for the better.

Peter Reid has not changed. He still understands the importance of football clubs to communities. Despite his longstanding disappointment, he was still wringing positive effects from that day in May 1986 a quarter of a century later.

In 2011, he auctioned his cup-final runnersup medal to raise money to pay Plymouth Argyle staff when the team ran out of cash. It helped keep the near-bankrupt club alive.

Argyle sacked him within months. It's impossible to keep Reid down, though; he remains an important figure around Goodison Park and his punditry is always worth listening to.

The People's Game is now a largely televisual event for its mass audience. But it can still generate excitement and fanaticism. The feeling of going to a stadium for the match remains one of the great experiences. Football has changed but it has not lost its allure.

Selected Bibliography

John Belchem, *Irish, Catholic and Scouse: The History of the Liverpool–Irish, 1800–1939*, Liverpool University Press, 2007

Eric Dunning, Patrick J Murphy and John Williams, *The Roots of Football Hooliganism: An Historical and Sociological Study*, Routledge, 2014

Diane Frost and Peter North, *Militant Liverpool: A City on the Edge*, Liverpool University Press, 2013

Howard Gayle, *61 Minutes in Munich: The Story of Liverpool FC's First Black Footballer*, DeCoubertin, 2016

David Goldblatt, *The Ball is Round: A Global History of Football*, Penguin, 2007

Howard Kendall, *Love Affairs & Marriage: My Life in Football*, DeCoubertin, 2013

Anthony King, *The End of the Terraces: The Transformation of English Football*, Leicester University Press, 1998

Tony McDonald and Danny Francis, *Boys of '86: The Untold Story of West Ham United's Greatest-Ever Season*, Mainstream Publishing, 2001

Gary Shaw and Mike Nevin, *On the March with Kenny's Army*, published privately, 2011

Peter Taaffe and Tony Mulhearn, *Liverpool: A City that Dared to Fight*, Fortress, 1998

Rogan Taylor and Andrew Ward with John Williams, *Three Sides of The Mersey: An Oral History of Everton, Liverpool and Tranmere Rovers*, Robson Books, 1994

Pat Van Den Hauwe, *The Autobiography of the Everton Legend*, John Blake, 2012

The End, Every issue of the ground breaking 80's fanzine, Sabotage Times, 2011

Websites
Blue Kipper
Liverweb
Toffeeweb

TV
The Mayfair Set, producer Alan Curtis, BBC, 1999

Picture Acknowledgements

Every effort has been made to contact copyright holders where known. Those who have not been acknowledged are invited to get in touch with the publishers.

Page 1: Emily Place and Ben Johnson Street: both © City Engineer, Liverpool City Council; *Aquitania*: © National Museums and Galleries on Merseyside.

Page 2: Liverpool FC in 1892: © EMPICS/EMPICS Sport; National Dockworkers' Strike: © PA/PA Archive/PA Images.

Page 3: Tony Mulhearn and Derek Hatton and youngsters protesting: both © David Sinclair; Margaret Thatcher visiting Liverpool: © Mirrorpix.

Page 4: Kenilworth Road riot: © PA/PA Archive/PA Images; Heysel Stadium, 1985: © David Cannon/Getty; Valley Parade fire: © Hulton Deutsch/Getty.

Page 5: Howard Kendall and Gary Lineker: © Mirrorpix; Lineker with Adrian Heath: © Bildbyran/Press Association Images; Laurie Cunningham, Cyrille Regis and Brendon Batson: reproduced courtesy of Wolverhampton Express & Star.

Page 6: Frank McAvennie: © Jim Steel; McAvennie with Jenny Blyth: reproduced courtesy of Landmark Media; Craig Johnston and Kevin Sheedy: © Bob Thomas/Getty; Jan Mølby: © S&G/S&G and Barratts/EMPICS Sport.

Page 7: Ken Bates: © PA/PA Archive/PA Images; Kenny Dalglish: © David Cannon/Getty; extreme fans: © Mirrorpix; Liverpool celebrate: © Professional Sport/Getty.

Page 8: Gary Lineker walking off pitch: © Mirrorpix; Liverpool celebration bus: © Getty Images.

Index

ABOUT THE AUTHOR

Tony Evans is a former columnist and football editor for *The Times*, he is the author of *I Don't Know What It Is But I Love It*, and is now a writer and pundit. Before becoming a journalist, he spent his twenties following Liverpool FC and playing in bands, including a stint with The Farm. He lives in London with his wife and daughter.